Pretty Little
KILLERS

Pretty Little
KILLERS

*The Truth Behind the
Savage Murder of
Skylar Neese*

DALEEN BERRY
AND GEOFFREY C. FULLER

BENBELLA

BenBella Books, Inc.
Dallas, TX

BenBella
BenBella Books, Inc.
10300 N. Central Expressway, Suite #530 | Dallas, TX 75231
www.benbellabooks.com | Send feedback to feedback@benbellabooks.com

Printed in the United States of America
10 9 8 7 6 5 4 3 2 1

Library of Congress Cataloging-in-Publication Data
Berry, Daleen.
    Pretty little killers : the truth behind the savage murder of Skylar Neese / by Daleen Berry and Geoffrey C. Fuller.
       pages cm
    Includes bibliographical references and index.
    ISBN 978-1-940363-10-3 (paperback)—ISBN 978-1-940363-66-0 (electronic)   1. Murder—West Virginia—Morgantown—Case studies. 2. Murder--Investigation—West Virginia—Morgantown—Case studies. I. Title.
    HV6534.M778B47 2014
    364.152'3092—dc23
    [B]
                                                                            2014017783
Editing by Erin Kelley
Copyediting by James Fraleigh
Proofreading by Greg Teague and Cape Cod Compositors, Inc.
Cover design by Sarah Dombrowsky
Text design by Silver Feather Design
Text composition by John Reinhardt Book Design

Distributed by Perseus Distribution | www.perseusdistribution.com
To place orders through Perseus Distribution:
Tel: 800-343-4499 | Fax: 800-351-5073
E-mail: orderentry@perseusbooks.com

Significant discounts for bulk sales are available. Please contact Glenn Yeffeth at glenn@benbellabooks.com or 214-750-3628.

For Skylar's family—may you find peace.

And for today's youth, the first generation to grow up swimming in social media, and to their parents, who must help them navigate strange waters.

Contents

Relevant Individuals

The following people appear in the pages of *Pretty Little Killers*. This is not meant to imply cooperation with the authors' investigation or interview process, however—only that the individual played a role in the case.

The Neese Family

Skylar Neese | The only child of Dave and Mary Neese, Skylar was a University High School (UHS) honors student focused on her goals of earning a scholarship, attending college, and becoming a lawyer. The sunny sixteen-year-old was an informal counselor for many of her friends.

Mary Neese | Skylar's mother and an administrative assistant in a cardiac lab, Mary fought like a mama bear to find out what really happened the night of July 6, 2012. She fought equally hard for the return of Skylar's remains and for justice for her only child. Mary prefers not to speak in televised interviews, but she has been active on Facebook.

Dave Neese | Skylar's father and a product assembler at Walmart, Dave reluctantly took center stage before the media: discussing his daughter's murder, fighting for passage of Skylar's Law, and seeking justice for his little girl.

Dave's on-camera dignity, despite his visible grief and anger, has been widely commented on by the public.

Carol Michaud | Skylar's maternal aunt, Carol developed a special bond with Skylar when she was born that lasted until the teen's death. She read the Bible to her niece and took her to church, and the two loved to playfully argue and prank each other.

Kyle Michaud | Skylar's brainiac older cousin and Carol's son, Kyle was once like a big brother to Skylar. He watched as she grew into a popular, pretty teen and questioned her choice of friendship in Shelia, whom he called a "bad seed" when the girls were still in middle school.

Joanne Nagy | Dave's aunt by marriage, who lost contact with her ex-husband's side of the family after the divorce, Joanne had begun reestablishing connections with the Neeses when Skylar disappeared. Joanne was a great comfort to Mary and Dave, as well as a one-woman army when it came to coordinating volunteers to search for Skylar in the fall of 2013.

Rikki Woodall | A cousin of Skylar's who did not know her at all. This didn't stop her from posting a Facebook alert about Skylar's disappearance, however.

The Hunts | Jennifer and her son, Hayden, started the first and largest Facebook page, TeamSkylar<3. At first useful in the search for Skylar, TeamSkylar<3 degenerated into a forum for gossip and innuendo. Jennifer Hunt's claims to insider information became increasingly bizarre throughout the fall of 2013.

Skylar's Friends and Acquaintances

Shania Ammons | One of Skylar's closest friends, Shania is a fiery redhead and Clay-Battelle High School volleyball player. She hung out with Shelia Eddy and Skylar as much as Rachel Shoaf did. Because she came to Shelia's defense early on, she was viewed as a suspect in Skylar's disappearance and falsely accused by many local teens. She is still ostracized by them today.

Mikinzy Boggs | Rachel's ex-boyfriend, Mikinzy is a guitarist and vocalist who was head over heels in love with her. When he finally learned the truth about Rachel, he came to believe he had been lied to and used for months.

Darek Conaway | The older of two Blacksville brothers, Darek was indicted in September 2012 on five counts of third-degree sexual assault. He pled guilty to count one of the indictment and is now under home confinement. He was also a person of interest in Skylar's disappearance until Rachel's confession cleared him.

Dylan Conaway | The younger of two Blacksville brothers, Dylan was linked sexually with Shelia. Before moving to Morgantown in the early summer of 2012, he hosted small parties that Shelia, Skylar, and Rachel attended. Dylan was a person of interest in Skylar's disappearance until Rachel's confession cleared him.

Shelia Eddy | One of Skylar's two best friends, Shelia Rae, as her family calls her, is an only child. Pretty and intelligent, Shelia was an honors student at UHS until the fall of 2013. Shelia pled guilty to first-degree murder in January 2014 and was sentenced to life with mercy, making her eligible for parole in fifteen years.

Eric Finch | Because he was the last person known to have interacted with Skylar before she snuck out of her family's apartment on July 6, 2012, police questioned Eric early in her disappearance. He was also one of three teens called to testify at a federal grand jury.

Daniel Hovatter | Skylar's closest male friend, Daniel said Skylar was the first person he came out to. He was the only boy who was involved in social activities with Skylar, Shelia, and Rachel outside of school. He became obsessed with finding Skylar, and his unremitting pressure contributed to Rachel's confession.

Amorette Hughes | Skylar's partner in dance class. The pair texted each other for moral support when they realized they shared a common bond—they both had two best friends who were excluding them.

Morgan Lawrence | Skylar's oldest friend and an aspiring meteorologist, Morgan is the only child of a local doctor and his wife. Skylar was a daily visitor in the Lawrence home during elementary school, and the Lawrence family took Skylar with them on many day trips and extended vacations.

Hayden McClead | Another of Skylar's closest friends, the soft-spoken Hayden had distanced herself from Skylar because she didn't like Shelia. Hayden got Skylar a job at Wendy's. Not long before Skylar's murder, the two friends were becoming close again.

Brian Moats | A friend of Floyd Pancoast, eighteen-year-old Brian was driving the night Officer Teets pulled Skylar and her friends over for curfew violation.

Floyd Pancoast | Tattooed and with a buzz cut, nine-teen-year-old Floyd Pancoast was a brooding young man who confided in Skylar. They often went joyriding together.

Rachel Shoaf | Another of Skylar's best friends, Rachel was an honors student at UHS. The budding singer and actress broke down just after Christmas 2012 and was hospitalized at Chestnut Ridge Center. Upon her release, Rachel confessed, led police to Skylar's body, and pled guilty to second-degree murder on May 1, 2013. Rachel's confession implicated her best friend, Shelia Eddy.

Crissy Swanson | A distant cousin of Shelia Eddy, Crissy, twenty-one, was also like Shelia's older sister. She staunchly defended Shelia on Facebook and Twitter, which made her the target of false accusations from the public.

The Parents

Tara Eddy-Clendenen | During most of Shelia's child-hood, Tara was a struggling single mother. She works as an accountant for a car dealership. In October 2010, Tara moved with her new husband and Shelia from the eco-nomically depressed town of Blacksville to the more afflu-ent Morgantown.

Jim Clendenen | Shelia's stepfather, Jim is a foreman in a coal mine who sent his new wife, Tara, flowers every month on their anniversary date. Jim is rumored to have cashed in his retirement to pay $500,000 for Shelia's legal fees.

Greg Eddy | Shelia's birth father, Greg had a serious car accident that left him with a traumatic brain injury and permanent disability. He and Tara divorced in 2000. His family's land is near the murder site. Greg, who was devastated by his daughter's actions, loyally stood by her.

Patricia Shoaf | During much of Rachel's childhood, Patricia was a single mother. She works in communications. By turns lenient and controlling, Patricia believed presenting an image of perfection to the world was vital.

Rusty Shoaf | Rachel's father, Rusty works at an upscale men's store in Morgantown. He looked the other way as Patricia controlled Rachel, preferring to be his daughter's friend rather than her parent.

Law Enforcement (in order of appearance)

Officer Mike Teets | Teets stopped Skylar and her friends after curfew in the late spring of 2012. He released Floyd Pancoast and Brian Moats, both of whom were over eighteen. He called Shelia's and Rachel's fathers and drove Skylar home.

Officer Robert McCauley | A part-time Star City police officer at the time of Skylar's disappearance, McCauley is a veteran law enforcement officer who took the initial 911 report of Skylar's disappearance. McCauley turned the case over to Officer Colebank because it required a full-time investigator. He has since retired.

Officer Jessica Colebank | The first Star City police officer to work full time on Skylar's case, Colebank was obsessed with finding Skylar throughout the fall of 2012. She logged hundreds of hours on the case and was the first investigator to realize Shelia and Rachel were hiding something. Colebank insists the murder was a thrill kill.

FBI Agent Morgan Spurlock | An FBI agent and accountant, Spurlock is known for his boyish looks and ever-present backpack. He worked on the Huntington National Bank bank robbery case and Skylar's disappearance.

Corporal Ronnie Gaskins | The lead investigator on Skylar's case, the thoughtful, soft-spoken state trooper initially took an interest in Skylar's disappearance when he thought she could have discovered who the bank robbers were, resulting in them killing her. Gaskins enlisted the aid of Trooper Chris Berry and together, the two tracked down many of the key facts about the case.

Senior Trooper Chris Berry (no relation to the author) | A self-assured, brash state trooper, Berry transferred from the Fairmont detachment specifically to investigate the bank robberies. He took a personal interest in finding Skylar because he was so moved by the contents of her diary.

Chief Vic Propst | Chief of the Star City Police Department, Propst is a long-time law enforcement officer who functioned in a supervisory role in the investigation into Skylar's disappearance.

Monongalia County Sheriff's Deputy Timothy Hunn | A friend of Jessica Colebank's, Hunn procured ATVs for himself, Colebank, and Berry to ride during their off-hours as they searched the backwoods of the remote, tree-covered western panhandle of the county.

FBI Agent Tessa Cooper | An FBI victim liaison, Cooper helped guide the Neeses through difficult times after they learned their daughter had been murdered. She led the Neeses to the site where Skylar's remains were found.

Greene County Coroner Gregory Rohanna | An elected Pennsylvania official, Rohanna refused to release Skylar's remains in early July. His actions created a huge public outcry and focused even more media attention on the murder, as people threatened to protest on his office steps.

The Court

Monongalia County Prosecuting Attorney Marcia Ashdown | Ashdown has been prosecutor since 1996 and was lead prosecutor in *West Virginia v. Shelia Eddy*. Although she runs a tight-lipped prosecutor's office, she has been known to speak out on issues involving the rights of women and children.

Assistant Prosecuting Attorney Perri DeChristopher | Known as an effective litigator, DeChristopher just completed a two-year term as secretary of the West Virginia Prosecuting Attorneys Association. She functioned as the Neeses' primary contact about progress in the cases against Rachel and Shelia.

Mike Benninger | Shelia's defense attorney, Benninger is a big bear of a guy who got his start as a personal injury attorney. Benninger has a commanding demeanor in the courtroom. He reportedly told Shelia's parents his job was simply to keep her from receiving a life sentence.

John Angotti | Rachel's lead defense attorney, Angotti is known as a thorough and skilled criminal lawyer, and is the son of former Monongalia County prosecutor Sam Angotti. He is experienced, well-connected, and smart.

Monongalia County Circuit Judge Russell Clawges Jr. | Known as a deliberative and fair judge, Clawges has held the position since 1997. He and his wife reared two daughters.

University High School Faculty

Shari Burgess | The new UHS principal at the time Skylar disappeared, Burgess mandated that faculty and staff not discuss Skylar's murder or events subsequent to it. Her actions in the wake of Skylar's murder have been widely criticized by students and parents.

Pete Cheesebrough | An assistant principal at UHS, Cheesebrough was arguably the "face" of the UHS administration. He was well liked by UHS students.

Richard Kyer | A drama teacher at UHS, Kyer took a personal interest in his students and was viewed as a saint by many of them. He consistently defended Rachel, telling other students to leave her alone.

Dan Demchak | A UHS science teacher at the time of Skylar's murder, Demchak taught the class in which students say they overheard Rachel and Shelia discussing the best way to dispose of a body. He has since retired.

Skylar's Law

Becky Benson Bailey | Becky went to school with Dave Neese and was ranting one night over the inaction in Skylar's case when she came up with the idea to expand the AMBER Alert program. Skylar's Law requires police to contact the AMBER Alert system and to treat all missing children and teenagers as actual kidnapping cases unless an investigation proves otherwise.

Tom Bloom | A Monongalia County commissioner and retired high school counselor, Tom is familiar with Skylar and many of the students involved in this case. He helped revise Skylar's Law and drew the attention of state legislators to the bill.

Chuck Yocum | One of Tom Bloom's former students, Chuck became interested in Skylar's disappearance and helped Bailey write Skylar's Law. He works in the Maryland public school system.

Charlene Marshall | An eighty-year-old state legislator, Marshall was largely responsible for getting unanimous support for Skylar's Law during the 2013 session of the legislature. The bill became the top priority for politicians and sailed through with bipartisan support in just one session.

Preface

The death of a child is every parent's worst nightmare, but a child's disappearance can be even worse. Not knowing what happened—did she run away or was she kidnapped?—can stretch into hours or days or months. Every minute until her return, the parents experience a helter-skelter of emotions that swerve from worry to fear to anger.

Like many people in Morgantown, West Virginia, we began following Skylar Neese's story because we are parents. Geoff's stepdaughter Celeste was the same age Skylar was when she went missing, and Skylar's photo on the MISSING posters reminded him of Celeste. My experience is more emotional: I have four adult children—two of whom were once runaways.

We can appreciate how difficult it is to rear children today. Challenges exist when they are babies and toddlers, but parenting teens is entirely different. It's like learning Spanish for your vacation to Cancun—only to discover everyone there speaks Russian. Rearing teenagers in today's fast-paced, plugged-in world is so challenging that parents need all the help they can get.

Add crimes against children to the mix and it is easy to see why some couples decide never to have children. Yet, gone are the days when we imagined a stranger in a trench coat lying in wait to snatch an unsuspecting youngster. In today's society, law enforcement has found that most children go missing because a family member has taken them and a custody dispute is at the root. In these cases, the child's whereabouts usually become clear quite quickly.

When it comes to stranger danger in the twenty-first century, we picture someone far sinister: the internet predator. Today we are much more concerned, and rightly so, about who our children befriend while surfing online. However, Skylar's murder reminds us the biggest danger to our children comes from people they know—and often know intimately.

***

In the last ten years, ninety-six West Virginia teenagers have gone to prison for murder or manslaughter. Most of these cases involve teens whose young lives have been impacted by violence, neglect, drug use, or early exposure to pornography. In that respect, these two killers are no different: their families have a history of drug or alcohol addiction.

However, when Shelia and Rachel planned and then carried out Skylar's brutal murder, we knew this type of crime was a first for our tranquil state. Mountain State teens are not hardened killers. Girls, especially, do not kill in cold blood. According to the West Virginia Division of Juvenile Services, when it comes to murder the majority of incarcerated teens are there because of gang-related offenses—or else they killed a family member who abused them.

Murders committed by West Virginia teens are "not generally as premeditated and calculated as this one," Acting Interim Director Stephanie Bond said, "not where they took someone away and (then) helped search."

Due to these unusual factors, Rachel and Shelia were transferred to adult status. That is a rarity as well, and speaks of a heinous criminal act that carries the capacity to shock us.

***

Geoff and I were children when Charles Manson and his followers murdered seven people. As adolescents, we both read *Helter Skelter,* the story about the Tate-LaBianca murders and Manson's subsequent trial. That book provided insight into the controlling behaviors that led up to Skylar's July 6, 2012, disappearance.

We believe the criminal case involving the Manson family also hinted at the motive behind Skylar's murder, so her story captivated us from the outset. Later, Rachel Shoaf's confession and Shelia Eddy's chilling courtroom behavior echoed themes seen in the Manson case.

We realize how difficult it is for teens to understand that parents really *do* know best, when we warn them an acquaintance is bad news or require them to follow rules. We're not being mean when we insist on consequences for wrong conduct. Most rules have reasons behind them. The problem is, teens don't like to listen to their parents, whom they often consider hopelessly uncool.

This problem is compounded by something that only happens to adolescent girls. In *Reviving Ophelia*, author Mary Pipher, Ph.D. said our culture sexualizes young girls and overemphasizes their looks, while pressuring teenage girls to assume a false persona to please their parents. Then, when they are in much need of parental support, these adolescents become secretive and turn to their peers. "They are self-absorbed and preoccupied with peer approval," Pipher said.

That's what happened to my daughters. Mileah was 14 when she began hanging with the wrong crowd. In fact, Shelia Eddy reminds me of Mileah's friend Debbie. She came from a troubled background, so I tried to keep Mileah away from her. But Mileah was like Skylar, fearless and willful, and determined to be with the friend she admired.

As a news reporter, I worked with local law enforcement, so the Preston County Sheriff's Department quickly dispatched an officer to search for my daughter when she ran away one night. He found her at Debbie's house within hours. After he cautioned Mileah about the dangers of running away, I took her home.

When my second daughter, Trista, ran away four years later, we were living near Oakland, California. As soon as I realized she was gone I called the police, but California's AMBER alert program was being tested on a regional basis in 1999 and didn't go statewide until 2000. Even if it had been in place, the system wouldn't have been activated in Trista's behalf. She simply didn't meet the criteria.

So I did the same thing the Neeses did: I designed a MISSING poster, planning to make hundreds of copies and personally recruit every friend I could find to help me cover an area that held almost half a million people. Fortunately, a beat officer recognized Trista and brought her home late that same night.

For a few hours, I understood what it felt like to be Mary and Dave Neese, to not know where your daughter is or if you will ever see her again. In the case of Mileah and Trista, my worry and fear lasted less than one day. I lived through two brief episodes—nothing nearly as extreme as the Neese's prolonged anguish—and my heart aches for any other parent who feels that kind of terror.

———

Not long after Skylar disappeared, Trista, then thirty-one, and I were walking on the rail-trail that circles Morgantown. We were in Sabraton when I wondered aloud if we would see Skylar. Rumors ran amok, saying the 16-year-old had been seen there. Was she really another runaway, hiding out with her boyfriend? Thinking of the gruesome cases I've covered, I hoped that was all that had happened, and prayed Skylar wasn't somewhere being tormented by a psycho. When Geoff and I learned Skylar's close friends had planned and then brutally murdered her, we were as stunned as everyone else. As we began investigating, we concluded that the three-way relationship between Skylar, Shelia, and Rachel was toxic. It wasn't unlike many romantic relationships or marriages where everyone else sees the red flags except the victim; neither

Skylar nor Rachel recognized the danger that came from being close friends with Shelia.

During interviews, many teens said either they didn't have a good feeling about Shelia, or their parents didn't want them involved with her. Those same teens tried to convince Skylar and Rachel that Shelia wasn't a good person. After noticing changes in their daughter's behavior, even Mary and Dave repeatedly tried to pry Skylar away from Shelia. Skylar wouldn't listen.

At the same time, Shelia, Rachel, and Skylar's relationship was already deteriorating. The trio turned mean, and their online fights later became fodder for the public who would follow the unraveling story. Their behavior might not have seemed serious, but it was. "The way girls handle the problems of adolescence can have implications for their adult lives," Pipher said.

These malignant relationships all look alike. It is only after victims escape that they often say in retrospect: "Everyone else was right. Why didn't I see it?" There is some evidence indicating Skylar was starting to see the inherent dangers in that friendship—but she didn't escape in time.

Talk about dire implications: three years after the trio began fragmenting, Skylar is dead, and Shelia and Rachel are in prison.

To see how damaged Shelia Eddy is, simply look at her behavior following Skylar's murder. She inserted herself into the investigation, helped Mary and Dave search for Skylar, and even distributed the MISSING posters around town. People were appalled and wondered how Shelia could do something so brazen, but this activity seems to be a hallmark of a certain type of criminal.

Over the last several years, many other high-profile cases involved killers or kidnappers who helped families hunt for their loved ones. It isn't at all unusual, especially when the case features a missing wife or ex-wife, such as occurred with two women named Peterson. (Lacie in Modesto, California, in 2002, and Stacy in Bolingbrook,

Illinois, in 2007.) Scott Peterson and Drew Peterson (not related) both helped pass out flyers and canvass neighborhoods looking for their missing wives.

So did Ariel Castro, the notorious kidnapper and rapist who held three Cleveland girls captive in his home for ten years. Some criminals simply cannot stay away from the spotlight that shines on their victims—which makes them especially dangerous.

————————

While working on this book for the last year, it's become apparent that many area teens were traumatized upon learning their fellow classmates had murdered a childhood friend. Other teens experienced emotional distress such as panic attacks, nightmares, and depression, because they defended the two teenage killers. Some of these youths still cannot talk about the murder. If nothing else, we hope their parents will recognize such signs and seek therapy for their teens.

After we learned about Skylar's disappearance and later, her murder, our hearts went out to the Neeses. As we learned more details of what happened, we became fascinated by the case.

It was Mary Neese's love for her daughter, though, that made us determined to tell Skylar's story as candidly as we could. Mary said she was content knowing she "created something that good. [Skylar] was just awesome."

We hope this book honors her memory while highlighting the serious dangers facing today's teenagers—and their parents.

Daleen Berry
Geoffrey C. Fuller

one

Where the Children Play

The murder plot started out as a sick joke.

They never intended to carry it out, never dreamed they would actually go through with it. But they did, after something went terribly wrong. It took investigators more than a year to figure out what that "something" was.

Even then, they didn't have *the* answer—the answer to the question everyone has clamored for since May 1, 2013—when Rachel Shoaf and Shelia Eddy, two beautiful teenage West Virginia honor students, were arrested for their part in Skylar Neese's murder.

It was the same question that fell from Skylar's lips as she was being savagely stabbed to death:

"Why? Why? Why?"

Why did two teenage girls brutally kill their best friend?

People who know the Shoaf and Eddy families say they are all good people. In the case of the Shoaf, Eddy, and Neese families, several dynamics were at play: each family had borne at least one tragedy, each had some history of drug or alcohol use, and all three families had only one child—a little girl who, for various reasons, was accustomed to getting her way.

Many families experience similar problems but they don't end in murder. What made this situation end differently?

The answer is complicated, and the investigators who took on the missing teen's case in July 2012 had no idea that it would turn into one of the most complicated murder investigations they had ever undertaken, or that it would span two states and miles and miles of rural Appalachian backwoods. Nor did they have any idea how two popular and pretty sixteen-year-old girls could go from cracking jokes in biology class to plotting how to dispose of another student, someone who believed she was their best friend. Police found two options the girls entertained particularly chilling: "dunking her in a barrel of acid" and "feeding her to the pigs."

The story of Skylar's disappearance and murder looks at the huge role social media played in helping to expose her killers, and how broad inferences can be amplified fiftyfold by Facebook, Twitter, and other social networking sites such as Instagram. It's a story of how an online group convened to search for Skylar and comfort her parents instead deepened their grief. This account explains why the FBI was on the case like lightning, a scant two days after Skylar was reported missing, and the rumored connection between Skylar's murder and a rash of bank robberies in the region. It also tells how law enforcement managed to log thousands of hours on the case—until they put the killers behind bars.

Finally, this story is about whether killer Rachel Shoaf's stated motive for murder, "We didn't want to be friends with her anymore," carries any validity at all, or if the real reason can be found in the rumors of a lesbian love triangle—or something entirely evil.

Skylar Annette Neese was the only daughter of Mary and Dave Neese, parents who struggled to provide her with the bare necessities. Extras weren't always possible but when they were, Mary and

Dave made sure Skylar had them. Even though life's luxuries were often out of their reach, the Neeses provided Skylar with something many children never receive: unconditional love.

Mary, Dave, and Skylar, age 6.

Years before Skylar was born, Mary had a long-time crush on "DJ Dave," a local disc jockey who played on the Morgantown bar circuit. She didn't know if he knew her, but she always tried to dress up in case he glanced her way. With his longish brown hair and leather jacket, Mary thought he was cute, but it was his wide smile that made Mary really want to get to know him. With a mischievous sparkle in his eye, Dave looked like he would be a lot of fun.

One night after the music ended, Mary and her girlfriends were leaving a local bar where they had gone to celebrate someone's birthday. They noticed a large crowd gathering outside and saw Dave on the ground, blood pouring from his mouth.

Mary pushed through the crowd, demanding to know what had happened and who was responsible. Someone said three rough-looking men had jumped Dave as he was walking to his car.

From what Mary could tell, they had done their best to mess up his face. She leaned over and told Dave she was taking him to the hospital. He didn't argue.

Once there, sitting inside a little exam room, a doctor said Dave's injuries weren't serious. He wouldn't be talking for a while, though, because his jaw was broken and they had to wire it shut while it healed. Perhaps because he didn't have to worry about spinning tunes for an audience, Dave could focus on Mary. He felt like he was seeing her for the first time. With her thick black hair and big blue eyes, he thought she was the prettiest woman he had ever seen.

"Well, since I won't be talking for a while, I should go ahead and ask you now. Would you like to go see a movie?"

Mary blushed, realizing her dream of dating the cute DJ was coming true. Dave didn't waste any time, either. As soon as he was released he took Mary to that movie. Even though he couldn't talk for the next three months, Mary knew he was the man for her.

"Ladies, if you don't stop talking, I'm going to separate you."

It was easily the rowdiest class he'd ever had, probably because the boys outnumbered the girls three to one. Every day another student was tardy. Most days, many students came to class late. Usually it was the two girls he was trying to silence that day in the autumn of 2011.

Ignoring the bearded man at the front of the class, the two pretty teenagers—one a brunette, the other a redhead—did not stop talking. They prattled on as if they were deaf. Mr. Demchak's sophomore biology class wasn't anything special, but students liked him because he was known as an easy teacher with lax discipline. They described him as one part Santa Claus, because of his legendary long white beard, and one part absent-minded professor.

"Hey, do you know how to dispose of a body?" Shelia Eddy asked the student behind her.

Nick Tomaski shrugged. "I dunno. That show *Breaking Bad* has stuff like that on there." He was more interested in drawing in his notebook than in anything Shelia said. Besides, he knew she was a flirt.

"We want to figure out what to do with Skylar," Shelia said. Nick just looked at her like she was stupid.

"Shhh!" Rachel Shoaf, the redhead, whispered. "No names."

According to students in class that day, Shelia's question came on the heels of several negative comments she and Rachel made other days in the same class, about how much they hated Skylar.

"What kind of acid would you dispose of a body in?" Shelia asked the biology teacher. One student in particular insists Demchak heard this question that day and that he said it could amount to something like conspiracy.

Demchak barked his reply at both girls, according to that student: "How dare you ask that? Get out of my class. Go to the office right now."

The student said the girls did as instructed and, once there, they reportedly spoke to an administrator who sent them back to class. Since the girls weren't gone long their fellow students assumed they hadn't even been reprimanded.

This is where accounts differ. Mr. Demchak says he never heard Shelia and Rachel casually ask that specific question or mention Skylar's name in connection with it. He is adamant he never commented on a possible "conspiracy," and said school policy would have required he write up a report if he had. What he did say was, as he had been instructing students about DNA, that it was "very possible" the girls could have asked such a question.

Whatever Demchak did—or didn't hear—that day, it was the last time either girl brought up the subject in class.

When Mary discovered she was pregnant, she was not happy. The thought of raising a child terrified her because she believed she would be a horrible mother. Still, she wouldn't end the pregnancy and when Skylar was born, Mary fell in love with her.

"The first time I saw her, yes, that was the greatest moment of my life. It was instant love," she told Andrea Canning on *NBC Dateline* in 2014.[1]

Even with a newborn daughter, Mary wasn't sure she wanted a husband. Dave was persistent. He kept proposing, and Mary stubbornly kept putting him off. She hesitated when he said they should move in together. After Skylar's birth, though, Mary had a change of heart, and she and Skylar did move in with Dave.

Mary became the glue that held the family together. Her humor and playfulness created the bond; her will and determination made it stick. As the years passed, Skylar became a miniature version of Mary. People even used the same words to describe them, right down to their unfailing senses of justice, iron stubbornness, and occasional flares of temper. Where Dave and Skylar were best buddies, Mary and Skylar were intertwined in the way only mothers and daughters can be. Their family photos bear this out: Skylar possessed the same bright blue eyes as her mother and occasionally flashed a similar cynical smile.

The DNA discussion could have occurred at the same time students later told police Shelia and Rachel had asked their question. Classes were abruptly dismissed early on October 6, 2011, after students were told there was a gas leak. In reality, they were sent home because police had found a body in the woods behind the school.[2]

---

[1] As heard on the episode "Something Wicked," which aired March 7, 2014.

[2] The body was later identified as Christina Nicole Terry, 33, of Fairmont, West Virginia. In July 2013, Kevin Utter, a Morgantown man, was sentenced to forty-three years in prison for strangling her to death.

When classes resumed and students learned about the dead woman, Demchak said his class discussed DNA evidence and analysis. He believes this is the most reasonable explanation for the two girls' questions.

Whether Mr. Demchak is correct, or they asked that question with a more devious motive in mind, other students said Skylar's name came up in connection with the idea of disposing of a body. Rachel confirmed this when she later told police the plot to kill Skylar was hatched that day during Mr. Demchak's sophomore biology class.

When Skylar was a baby, Dave would lift her above his head and toss her onto the bed, never letting her go until his hands touched the linens. Skylar would squeal and laugh, and Dave would repeat the game over and over. He called it "Baby Body Slam." The game soon became their favorite part of the day.

During Christmas Day the year Skylar turned three, Mary and Dave videotaped their baby girl when she found her gifts. Skylar squealed as she jumped up and down, her blond curls bouncing in time to her steps. Racing around the living room and then running toward the camera, Skylar yelled, "I love you, Daddy!"

Daddy keeping watch while Skylar (age 3) tells him stories.

The constant, daily affirmation that came from the heart of a toddler would become Skylar's best gift to Mary and Dave—and what her parents would miss the most after Skylar was gone.

_____

When the two teens didn't stop talking, Mr. Demchak spoke up again.

"All right, Miss Eddy, Miss Shoaf, one of you needs to move." He gestured to a male student. "Miss Shoaf, you and Trent switch seats."

Shelia rolled her eyes at Rachel as she and Trent traded seats. Despite the relocation, she and Rachel continued to chat.

Demchak would later describe having had two murderers in his class as "the most bizarre thing I ever experienced in my teaching career." At the time, though, he thought they were two girls acting out for attention.

Regardless of when the two girls asked their bizarre question, none of the people who may have heard it—Mr. Demchak, Nick, and the three other students within hearing—had any way of knowing what they actually witnessed that day in the fall of 2011 was the birth of a murder plot. They had no idea Shelia Eddy and Rachel Shoaf, fifteen-year-old University High School sophomores, were planning to kill Skylar Neese.

_____

Love was always a constant in the Neese household, but money wasn't. Skylar's parents lived paycheck to paycheck all her life, which explains why they didn't take their first family vacation until the summer of 2000 when Skylar was four years old. They chose Ocean City, Maryland, six hours away, so Skylar could experience the beach for the first time.

The family could afford the vacation only because Mary had nearly been killed the previous year. A few days before Thanksgiving 1999, Mary dropped Skylar off at Pleasant Day Daycare. On her way home, Mary found herself behind an

O. C. Cluss lumber truck. The truck missed its turnoff, stopped abruptly, and began to back up.

Mary blared the horn and tried to put her green Mercury in reverse, but she wasn't quick enough. When the truck began to climb her hood, she threw her left arm up in reflex and the airbags engaged, cleanly snapping her forearm. Seconds later when she came to, her left arm was hanging awkwardly over the steering wheel and dripping blood. She had to lift it off the steering wheel with her right hand. When she noticed the impact had knocked the car's ashtray into the back seat, she was instantly relieved Skylar hadn't been in the car.

One metal plate, two operations, and several months later, Mary's arm was functioning at nearly 100 percent. In addition, the insurance company agreed to a settlement to cover the medical expenses and pay restitution. It was not an extraordinary amount, but would be enough for a frugal trip to the beach.

While Skylar later became a big fan of the ocean, she didn't like it during her first visit; she was small and the waves kept knocking her over. However, she loved the hotel's swimming pool. One afternoon as Mary laid her towel on a chaise lounge and Dave stripped off his shirt, Skylar stared at the pool, an inflatable seahorse around her waist and floaters on each arm. She waddled toward the pool's edge, peering intently at the sparkling water.

"Daddy's not ready for you yet, honey," Dave said. "Daddy'll help you. You don't know how to swim."

"I can so swim!" Skylar shouted. To prove it, she jumped in the water. Dave panicked and leaped in after her. Mary laughed at them.

"It's okay, Daddy!" Skylar sputtered, slapping the water with her floaters while kicking her legs. "I can swim!"

"You can't swim, honey!" Dave grabbed at her, but the small child kept squirming.

"I can so!"

Dave had to admit the floaters gave Skylar the confidence to swim just fine. That was the moment when he began to think of his daughter as fearless. In new situations, she was watchful and held back—until she plunged right in.

Skylar was also willful: *she* would decide what she would or wouldn't do, no matter what her parents or anyone else said.

――――――――

Skylar didn't believe it for a second. Shelia and Rachel would *never* do that.

"I'm just telling you," Nick said the next time he saw Skylar, "I heard them ask how to dispose of a body. Then they said how much you get on their nerves, and they didn't like you."

Unconvinced, Skylar flashed Nick a sweet smile. "They were probably just playing a game. We always play that game, you know, 'Would You Rather.' We play with weird stuff, like, which way would you rather die."

Nick shrugged. "Whatever. Might wanna ask them about it anyway."

She, Shelia, and Rachel had every class together but biology, where students later told police they heard the exchange. According to students who heard it, Skylar did question Shelia and Rachel.

"Hey, Nick said you two were making jokes in biology class about wanting to kill me. What's up with that?" Her voice was even, but her eyes were steely.

Shelia gave Skylar a blank stare as Rachel's eyes darted around.

"Why would we do that?" Rachel asked, laughing.

"That kid has been smoking too much weed," Shelia said. "See? Now there's a lesson for all of us. Don't smoke so much weed you think people are out to kill you."

"Yeah, you know you can't trust a stoner anyway," Rachel said, laughing.

two

Early Years

As a result of the unconditional love she received, Skylar had a deep and unbreakable bond with her doting parents. Although it seems she was a "daddy's girl," Skylar's world revolved around her mother.

"My mom, of course is the most important person in my life," Skylar wrote in her English journal.[3] "She not only cares for me, but she also listens to me and I know I can talk to her. I think it's important for parents to not only take care of their children, but to also make sure their kids can talk to them."

It mattered little to Skylar that she didn't have as many toys and clothes as other kids, or take as many trips as other children did with their families. In fact, having fewer possessions seemed to ground Skylar, making her care more than many of her peers about social problems like bigotry, global warming, and racial discrimination.

Skylar also hated injustice and was blessed with an abundance of empathy. At an early age she became a champion of the underdogs she met in her short life. When Dave used to make fun of gays, Skylar would reprimand him and tell him to knock it off. Sometimes

---

[3] Dated September 20, 2011, the journal entry came from Skylar's sophomore Honors English portfolio.

she would even punch him in the shoulder and say, "Stop it, Dad. They're people too, you know."

Her capacity for empathy and compassion could also be seen in her schoolwork. In her Honors English class, the big-hearted teen wrote a poem for Ryan Diviney, the former West Virginia University student who was beaten so badly in November 2009 he remains in a vegetative state today.

Skylar at age 11.

Skylar's earliest friend, Morgan Lawrence, also knew about uncondi- tional love, a feature in her home from the day she was born. Long before Skylar met Shelia or Rachel, she and Morgan, also an only child, were best friends. The two blonde toddlers first met at preschool and then reunited as kindergarteners at Cheat Lake Elementary. The first day of school the two towheads passed each other in the hall, made eye contact, and sensed they knew each other from somewhere.

"We just never stopped being friends after that," Morgan said.

Unlike Skylar, Morgan's father was a white-collar professional: a physician, the chief of the Monongalia General Hospital Emergency Department. Having money meant that, unlike Skylar's parents, Morgan's mother was usually available to pick up the kids after school.

Cheryl Lawrence became like Skylar's second mother. All through kindergarten, she brought Skylar home with Morgan and kept her until Mary picked her up. Inside the Lawrence home, the two little girls played together—until one of them wanted a toy the other child had. Then a fight ensued. Cheryl would separate them, sending Morgan to her room. Skylar was left behind with all the toys and the TV, and Morgan soon learned Skylar really enjoyed having everything to herself. Such is a trait of many only children, Morgan later said, "including me."

For all their advantages, David and Cheryl Lawrence were about as grounded as it gets. That's one reason they felt so comfortable with Skylar and her parents. They recognized the Neeses shared the same family values. They also viewed Skylar as a good influence for their daughter.

In fifth grade Morgan believed she and Skylar would be best friends forever. A poll they later read in Honors Science class said by age eighteen, only 5 percent of people would still have contact with their first friend.

"We were like, 'Boo! Boo! That's not going to be us. We're lab partners, and we have classes together,'" Morgan said. "I remember looking back and being, like, 'Suck it, world, 'cause that's not us! We're still in contact.'"

What Morgan was most looking forward to with Skylar, and Skylar with her, was when they would be bridesmaids at each other's weddings. It was a promise they made to each other as little girls— and they intended to see it through.

The year after kindergarten, Skylar and Daniel Hovatter were in first grade together at Cheat Lake Elementary School. Daniel later became

Skylar's closest friend and confidant—when she confided in anyone at all. Even as a child, Skylar showed signs of being a private person. She didn't share much with anyone, not even her parents.

Skylar and Daniel's friendship grew stronger because Dave did handyman work for Daniel's mom while his dad worked overseas as a military contractor. When Dave came by he'd bring Skylar along, and the two children would entertain themselves playing Life or Battleship for hours on end. When they suspected Dave was about finished, they'd take their game inside a closet, furtively hiding so they could keep playing.

Shelia Eddy entered Skylar's life when they were second graders. During summer, the two girls spent weekdays at the pool together at The Shack Neighborhood House, a community center outside Morgantown. Their play dates continued almost every weekend during the colder seasons. Usually Shelia's mother, Tara, would take Skylar home with her after work on Friday, to save Mary and Dave from making the twenty-mile trip to Blacksville. During the school year, Skylar spent her afterschool hours at Morgan's home, but during summertime she was often a visitor in Shelia's home.

It wasn't a surprise the two little girls ended up becoming fast friends at such an early age, because their mothers, Mary Neese and Tara Eddy-Clendenen, were close to the same age and had known each other when they were teens.

Like Skylar, Shelia was an only child. Also like Skylar, her parents came from small West Virginia towns and didn't have much money. When Shelia was about two years old, her father was in a severe car accident. Greg Eddy sustained brain damage and was left partially crippled. A family friend said Greg "has made mistakes as we all have but he has a good heart." As a single parent, Shelia's mom struggled. She worked in Morgantown, but wanted a better life for her daughter, so she took college classes to become an accountant.

When Shelia rode in her parents' car as a little girl, she often passed Kent's Chapel, a church across the state line in Brave, Pennsylvania. A few miles north of Blacksville, West Virginia, where the Eddys lived, Brave is tiny—with its 201 residents—and is part of Wayne Township in Greene County. Before Skylar's murder, it was an idyllic town where people left their doors unlocked and lived without fear of what would become of their children. One resident said, "The community of Brave was a picture-perfect place."

Kent's Chapel is a little white church on the same road where Skylar was murdered. Although the Eddys didn't often attend, Greg sometimes helped out with the youth in the church; congregants recall many mornings when he fixed breakfast for the young people there. His Sunday breakfasts became a thing of the past after Skylar's body was discovered.

Back in 2002, Shelia and Tara took part in a religious service at Kent's Chapel. Tara read from Scripture while Shelia held up a chrismon[4] before the eyes of everyone gathered in the small chapel. As Shelia hung her chrismon on the church's Christmas tree, Tara explained it meant "new birth." Shelia was just seven and her chrismon was a butterfly.[5]

That's about the time Shelia showed signs of having a personality trait the public would later witness during her court appearances: she craved attention. Crissy's mother babysat Shelia when she was an infant. Tara and Greg were separated and Tara didn't have much money, so Crissy's mother "bought her diapers...formula...everything," Crissy said.

When Shelia was seven or eight they began to notice her eccentric behavior. As Crissy described, "One time we were out [at a restaurant] eating...and everything was fine and Shelia just stood up and she was eating, and my mom's like 'Shelia, what are you doing? Sit down.'

---

[4] A handmade gold or silver object that is said to symbolize the Christ child.

[5] Tara Eddy-Clendenen declined to be interviewed.

"'I like to stand up when I eat,'" Crissy said Shelia replied.

No matter how many times her mother asked Shelia to sit down, she refused. Crissy believes Shelia's actions were designed to get attention from everyone around her. Those odd mannerisms continued to define Shelia as she grew older, but her loved ones explained them away, saying she was an only child and the center of her mother's life.

Unlike Skylar's parents, Shelia's parents divorced before she ever entered school. By the time Skylar was murdered in 2012, it appears the double tragedy—losing her father twice—might have taken its toll on Shelia. By then, she and Skylar had been friends more than half their lives.

Not too far from the Neeses' home in a nearby section of Morgantown known as Evansdale, another little girl was growing up. Rachel Shoaf was the only daughter of a merchant father—Rusty Shoaf owned and operated Reiner and Core, an exclusive clothing boutique in town—and a stay-at-home mother, Patricia. Rusty's first wife had succumbed to cancer, leaving him a widower with a young son and the proceeds from her life insurance policy. When he met and married Patricia, an outsider from Hampton, Virginia, his family thought he was rushing into a new relationship too soon.

The Shoafs soon had a baby girl. One family friend said she became "the sun, the moon, the stars" to her parents. Before long, Rusty's store went out of business, he and his son, Kevin, moved out, and the marriage ended in divorce. Rachel, whose favorite pastime then was playing Blue's Clues on the family computer, was four years old.

People who have known the Shoafs for many years said they have big hearts—sometimes too big, allowing people into their lives who later take advantage of them. Patricia Shoaf's closest friend, Liz,[6] recalled how she struggled as a single mother and how Patricia came

---

[6] Liz is not her real name.

to her aid. Liz's daughter Karen was two years younger than Rachel, but because Patricia gave her all the outfits Rachel outgrew, Karen was the best-dressed child in school.

The Shoafs did not move in the same social circle as the Neeses or the Eddys, so Rachel didn't know either girl. Instead, by the time she began school, Rachel was friends with children from the more affluent families in town. Liz said Rachel was a nervous child when at home. Away from home, though, she often lovingly tended to other children and later, as she grew older, regularly volunteered with the Special Olympics. "Rachel was the first person to defend those kids and wouldn't let anyone be mean to them," Liz said.

Skylar had always seemed sensible to Dave—sometimes irritatingly so. Many years after the Neeses' vacation to Ocean City, when Skylar was a teenager and the family lived in the Cheat Lake area, she called her father to task for his excessive behavior during televised sports events. Dave was an unabashed fan of West Virginia University football. The team has never won a national championship, but the promise has often dangled. For a rabid fan like Dave, their performance has been exhilarating and frustrating. Dave watched every game, often yelling at the screen.

One day, Dave recalls, when they still lived in Cheat Lake, Skylar came downstairs to the living room where Dave was watching the game. She stood for a few seconds, observing how wrapped up in it he was.

"Daddy, what do you care? So they lose. Why get all worked up about it?"

"Did you see what Slaton did? It's like he just gave up and fell down!"

"How does that affect you? How is your life going to change if they lose? Or if they win, for that matter?"

Something about hearing those questions from his fifteen-year-old daughter brought Dave up short. She was right, and "Ohh—go upstairs with your mother," was all the frustrated father could say.

Dave went back to watching the game, but Skylar had planted a tiny seed that would germinate inside him and change his outlook on WVU football. He still watched the games but was more objective. Skylar planted many seeds in her dad, changing his views on subjects important and trivial. She was that kind of kid, and he was that kind of father.

As early adolescence approached and cell phone coverage improved, Skylar and Shelia called or texted each other whenever they weren't together. The summer before Shelia moved to Morgantown, Skylar often stayed with Shelia.

Shelia's neighbors said they didn't see anything out of the ordinary during those visits. Skylar seemed friendly and sociable, and the two girls would often walk to the nearby Bell's Grocery store, or they would hang outside on the front porch with local boys who dropped by—usually when Tara was at work.

Neighbor Ted Bice said Shelia was quiet and shy, and would often walk in her bikini through the backyard, where she would sunbathe. He would spray Shelia with a water hose if she was outside when he was washing his truck.

He remembers hearing Tara and Shelia yelling at each other "several times." That could have been around the time Tara began dating Jim Clendenen, since several people have said Shelia didn't like her mother's new beau.

Even though he mined coal for a living, Jim wasn't your average coal miner: Crissy said he wore jewelry and got pedicures, so she and Shelia often teased Tara. Men in rural West Virginia rarely engaged in such pampering.[7]

Shelia did find one reason to like Jim: he was generous.

---

[7] Jim Clendenen declined to be interviewed.

"Jim was so gracious with his money, so gracious," Crissy said. "He just gave and gave and gave and gave, and if Shelia wanted the best, she got the best."

Once, possibly during a heated argument over her mother's boyfriend, Bice heard Shelia threaten to kill Tara. "I don't know how many more times she flipped out on her mom," he said. "She was, like, really getting wild."

Other neighbors said Shelia seemed odd. An older girl across the street from Tara's old apartment said Shelia was also mean, calling her a "whore" after the teen neighbor got pregnant.

"[Shelia's] always been a little weird, stayed in the house a lot," a neighbor named Lee Barker said.[8] "She acted like she didn't want to be seen in public, 'cause she'd have her dad stop down and go to the store for her and bring stuff down while her mother was at work."

Crissy said Shelia didn't have a good relationship with her father, but Greg clearly loved his daughter and was more than happy to run errands for her. Greg was often a regular at Dunkard Valley Golf Course, where he and his father would play golf.

"He would come in about three times a week," Kristen Miller said, "and say he had to get his 'little girl a sodie pop.'"

Miller, who worked at the golf course restaurant, said none of the staff even believed he had a daughter—because they never saw her. When staffers later heard the news and learned Greg's daughter had been charged with killing Skylar, Miller said they were shocked to learn she was a teenager. "He always talked about her like she was a little girl."

It took, of all things, a wedding to set in motion a chain of events that would bring the three girls into almost constant contact—and alter the course of their lives forever.

---

[8] Lee Barker is not his real name.

Tara's decision to marry Jim ushered a number of changes into Shelia's life: a new stepfather, a well-appointed townhouse located outside Morgantown, and city living. In addition, gaining a new husband who worked as a foreman for a union coal company meant Tara could say farewell to difficult financial times. So could Shelia.

Jim's generous income added luxuries to the lives of mother and daughter: he sent flowers to his new wife every month and Shelia could finally wear the expensive labels she'd always coveted. She could also get her hair styled and go to the mall for manicures. Even so, Shelia didn't have the same status as the daughters of the local business moguls or the sons of prominent lawyers.

The move did allow Shelia to attend UHS, five minutes away, and her new home was only ten minutes from the Neeses' Star City apartment. Shelia and Skylar were excited about the prospect of being together all the time. That prospect became a reality in October 2010 when Shelia transferred to UHS as a ninth grader and immediately requested a class schedule identical to Skylar's.

Aside from her family, Skylar's life had three constants: Morgan, Daniel, and Shelia. Rachel didn't enter her life until both girls were fourteen and freshmen at UHS.

By then Skylar's friendship with Shelia seemed to grate on the nerves of all her other friends. Those girls said Shelia was "mean" and "controlling." Sadly, they saw the same thing as Mary and Dave—a change in Skylar's behavior—which they attributed to her close association with Shelia. It impacted her other friendships so much that by the end of middle school, even Morgan and Skylar weren't hanging together very often.

"Hey, just tell Skylar we're not going to go," Morgan's friend said.

Earlier that day in the cafeteria, several UHS freshmen had made plans to see a movie. Skylar was there at the time so Morgan assumed she was included. Most of the teens were good friends with Morgan but none of them were close to Skylar.

It happens in high schools and everywhere else in society: people associate with other people who are like them. Often that means economic and cultural similarities. Morgan's father was a doctor and many of her friends' parents were white-collar professionals as well—lawyers, consultants, accountants, and professors.

"No, no," Morgan said. "That's not how that works. Either we're both going, or I'm not going at all. Skylar and I'll do something, 'cause I'm not doing that. That's stupid."

"I think it would be awkward if she went," her friend replied. "This could be weird. We're not that good of friends with her."

"Well, I am. I'm friends with all of you."

Morgan didn't think it was a conscious choice on her friends' part. They weren't trying to exclude Skylar because her family didn't have money; they just weren't on the same wavelength.

Class differences weren't always fueled by snobbery, but the effects could be equally divisive. Especially when it appeared snobbery was alive and well at UHS. Whether or not this attitude of entitlement affected Morgan's friends, Skylar must have been aware of it. How could she not be? It was all around her. Students say some of the wealthier teens, the more mean-spirited ones, actually referred to the rural kids or those from working-class backgrounds as "the dirty kids" or simply, "the dirties."

three

The Lesbian Connection

Skylar and Shelia met Rachel when the three had a class together and the next thing Skylar knew, wherever she and Shelia were, so was Rachel. This was fine by Skylar, who made friends with everyone. While they were freshmen, Shelia, Rachel, and Skylar became a well-known trio who turned the heads of other students they passed in the UHS hallways.

Skylar was ecstatic when Shelia Eddy—*her* Shelia—transferred there from an outlying rural area. Skylar and the tiny brunette had been friends since second grade, and she could imagine how fantastic it was going to be. Although Shelia was boy crazy and always on her cell phone, she had connections and could get weed.

Slender and sharp-tongued, Shelia had been popular at her old school, Clay-Battelle. But at UHS, she was an unknown. Except for Skylar, all her childhood friends lived in Blacksville. When Shelia didn't become popular at UHS, she used her budding sexuality to make friends and influence people. UHS teens say Shelia was the least liked of the three.

Unlike Shelia, Rachel was surrounded by her childhood friends, many of whom also came from Saint Francis, a parochial school. Unlike Skylar, Rachel had money, and her parents were considered more white-collar workers than blue-collar. A popular redhead, Rachel was known for her staunch Catholic faith and her volunteer work during Special Olympics. A songbird and aspiring actress, Rachel was the most talented of the three.

Finally, there was the five-foot-two blossoming environmentalist and champion of the underdog. The girl whose every step became a bounce, who smiled all the time, aced every exam, did her friends' homework, and insisted she was going to law school. That, of course, was Skylar. A likable honors student, she was the smartest of the three.

By the time they became fast friends, they were inseparable: the brunette, the redhead, and Skylar, the beautiful girl with Bette Davis eyes.

Despite the three girls' desire for excitement—or perhaps because of it—their relationship would soon be marked by tension, distrust, and one fight after another.

During those two years, Skylar must have assumed the social payoff was worth the occasional drama. She either wasn't bothered by the shifting alliances and two-on-one disputes that can occur between three close friends, or she tolerated the problems for the sake of having fun and partying. It was the worst mistake she ever made.

Fellow students wouldn't forget Skylar after they saw a firsthand glimpse of her stubborn streak during band practice early in the fall semester 2010.

Skylar and the rest of the UHS marching band had gathered in a parking lot downtown, preparing for a parade. It was the beginning of the school year and quite hot outside when the band got into position. Ariah Wyatt, Hayden McClead, and Skylar were all in the flute section.

As Ariah later described it: "We'd always practiced like that, every single time, the same order." As performance time neared, however, the upperclassmen decided to switch up the order. The freshmen didn't like it.

"We'd already told our parents," Ariah recalled, "so they're . . . ready to watch us march by. We were all not wanting to move."

The upperclassmen insisted on the order change but Skylar would have none of it. As the older students physically moved people, Skylar got angry. "No, this is where I told my family I was gonna be, this is where I'm gonna to be," Ariah remembers Skylar saying.

"Skylar stood there with her flute in her hands," Ariah said, "clutching it to her chest, going, 'I swear, if one of them touches me, I am going to flip out!' She was so mad, all the upperclassmen backed off as soon as she said that."

At that instant they knew: Nobody messed with Skylar Neese when she was angry.

———

Rachel's voice defined her freshman year at UHS. The first time students heard Rachel sing, their jaws dropped. "Oh, my gosh," one student said. "She's a freshman. She's gonna be so good!"

Richard Kyer, the UHS drama teacher, wanted to gauge the incoming freshmen so he held an informal audition in drama class at the beginning of each school year. The event told him who could sing—and who couldn't.

"Who wants to come up and sing?" Mr. Kyer asked.

Rachel volunteered and practically ran up on the stage. Students knew instantly they were watching someone who likely would land lead roles.

———

Other than her childhood friends, the only students who spoke well of Shelia were a few boys who considered themselves modern-day hippies.

One of them was a UHS student named Frankie.[9] He had known Shelia since third grade. "She was just like the sweetest girl," he said.

Frankie said he and Shelia smoked weed, did coke, and took Roxicet—a form of oxycodone—many times. They also slept together. Frankie believed Shelia's unpopular status had more to do with her arrest than people were willing to say. "She was cool," he said. "She was funny, and nice. I'm probably the only one who would admit it."

Many students liked Shelia before Skylar disappeared, Frankie said. But later he believed they were afraid to say they'd ever liked her, because she'd been labeled a murderer.

―――――――

As did Shelia, Daniel remained fast friends with Skylar through-out elementary, middle, and high school. Although Daniel often found Shelia annoying, her presence never seemed to interfere with Skylar and Daniel's friendship. Because he was a boy, it was pos-sible Shelia didn't see Daniel as competition, which she might have with Skylar's female friends—many of whom said Shelia tried to push them away.

Later on, Daniel often joined Skylar, Shelia, and Rachel on their weekend joyrides. He also hung out with the trio on a regular basis before classes or during lunchtime, and he and Rachel performed in high school plays together.

"We never argued," Daniel said about his calm and steady bond with Skylar. "I cannot think of one argument we were in. We would get irritated with each other, but we never had an actual argument where we didn't talk to each other."

By the time they turned into teenagers and entered high school, Skylar's relationship with Shelia—and later Rachel, once she joined the Skylar and Shelia club—came to dominate her world. Rachel's

―――――――

[9] Not his real name.

friends said it seemed Shelia was trying to control Rachel, and said they could see the bad effect Shelia was having on her.

Skylar's friends echoed those sentiments and were equally troubled about Skylar, but both girls brushed off their friends' concerns. In the process, Rachel and Skylar drew even closer to Shelia—until the three-way friendship turned tumultuous, leaving Skylar the odd girl out.

Skylar had snuck out when the Neeses still lived in the Cheat Lake area. Mary worked at Ruby Memorial Hospital then, but Dave only worked part time, making advertising signs for company cars. Times were lean for the Neeses.

On a warm spring night Skylar engineered a plan to go joyriding with Shelia. Joyriding is what today's teens call riding around aimlessly in a car, talking and texting and tweeting and sometimes getting high. Skylar and Shelia had gone joyriding many times, but Mary and Dave didn't know that.

Because neither girl had a license, Skylar had talked Floyd Pancoast, a friend of hers, into taking them. Pancoast, age nineteen, was a brooding young man, but Skylar liked him anyway. Skylar was his sounding board, as she was for so many teens at University High School.

Floyd's eighteen-year-old friend Brian Moats ended up driving. They also picked up Rachel and Shelia, who lived just a few minutes away from Skylar. The car with its five teenage occupants was cruising a little too fast down a long hill in Star City when Officer Mike Teets noticed their speed and took off in pursuit. Star City had a strict 10:00 P.M. curfew for anyone under eighteen, and the officer thought some of the car's occupants appeared quite young. When he strolled up to the driver's window after pulling them over, his suspicions were confirmed: the girls were underage. Officer Teets released Pancoast and Moats. He drove the three girls to the Star City police station, then called Rachel's and Shelia's fathers to come get them. The two teens had intentionally not given him their mothers' cell phone numbers. Rachel said her mom would get violent; Shelia knew her dad would go easier on her.

Neither mother immediately knew what happened because both dads snuck their daughters back into their respective homes. But Skylar didn't realize that. The Neeses didn't have a home phone then, nor did either of them have a cell—although they made sure Skylar did in case of an emergency. Since Officer Teets had no way to reach her parents, he loaded Skylar into the back of his patrol car and drove her home himself.

According to Mary, Skylar was nearly hysterical. She was inconsolable, saying Rachel's mom would beat her daughter up because she snuck out. Rachel had repeatedly told Skylar and Shelia about beatings she said she received from her mother.

"It's all my fault!" Skylar gulped through her tears. She had been the instigator of the plan, and Mary thought the chastised teen's guilt was appropriate.

"Yes, it is. You can't be doing that, Skylar!" Mary said. "Do you even know these boys that well? What if they hurt you? What if they raped you, killed you?"

"Rachel's going to be in such trouble!"

"As she should be. Now off to bed."

Mary and Dave both agreed Skylar had punished herself enough, so they didn't ground her or administer any other discipline. They believed she had learned her lesson.

Looking at events leading up to the murder, two facts are certain: Skylar's personality had begun changing, and she was growing angrier. Anyone who knew her well knew that. It is possible Skylar's temper was due to her personality change. Dave bragged she once punched him in the face so hard he was surprised she didn't knock him out. She and Shelia were always feuding, many times because Skylar was angry at Shelia when she didn't get her way. Then there were all those angry tweets Skylar sent out for the world to see, which she tweeted steadily in the late summer and fall of 2011.

Skylar was angry at Shelia, as evidenced by their frequent online fights. The bickering seems to have begun in late summer of 2011. In fact, June, July, and early August may have been the high point of the relationship among the three teens—both figuratively and literally.

Skylar's tweets from this time are positively giddy. Just after three in the morning on August 4, she tweeted to Shelia, *ima pass the time by blowing up yo shitt* and two minutes later, Rachel: *i have a story for you tomorrow. text me when you wake up! you can help my boredom on the ride to the beach :))*. And not long after: *OMGOMGOMGOMGOMGOMGOMG*.

Clearly Skylar was pleased and excited—until the big blowout at Rachel's home. Based on written documentation, the fight happened on August 16, just before the girls returned to school. It was loud enough to wake Rachel's mother, who separated them.

Rachel invited Shelia and Skylar for a sleepover. It was the first and last time they stayed with her. Sometime after Patricia fell asleep, the girls began drinking from the bottle of vodka they had somehow gotten their hands on. Before long all three girls were drunk, which is apparently when they started snapping photos of each other and kissing.

Skylar may have taken part in the drunken kissing, but based on what is known about her public displays with the same sex, that's probably all she did. For a while now, rumors have floated around she took pictures of—and some students say she even videoed—what happened next.

That is, Rachel and Shelia undressed and began having oral sex, and then scissored.[10] Skylar, who was in an unfamiliar home with a parent Rachel claimed could be violent, was unlikely to have felt comfortable enough to leave the bedroom. So she was trapped, forced to watch.

---

[10] Slang term for tribadism, or *tribbing*, which is genital-to-genital stimulation between females.

Afterward all three girls slept in Rachel's bed. Or they tried to. Shelia ordered Skylar to "move over, so I can cuddle with Rachel."

Shelia's request angered Skylar, who began complaining. A loud and rowdy fight ensued between the two girls. The next thing they knew, Patricia burst through the door. "What's going on down here?"

"I don't know, Skylar and Shelia—" Rachel began, then stopped. "They just started fighting."

Patricia told them to keep it down and took Rachel upstairs to sleep in her bedroom. But Shelia and Skylar continued fighting, so Patricia was forced to return at least once more to quiet the two girls.

This secondhand account comes from another friend, Shania Ammons, to whom Skylar related the events.[11] But Mary Neese verified the incident, when she later said Skylar wrote in her diary about Shelia and Rachel having sex.[12]

"Skylar... didn't seem happy about it," Shania said.

Shania didn't discuss Skylar's version of events with Shelia. "I pretend it never happened. I don't want to talk about it," she said. "I don't have anything against it.... It was just like, Shelia and Rachel. It was weird."

---

[11] Shania spoke about the incident during a February 24, 2014, taping of Dr. Phil.

[12] Mary verified the story during the same February 24 taping.

four

Big Girls Do Cry

According to one investigator who read Skylar's diary, she said very little about Shelia and Rachel having sex and seemed more upset about the fight she and Shelia had afterward. Skylar claimed she was mad at Shelia because whenever another person was around, Shelia favored that person.

As their sophomore year approached, a stronger note of the discord simmering beneath the unstable three-way relationship crept into Skylar's furious tweets: *yet ANOTHER reason to fucking hate you. youre realllly starting to push it. #idareyou to give me one more.*

The identity of the person (or people) Skylar kept subtweeting[13] is uncertain, but Shelia and Rachel are the most likely candidates. By then, they were the two friends Skylar was most concerned with.

However, she wasn't ready to let go of the relationship and seemed torn by her feelings for both girls. This was apparent by the end of August, when Skylar was waxing nostalgic, writing about the good times they had together sneaking out: *missinn the old daysss with @_sheliiaa @rachel_shoaf96 #fuckgettingcaught :(((.*

---

[13] It was a subtweet, the modern version of talking behind someone's back.

Even so, Skylar was becoming angrier and her outbursts more vocal. She seemed to blame the girls for problems that might have impacted her: *people who start shit for no reason at all #pathetic* and *hmmm even bigger whore than i thought? #notsurprising.*

Of course by then Skylar knew Shelia's affection for Rachel was more than platonic. She must have sensed she was being replaced by this newcomer, this upstart, this *intruder* in a relationship going back to the second grade.

She took to Twitter on August 21, lamenting, *its almost ridiculous how i somehow find out everything.*

By September Skylar tweeted what sounded like it could have been a threat, but was probably more her blowing off steam—however, it is possible the other two girls began to worry she *did* intend to expose their relationship.

Whatever was going on behind the scenes, Skylar was extremely upset, as shown by this August 23 tweet: *i forreal need to quit wishing death on people. #thatsterrible #karmasabitch.*

Either Shelia or Rachel—or both—were wearing on Skylar's nerves when she tweeted on September 5: *she found out shes got no soul but it reallly doesnt bother her <3.*

Then came the tweet many people say indicated Skylar was threating to "out" her two friends. On September 6 she wrote: *id tell the whole school all the shit i have on everyone, which is a lottttt #IfICouldGetAwayWithIt.*

It hardly seems a coincidence that one month later, Rachel and Shelia began to joke about killing Skylar.

People on the outside looking in might wonder why the three girls didn't just go their separate ways. It's not an easy question to answer, but part of the explanation could be the fact that Shelia Eddy had something Rachel and Skylar did not: a car.

Shelia's car played a crucial role in the dynamics of the girls' relationship the entire time they were a trio. Shortly after they became sophomores, Shelia turned sixteen and received the gift from her mother and stepfather. Some teens have speculated she used the vehicle to control Rachel and Skylar.

Having transportation meant freedom from parental oversight. Rachel didn't have a car because she didn't get her learner's permit until late, and Patricia's friend Liz said Rachel's dad eventually planned to buy her a used car. However, once Rachel began acting out, her parents refused to let her have a vehicle.

Skylar knew her family's financial situation meant she wouldn't have a car until she earned enough money to buy one. Mary and Dave might have wanted to provide their only daughter a vehicle, but it was beyond their means.

Possibly because of that desire for independence, and knowing Shelia had the transportation to provide it—or out of an impulse to heal a broken relationship, or maybe based on a need for emotional support—Skylar began reaching out to Rachel.

It's possible Skylar knew Rachel would get her to Shelia, and Shelia's wheels. Or it could show that Shelia was the intended target of all those angry tweets, whereas Skylar wasn't giving up her friendship with Rachel. Skylar did this in friendly tweets the end of August, when she tweeted to Rachel and another unnamed person on August 28, *@rachel_shoaf96 i heard ! im very excited for you both lmao :).*

The same day Rachel tweeted to Skylar about a gift Skylar bought her; Skylar retweeted it, *@rachel_shoaf96 my gaga shirt that my wonderful friend skylar got me.* Skylar also tweeted to Rachel about how much she liked her, *@rachel_shoaf96 hehe number 1 fan. no doubt.* While Skylar was playfully interacting with Rachel that day, her tweets show she clearly blamed Shelia for the serious rift that had developed: *LAST TIME. @_sheliiaa hate you.*

This back-and-forth, love-hate relationship—apparently toward both girls—continued throughout that fall, as Skylar's tweets grew increasingly negative. More and more, the subtext of her tweets spoke of jealousy, a failing relationship, and the nostalgic sadness of being left out:

> life would be so much easier if jealously didnt exist. #getsthebestofme summers spent in blacksville with @_sheliiaa. #momentsillnever forget.

Even though she seemed angry and hurt, Skylar missed the friendship—and kept hoping the situation would improve:

> those songs that remind you of how it used to be.. #happensforareason. everytime i see people talking about how sad it is to have your best friend slip away i get more greatful i never have to worry about it… #iloveyou because i couldnt imagine life without you.

Interestingly, from November 29 to December 9, Skylar had no tweets to, from, or about either Shelia or Rachel. Either she deleted her tweets during that eleven-day period, or a deep freeze had set in between all three girls.

Moodiness may be a normal part of adolescent development, but there was much more going on beneath the surface for Skylar. After Shelia moved to Morgantown, Skylar wasn't as bubbly and carefree as she once was. It's difficult to say how much of that change could be attributed to Shelia's negative influence, factors from within Skylar's own family, or the addition of Rachel to their little clique.

Daniel recognized there were issues between Skylar and Shelia, even though Skylar didn't talk about them. She didn't complain about Rachel, either, for that matter. Still, he sensed the friction lurking beneath all the laughter. It would bubble to the surface regularly in the form of heated arguments, which seemed to pass as quickly as they came.

Daniel saw the contention one day when another tiff occurred after Skylar reprimanded Shelia. He was with the three girls when

Skylar told Shelia she shouldn't have inappropriately touched a male student in history class. It wasn't a huge blowup, but Daniel said Shelia seemed annoyed that Skylar chastised her.

———————

Then there were the "really nasty fights" Daniel witnessed between Shelia and Skylar. It didn't seem like Rachel was directly involved, though.

One day when he and Rachel were waiting to go onstage to practice their roles in the school play, *A Midsummer Night's Dream*, they were hanging out in the school cafeteria. Except for them, the large room was deserted. Daniel said Shelia called Rachel and then added Skylar in a three-way call. Shelia deliberately didn't tell Skylar that Rachel was listening. Rachel muted her phone so Skylar wouldn't know she had an audience. Evidently, Shelia's plan was to provoke Skylar, so she and Rachel would be treated to some of Skylar's fireworks.

Rachel pushed the speaker button and encouraged Daniel to listen when Shelia and Skylar began screaming. "At first [Rachel] was crying [and saying], 'I can't believe they're fighting like this,'" Daniel said.

Then Rachel's tears quickly turned to laughter as she listened to her two best friends go at it. "Ha, did you hear what she just said?"

"I couldn't believe it," an incredulous Daniel said. "I thought, whoa, girls get nasty."

———————

Daniel wasn't the only person who knew about Shelia and Skylar's fights. Crissy did, too. She said she heard that the two girls repeatedly got into fistfights after Rachel joined their group. Crissy said she and her mom believed that Shelia and Skylar were fighting over Rachel.

While there is no evidence Rachel physically fought with Skylar or Shelia, her indirect actions may have helped to accelerate the slow burn between the other two.

It was about this time when Daniel recognized Shelia and Rachel were sending mixed messages. He saw this firsthand and wondered about it, and realized Shelia and Rachel always had to be next to each other when Skylar wasn't around.

"They were awkwardly too close to each other," Daniel remembered, saying Shelia and Rachel seemed more emotionally intimate than when Skylar was present. They made references their friends didn't understand, peppering their conversation with inside jokes. They were also physically closer, with lots of hugging and playful pushing.

"They were always touchy-feely," he added. "If we were smoking or something, Rachel would get all up on Shelia."

Daniel sometimes wondered if they were a couple. He began to notice they seemed more drawn to each other when Skylar was absent, than when all three of them were together.

Although Skylar never witnessed any of this—and she and Daniel never talked about it—she was aware of the dynamic. Skylar told people she was disappointed Shelia and Rachel had grown closer than she and Shelia originally were. More and more, she said, she felt like a third wheel.

five

The Game of Death

By the time the trio had been together a little more than a year, their roles were clearly defined. Shelia was the leader, even though she sometimes deferred to Rachel, whose popularity with the artsy and apparently more wealthy students opened doors for them both. This didn't appeal to Skylar; she didn't seek wealth or status and only wanted to have fun with her friends. This carefree attitude weakened her link within the trio.

Shelia loved being the leader of the pack. She excelled at it. As Shelia's goals and dreams became more entwined with Rachel's, she became mouthy with Skylar, who chafed at Shelia's attitude. Skylar couldn't stand being ignored or mistreated. She was used to speaking her mind and getting her way, and when she didn't, she could throw a tantrum. At times, though, when Skylar let her guard down, when she yearned to be accepted and included, she was perfectly content to be a follower. It was as if Shelia, the one who could see, was leading Rachel and Skylar, who were blind.

The trio's dynamics are easily seen on the video Skylar shot and uploaded to the internet just six months before she was killed. In the video, Shelia is leading—and Rachel and Skylar are clearly her followers.

The disturbing video begins in the middle of a conversation after Rachel or Skylar teased Shelia about peeing on the couch. Shelia denied it, her tone playful and joking.

"That's not my pee," Shelia said. "I had a grape popsicle, and that's not my pee." She gestured as she spoke, arms wide, one hand holding what looked like a mixing spoon. Her gestures and head tilts were self-conscious—a teenager aware she was being videoed.

Shelia is clearly the star, performing for a mostly offscreen Rachel and Skylar in the basement of Tara and Jim's townhouse.

"It's a grape popsicle, dude," Shelia continued. She pointed the spoon at Rachel. "You remember when you said 'grape stain on the couch'?"

"Yeah," Rachel said, "but that was way over here because my butt got wet."

"You said it two times." Shelia spoke as an authority, as if she was right and everyone knew it.

"'Cause my butt was freezing," Rachel whined.

Shelia abruptly changed the subject: "Would you guys rather suffocate or get shot?"

It appears they had played the game so often Shelia didn't have to explain the rules.

"Shot," Rachel said immediately, with Skylar's "Shot" following closely.

"Wait," Rachel said. "Depends on where."

"In the head," Shelia said, crossing her arms.

"Shot," Rachel and Skylar said in unison.

"There would be no suffering at all," Rachel added.

"Eaten by ants or suffocated?" Shelia asked, arms still folded across her chest.

"Suffocated," Rachel and Skylar's voices chimed.

"Drowning or suffocating?"

"Suffocate," the two friends said, again in unison.

Skylar added another thought: "It's almost the same thing."

"I know, but it's not," Shelia said.

Shelia would know—because she was in charge—and it had been her idea to play "Which Way Would You Rather Die?"

All the kids were flocking to see the newly released movie *The Hunger Games*. So were Skylar, Shelia, and Shania one Saturday night in March 2012. On the way, Shelia was on her phone constantly—talking, texting, using social media—even though she was driving. For Shelia, using her phone was like breathing. Unceasing cell phone use is common among teenagers these days, but many UHS students spoke of Shelia's nonstop attachment to her cell.

They were on their way to the theater when they passed a farm, and the foul scent of dung wafted into the car. Shelia held her nose with one hand and steered the car with the other. Riding with Shelia was always an adventure as she juggled the phone, steering wheel, radio, and whatever else attracted her attention. Riding with Shelia was fun *because* it was dangerous.

Along the way Skylar asked Shelia who she was texting. Shelia wouldn't say. She almost never did, even though Skylar constantly nagged at Shelia to learn what she was doing or who she was talking to.

The girls made it up the winding University Town Centre Drive and around to the Hollywood Stadium 12 theater. They went inside and found seats; Shelia sat in the middle, as usual, and held her phone up, the light from the screen shining on her face.

"I heard this was a good movie," Shania said.

"Yeah," Shelia said, still texting.

"You need to put that away before the movie starts," Skylar said.

"Yeah," Shelia said, but made no move to do so.

"You talking to Rachel?" Skylar asked. If she was jealous it was all for nothing—Shelia was texting a boy she liked.

"Nope."

"Who *are* you texting?" Skylar asked, more insistent.

"Hang on," Shelia said, continuing to text even as the theater's lights dimmed.

"Tell me who you're texting." When Skylar wanted something, she rarely gave up. When she didn't get her way, she would pout. Sometimes she grew more aggressive.

"Hang on," Shelia repeated.

"Let me see!" Skylar grabbed at Shelia's phone. Shelia smacked her hand away. Skylar punched Shelia in the face with her hand half closed, more of a smack than a punch.

"You bitch!" Shelia yelled. She hit Skylar as she closed and pocketed her phone.

"Fuck you!" Skylar smacked at Shelia's face again. Shelia slapped Skylar's hand away.

An elderly woman near Shania whispered, "Can you get them to stop?"

Shania muttered, "What do you think I can do about it?"

By then Shelia had run out.

"Yes! Go!" a voice behind them yelled.

Skylar looked at Shania. "I didn't do anything," she said with a cool shrug.

"Skylar, I saw you hit her!" Shania hissed.

"Yeah, well, she was being a bitch."

"Let's go. Now." Shania turned to leave, but Skylar grabbed her.

"I can't. My flip-flop is missing."

The two girls searched the floor until they found Skylar's flip-flop. They made their way up the darkened aisle and out the theater door, Shania in the lead and Skylar right behind her, both of them silent. Shania didn't want to land in the middle of any fight between Shelia and Skylar, but she could tell Shelia was growing tired of Skylar acting like a bratty little sister.

Once outside, Skylar and Shelia continued arguing in the car while Shania sat on the curb. She didn't want to hear any of it. They screamed at each other for several long minutes and as suddenly as it had begun, the fighting stopped.

It was only a matter of time before the two girls came to blows again.

The great divide between Skylar and Morgan began in earnest when they became sophomores. At first the frequency with which they hung out slowed. Then it stopped altogether. Part of the problem was Shelia: Skylar always wanted Shelia to tag along, but Morgan wasn't comfortable around her.

"You and I can go hang out," she would say to Skylar, "but I really don't want to be a part of you and Shelia and Rachel." One time, Morgan voiced her concerns a little louder: "Skylar, I just don't think Shelia's a good influence. You're doing things I've never seen you do." She was referring to Skylar's new habits: smoking weed, sneaking out at night, and generally behaving badly, behavior she thought Skylar was doing to imitate Shelia.

"Oh, it's fine," Skylar said, waving away Morgan's concern. She wasn't angry, she merely thought her friend was wrong. "It's just high school."

At the same time, Morgan's friend Alexis was equally troubled by Rachel's behavior. She had known Rachel for a long time, and when Alexis and Morgan compared notes, they found Alexis knew things Rachel had done and Morgan knew things Skylar had done—and both girls realized Skylar and Rachel's behavior was totally unlike them.

Morgan and Alexis discussed it, wondering if Shelia was to blame. "Shelia seemed like she could do whatever she wanted," Morgan later said, "and there were no repercussions."

Everyone who saw Shelia at UHS said she controlled Skylar and Rachel. Even Daniel Hovatter was influenced by her magnetic pull, when she convinced him to steal test answers from a teacher's desk.

When Morgan learned this, she wasn't surprised at all. "She did that kind of stuff all the time," Morgan said. "Stuff like that didn't bother her. She just wanted an A. She just wanted to stay out late. When she wanted something, that was what was going to happen."

Got any weed?

Daniel was at home when he received Skylar's text.

Some.

Wanna get high?

Daniel knew Skylar wasn't alone. She couldn't drive except to and from work. Shelia must have been driving and Rachel was probably with them, too.

Sure, he texted.

Be right there.

I'll walk to the church. Daniel's driveway was long and difficult so his friends usually picked him up in the church parking lot a hundred yards down the hill. By the time he got there, they were waiting for him. He assumed they had been close, maybe picking up Rachel.

Daniel climbed in the back with Skylar and away they went. Shelia turned off the main road and onto a smaller one that wound among a few houses. Mostly they were surrounded by trees. There was little traffic and no cops—perfect for what they had in mind.

At a pull-off they'd used before, Shelia parked the car. Daniel packed his small bowl with some weed, as Skylar did. Shelia and Rachel turned to sit cross-legged on the front seats, facing the back.

The four took a few minutes to get high, and then drove around.

"I still got homework," Daniel said after a bit, more bored than anything. He liked seeing Skylar, but Shelia and Rachel seemed even more into each other than usual. He was surprised because Skylar was there.

"Just going to get us high and get rid of us, huh?" Shelia teased. Daniel knew it was the other way around—they wanted to get high and get rid of him—or at least Shelia did, because she was always doing shit like that.

"That's pretty much—" He was interrupted by a booming sound as the car gave a terrible lurch. "I saw that!"

"Twenty points!" Shelia was laughing. Daniel didn't want to look back, but he couldn't stop himself. He felt sick to his stomach. It was a bunny.

"Shelia!" Rachel yelled, too loudly for the small car. "Don't hit the fucking animals!"

Skylar and Daniel looked at each other; they both hated it when Shelia did that.

"Oh. My. God," said Daniel, burying his face in his hands.

Skylar patted his shoulder. "There, there, bud."

"I swear she did it on purpose," he whispered to Skylar.

Daniel saw fissures beginning to form in the trio's friendship long before Skylar was murdered, but he didn't fully understand what he witnessed. He wasn't the only one; Amorette Hughes, who knew Skylar from dance class, saw the same thing.

By the time she met Amorette, Skylar's baby curls were long gone and she was "obsessed with Shelia," as Mary would say after reading her daughter's diary. Skylar was coloring and straightening her fair hair so she would be a brunette like Shelia, and Mary said Skylar had written extensively about Shelia throughout her diary. In fact, people who have read it, including police officers who worked the case, say Skylar seemed to be living vicariously through Shelia, writing all about Shelia's life—but saying nothing about her own.[14]

Amorette was a senior and Skylar a sophomore in the spring of 2012 when her relationship with Shelia became more contentious and the trio was in tumult. Amorette and Skylar soon found they shared the same perplexing problem.

---

[14] The Neeses declined to let the authors see Skylar's diary.

"I had two best friends," Amorette recalled, "and she had the two best friends. We were going through the same thing at the same time."

Having two best friends instead of one may not seem like a problem, and maybe it isn't for teenage boys, but more than one girl spoke of having a similar experience.

"Sometimes I would see that Rachel and Shelia would match," Amorette said, "and Skylar wouldn't. They'd both wear jeans and a pink shirt and Skylar would be in yoga pants. My friends would do that to me."

Amorette and Skylar grew close throughout the 2011–2012 school year and frequently confided in each other. They bonded over their struggle with their two best friends.

They're doing it again, Skylar texted Amorette one day after Shelia and Rachel made plans without her. Amorette encouraged Skylar to hang in there. Skylar did the same for Amorette whenever she felt sad and slighted.

I know, let's get together after school lets out, Amorette texted Skylar one day. *We can be BFFs.* Skylar thought it was a great idea but both girls were too busy to connect that first month of summer vacation.

Amorette wished they had taken the time to get together. She believed Skylar might still be alive if they had.

six

She'll Tell Our Secrets

A month before classes dismissed for summer break, Wendy Evans[15] was studying during lunch in one of the rooms off the library when Rachel came in. Wendy was one of the friends she had ditched for Shelia. It didn't take Wendy long to realize Rachel wanted to vent. Rachel closed the door so they were alone. She seemed exasperated—or angry.

"I can't stand Skylar," Rachel said suddenly.

Wendy shrugged. "Why not? I thought you all were best friends." She remembered how little she had seen or heard from Rachel since she, Shelia, and Skylar had become fast friends. Even so, Wendy knew Rachel and Shelia talked badly about Skylar behind her back. They bad-mouthed everyone, including Skylar.

"I can't stand her," Rachel repeated, her eyes hard, "but I can't not be her friend."

"Why?" Wendy asked. "Just don't be friends with her."

"She's like, so mean," Rachel said. "She'll blackmail us and tell all our secrets if we stop being friends with her."

---

[15] Not her real name.

Wendy smiled, thinking Rachel was being overdramatic. No wonder she was in theater. "What secrets?"

Rachel didn't answer. Instead, her eyes narrowed and a scowl formed on her face.

"At this point," Rachel said, "I wouldn't mind if she died."

———————

Shelia and Rachel laughed as Daniel and Skylar got into the car. They had changed out of their uniforms in the bathrooms at work, so they were ready to go. It was a summer Saturday afternoon, with Rachel in the front passenger seat, Skylar and Daniel in the back seat. Shelia wanted to treat herself—and Skylar and Daniel had gotten their paychecks.

"Hang on," Shelia said as she finished a text. "Cool Ridge?"

"I haven't been there in, like, forever," Rachel said.

Cool Ridge was the head shop on High Street in downtown Morgantown.

"Wait, wait!" Skylar said as Shelia pulled out of Wendy's parking lot. "I need an ATM."

Since they were new employees, Wendy's paid Daniel and Skylar with a type of debit card. The two teens could get cash with their cards and purchase whatever they wanted. Of course they needed cash for weed. They could get a cut for $60.

A quick stop at the gas station across Cheat Road and they were off to Sabraton, the next exit off I-68. Daniel knew a place. Shelia, Rachel, and Skylar waited in the car. Daniel was in and out in less than five minutes.

"Next stop—Cool Ridge!" Shelia said as she pulled back on the Interstate.

Daniel was packing a pipe and Skylar had her lighter in her hand. Rachel peeked over the passenger seat.

"Time for dementia hits," she said quietly in a high-pitched, mock-singing voice. She and Shelia said that a lot, laughing afterward.

Cool Ridge is like any other head shop around for the last forty years. They sell incense in assorted shapes and scents, bongs, colorful bracelets, and beads galore. Celebrity, movie, and video posters. Odd musical instruments, like didgeridoos. They also sell lots of T-shirts. It was the trio's favorite store, as it was Daniel's.

The four teens browsed for a while. Stoned, they weren't in any hurry. Skylar spent quite some time trying on bracelets. Daniel liked the T-shirts. Shelia and Rachel lingered near the incense, sniffing the ones that smelled especially good—or really bad.

By the time they were ready to go, Daniel had paid for a black T-shirt with an image of a marijuana leaf. Skylar had picked out a cool bracelet and some incense. Rachel didn't buy anything, but as the clerk rang up Skylar's purchases, Shelia handed Skylar the incense she had chosen.

"Mom wants me to bring home some milk and stuff," she said to Skylar.

"Sure," Skylar said, signaling the clerk to ring up Shelia's incense. Skylar and Daniel exchanged glances. They had talked about this many times in the last few months, how whenever they went shopping, saw a movie, or bought weed, Shelia never paid. Not since they had started working at Wendy's. They always just went along with it, but it was starting to bug them. The majority of the time, Skylar and Daniel blew their entire paychecks in one short weekend, paying for all four teens' purchases.

It was one of the last times the trio and Daniel partied together. The girls' relationship was deteriorating so fast it happened before they knew it. During the last few months Skylar was alive, her negative tweets toward Shelia and Rachel slowed considerably. They didn't stop, as evidenced by a February 2012 subtweet, *omg the number of times you do shit to piss me off throughout the day keeps going up and up. im not oblivious fyi.* But Skylar's Twitter traffic was not dominated by the dynamics of her relationship with Shelia—and Rachel—like it had been the previous autumn.

This matches Mary's belief that Skylar was pulling away from Shelia, disengaging. She was reviving old friendships—with Hayden McClead, for instance—and trying to start new ones, like the one with Amorette. Skylar was building a new life, one that invited old friends back into her world.

Some of Skylar's tweets showed her disdain for Shelia and Rachel; others showed they weren't on her mind at all. By May 10 she was tweeting, *obsessive girlfriends and ex girlfriends are my favorite. congrats on looking fucking pathetic.*

Her Honors English portfolio paints a picture of a girl who was maturing and coming to acceptance during her last few months of life. In a poem she titled, "Different," Skylar wrote about the loss of her childhood friend.

> *You were once friendly, funny, and flamboyant*
> *But now you're hopelessly needy, negative, and naïve*
> *A new boyfriend changed you for the worst*
> *But even claiming he was the apple of your eye didn't keep him*
>   *around*
> *From happy as a clam to sad as a skeleton*
> *You lost your friends and your spirit*
> *So now the only thing I have to say to you is*
> *I told you so.*

Skylar's words indicate she was trying to let go of Shelia—whom she blamed for giving up their friendship—but finding it hard to let her resentment fade away.

Tension and stress within the trio escalated again when their ongoing argument ruined Shelia and Skylar's trip to the beach the first week of June 2012.

By the time Skylar joined Shelia's family for their June beach vacation, as she had for the last several years, the tension between the two girls had turned their relationship quite volatile. No one knows what the fight was about, but people have speculated Shelia may have tried to put the moves on Skylar.

Perhaps this was an effort to test her control over Skylar, or merely an attempt to involve Skylar in the lesbian relationship she and Rachel may have had. It would have been a useful tool to Shelia: if Skylar played the same game, so to speak, she wouldn't dare reveal Shelia and Rachel's secret.

Regardless, something went very wrong during the trip. Shelia and Skylar argued the entire week. The fighting grew so intense, Shelia returned home and told Rachel they had to put their plan into action.

According to WVSP Corporal Ronnie Gaskins, the lead investigator, Shelia said, "Skylar has to die. Now."

Skylar's father believes if Shelia did make a sexual advance toward his daughter, Skylar would have rebuffed Shelia. Skylar was friends with everyone and especially disliked it when other people made fun of gays, but she wouldn't have been interested in Shelia sexually, Dave says.

It is very likely that's what Skylar's Twitter fight during the early hours of June 9 was about. But it might not have been. It's hard to say since the person with whom Skylar argued from 5:50 A.M. to 6:27 A.M. through subtweets has remained unnamed. Based on police reports that she and Shelia regularly argued online, however, it was believed Skylar was angry with her.

5:50 A.M.: *youre just as bad as the bitches you complain about.*
5:50: *and a liar.*

5:51: *"love"*

5:52: *well now im too fucking annoyed to sleep*

6:13: *yeeaahh..*

6:14: *fuucckk yoouu..*

6:15: *and no I do not type like that.*

6:27: *just know I know*

Star City police officer Jessica Colebank believes Skylar was arguing with Shelia and Rachel, but it is difficult to know what either girl said in return, since all of Shelia's tweets during the time the fight was taking place have disappeared from her Twitter feed, and Rachel's account has been deleted.

The single subtweet that stands out in Skylar's rant is the last one: *just know I know.*

It sounds like Skylar was warning someone, saying she knew something was going on behind the scenes, some secret Shelia (or she and Rachel) was trying to keep from her. Maybe Skylar realized that not only had Shelia and Rachel been sexual that time in Rachel's bedroom—but that they really were a couple.

Equally possible is this: Rachel was being very friendly with another girl while at Young Life church camp during this time, a fellow camper said. If Skylar heard that rumor and believed Rachel was cheating on Shelia with someone else, she could have been lashing out at Rachel—and threatening to tell Shelia. Given Skylar's fierce loyalty to her friends, this also seems plausible.

Or, is it possible that because of the trio's growing schism—as evidenced by oft-repeated and ever-increasing volatile arguments— Skylar had finally begun to believe the school rumor that Shelia might want to harm her? Or that both girls did?

———————

Gaskins said it was possible Shelia did make a pass at Skylar, but admitted the prosecution still had no way of knowing—because Shelia refused to say what the beach fight was about. The only information that police have comes from a witness, another student, who reported seeing Shelia and Rachel argue just after Shelia and Skylar returned from the beach.

The Twitter fight happened June 9 at the same time Rachel was returning from Young Life. That evening she and Shelia met in the UHS parking lot, where a male student later told police he overheard them arguing. He thought they were fighting over him and asked the girls about it. Shelia and Rachel were quick to dismiss his concern, saying their anger wasn't about each other or him.

They were upset, they confessed, with Skylar, over "something on Skylar's Twitter," the student told police.

Could it be because one—or both—girls knew exactly what Skylar meant, when she tweeted the ominous phrase: *just know I know*?

———————————

Rachel had left town with her Young Life friends midmorning on June 4, and was in Rockbridge, Virginia, through June 8. Several Morgantown teens were at camp, too, but only one other girl, Devon (not her real name), remembers anything remarkable about Rachel's time there.

Until Shelia came along, Devon said she had been quite close to Rachel, and she, too, had tried to warn her Shelia wasn't a good influence. Rachel never listened—until she and Devon went to church camp together.

While there Rachel, possibly having realized Shelia really intended to carry out their plan to kill Skylar, told Devon she was worried.

"I have to get away from Shelia." That was all Rachel said, and after returning home, she seemed to do just that.

"For a couple of weeks," Devon said, "Rachel was back with our Young Life group, hanging with us and not Shelia."

If so, it's doubly tragic Rachel finally saw the need to escape Shelia's sphere of influence—only to then be pulled back in. Or was it a case of hoping she could mislead her friends to make them believe she was trying to escape, so she could later convince them Shelia had killed Skylar?

Everyone agrees: Rachel Shoaf was a follower, not a leader. What was less clear was whether she let Shelia lead her into an act of murder—or whether she went willingly. Either way, less than one month later both girls' decision irrevocably changed their lives and those of their families.

It matters not whether Rachel followed Shelia because Shelia brainwashed her or because she was equally determined to kill Skylar. The choice to do so left the tiny town of Brave "unrecognizable," one resident said, and its people heartsick "that this kind of evil seeped into our midst."

———————————

Instead of celebrating her sweet sixteenth birthday with cake and candles, Rachel was helping Shelia plan Skylar's murder. So while no one knows what Shelia said in reply to Skylar's angry Twitter outburst—if she said anything at all—it isn't hard to figure out how Shelia felt about it. That very night, both girls viewed Skylar as a threat, and set a date to kill her.

Gaskins says that on June 10, after the two girls met in the UHS parking lot, they put their plan into action. First, they began researching the various ways to kill someone. Since neither girl had any experience shooting a firearm, they opted for knives. After all, they reasoned, they didn't even have to buy a knife—there were plenty in their mothers' kitchens.

They weren't sure how to go about stabbing Skylar to death, so they researched the best way to kill a person with a knife. After reading their options, they decided stabbing or severing the jugular vein was the surest way. No doubt during their sophomore biology class they would have learned this vein was a major blood vessel—and a deep wound there could easily be fatal.

Killing her, they imagined, would be the easy part. What about hiding her afterward? They tossed a couple of ideas around as casually as if they were playing a game of basketball. Perhaps they could get their hands on some acid somewhere. That would definitely do the trick. But they thought it might make people curious if they began asking about where to buy acid, so they quickly dismissed the idea.

Shelia, a big fan of TV shows like *Law & Order*, probably came up with the idea to feed Skylar to pigs. This is a commonly used device in television, as pigs are known for their strong jaws. In recent years episodes of *CSI* and *Criminal Minds* both featured victims who were fed to pigs.[16]

In addition, Shelia's father's trailer, her grandfather's house, and all the Eddy land out behind Blacksville were surrounded by coal mines and farmland. Finding a pig or two to eat Skylar after she was dead shouldn't be difficult at all. Of course, they probably worried they might wake up some sleeping farmer if they tried to drag her body over to a hog trough. They couldn't risk that.

In the end, it was much easier than either acid or pigs: they would take Skylar out to one of their favorite places to get high, smoke a few joints, and then bury her there behind the Eddy land. That place was so dark and deserted, no one would ever find the girl they had both come to hate.

---

[16] *Criminal Minds* season four finale; "To Hell...And Back," part 1, aired May 20, 2009; http://www.imdb.com/title/tt1422241/.

seven

Skylar Neese Must Die

Skylar had no idea of the evil awaiting her when she climbed out of her bedroom window at 12:31 A.M. on July 6. After stashing the bench around the corner of the apartment building, she hurried to a waiting silver Toyota Camry and climbed into the back seat.

Skylar was probably apprehensive about joyriding with Shelia and Rachel.[17] Her two best friends had ditched her more than once the previous week, and the girls' tweets told the tale. They were insistent, and said since a bad derecho in late June had caused Rachel's church camp plans to be rescheduled, it was a good night to sneak out and smoke weed before Rachel left.

For hours that evening, while at work, on her way home, even after she arrived home, Skylar and Eric Finch, a close friend Skylar met years earlier through Shelia, had been texting each other. In between Skylar learned something either Shelia or Rachel—or both girls—had done. It upset her and at 10:48 P.M. Skylar voiced her public displeasure when she tweeted, *you doing shit like that is why I will NEVER completely trust you.*

---

[17] Skylar's murder has been re-created based on the available evidence.

She continued receiving text messages from both girls, trying to get back in her good graces, and telling her they really wanted her to join them. They promised not to fight. Skylar still wasn't sure how well the night would go. Lately her friendship with Shelia and Rachel had been falling apart, and she wasn't sure how much longer it would last.

Skylar's childhood friendship with Shelia was as precious as her cell phone—it was her lifeline—and she couldn't stand the thought of losing it. She blamed the rift on Rachel and Shelia having sex together, because since then they had become inseparable. Skylar didn't like it, but she couldn't seem to do anything about it.

They must have convinced her, though, because a few minutes after 11 P.M. Skylar let her guard down. She was going to try not to be angry with them, and thought maybe—just maybe—she and Shelia could get back to the way they were, before Rachel came along and ruined everything.

She said as much at 11:15 P.M., when she retweeted her friend Jillian Molnar's tweet, *All I do is hope.*

———————

Sitting in the back seat, watching Rachel and Shelia laughing up front, Skylar may have thought about how things used to be. She may have remembered her Honors English journal entry from September 20, nearly a year ago, when she wrote she was closer to Shelia than anyone she had met, and she couldn't "imagine life without her." Perhaps she thought about how she and Rachel had "formed a bond that will last a lifetime," and how dull her life would be without Rachel in it.

She may have wondered about the beach trip she and Shelia had taken and how badly it ended. That argument between her and Shelia—the *most recent* argument, the one that ruined their six-day vacation at Myrtle Beach in June—still wasn't resolved. Skylar no doubt wondered what it would take to return to the days of their earlier friendship. Or if, by now, it was possible.

Rachel had been acting a little odd the last few days. She had grown distant and reserved. Skylar would have wanted to resolve whatever was happening among the three of them. The problem was, how? Bad feelings were poison to her, as she wrote in her English class and her diary.

As Shelia, Rachel, and Skylar headed away from Star City, past the Sheetz convenience store and across the four-lane bridge over the Monongahela River, Skylar probably looked out the side window, her earbuds in and her music loud, and pondered their friendship problems.

Maybe Skylar saw it first. Maybe Shelia, who was driving, or Rachel, sitting beside her, did. But as they headed north on Route 19, planning to turn left onto Route 7 and head west toward Blacksville, they suddenly came up short.

"Oh shit, Shelia, there's the po-po!" Rachel might have said.

"Fuck!" Shelia probably replied.

Parked near the intersection of Routes 19 and 7, in front of a Hot Spot gambling lounge, was a State Police car. It matters little who saw the car first, because all three girls immediately grew skittish: they were underage, breaking curfew—and they all knew they had weed in the car. What was important is that the trooper sitting inside his patrol vehicle didn't see the little car at all.

"Quick, turn around!" Rachel suggested.

Sure enough, Shelia saw the same circular entrance to Tirelady's Rainbow Tire that Rachel did, which allowed her to easily pull off the road and on again, quickly heading back toward Star City.

"That was close," Skylar, who would have removed one earbud as soon as she realized something was wrong, said from the back seat.

Shelia and Rachel stared straight ahead, each refusing to give in to the desire they had to turn to the other, eyes opened wide. But as Skylar stuck the little white bud back in her ear and turned to stare out the window again, not giving the police car another second of worry, their minds were on what was hidden in the trunk, and their thoughts were likely identical:

You have no idea, Skylar, no idea at all!

Once back at the intersection where Sheetz was, Shelia would have made an easy right turn while gliding through the traffic light. That late at night her little car was one of a few still on the road, and from there, it was barely half a mile to the I-79 on-ramp that would lead them north, and on an alternate route to Blacksville.

Shelia left the interstate six miles later at the Mount Morris exit, and drove through the tiny town until she came to Buckeye Road. She steered her car through the curves in the commonly traveled shortcut, which wound its way for a few miles along the narrow, twisty roadway. The night had cooled down to the midseventies, and the high, clear sky full of stars belied the violence of the storm less than a week earlier.

The road widened as they crossed the Mason-Dixon Line and then a big iron bridge that signaled the road's end. Shelia turned right at the intersection and followed Route 7 west to Blacksville past her old alma mater, Clay-Battelle High School, and finally, to the right turn that would take her and Rachel to their secret destination on Morris Run Road back in Pennsylvania.

The deeper they drove into this rural area, the more apparent the devastation from the recent derecho became. Both sides of the road were heavily forested and hadn't been completely cleared of toppled trees, broken branches, and general debris left behind by the eighty-mile-an-hour winds.

Skylar had only agreed to join them because she believed they were going to ride around for a while, chat, and get high. But a mile south of Shelia's father's house, on a dark stretch of road, Shelia pulled the little Toyota off at a place they all knew well. They'd smoked many joints there on the way to or from Shelia's dad's house. To Skylar, this was one more smoke break. She had no reason to suspect her two best friends had something much darker in mind.

Neither Shelia nor Rachel mentioned the real reason they invited her to join them on that midnight drive. Nor did they say a word about the paper towels, bleach, Handi Wipes, or clean clothes stashed in the trunk of the car. They didn't discuss the shovel Rachel had stolen from her father's house and hidden in the trunk. Concealed under their arms and beneath the folds of their hoodies, Shelia and Rachel each carried one of the knives Shelia had brought. The weapons had been in place since they picked up the girl they planned to kill.

Skylar never knew about any of that, so she never got the chance to restore harmony among them. The three got out of the car and walked a little ways down the road. Shelia produced the joint, but the lighter she brought didn't work. Skylar remembered she'd left her lighter in the car and turned in the road to get it.

The minute Skylar's back was turned, Rachel began counting. At the count of three, she and Shelia began stabbing. With each stab wound, they released their pent-up rage and anger—at the people who had wronged them, at the parents who had disappointed them, and at the girl who loved them both, but whose jealous temper tantrums had made them despise her.

Stunned and in pain, Skylar tried at first to run. But she didn't get very far, because Rachel chased and tackled her in the middle of the road. Both girls landed on the ground as Rachel and Shelia kept stabbing. Skylar was physically stronger and a natural scrapper, though, and because she knew she was fighting for her life, she managed to grab Rachel's knife. It was Rachel's turn to shriek when Skylar left a three-inch gash just above her right ankle.

Rachel recovered her knife, however, and as they continued stabbing, only one word fell from Skylar's lips, but she cried it out over and over: "Why?"

————————————

In the end, Skylar never had a chance. She was stronger and tougher than either girl, but the fight was two against one. Skylar was weakening from wound upon wound, while Shelia and Rachel became more frenzied, their attacks increasingly savage.

After they finally stopped, Skylar's "best friends" stood above her, victorious with their win, until she stopped breathing. They watched her die. The fight had been so vigorous, both Shelia and Rachel had accidentally pocket-dialed someone: Shelia, her own voicemail; Rachel, an old boyfriend who never got the call.

Together they dragged Skylar to the side of the road and tried to bury her near a creek, but the soil was too rocky. They covered her body with debris instead.

When they were certain no one would ever find her, they got the paper towels and Handi Wipes out of the trunk, stripped naked, and put their bloody clothes in a trash bag. The murder, cleanup, and burial under rocks, dirt, and fallen branches took just over three hours.

Then Shelia and Rachel, filled with a sense of mutual accomplishment and excitement from the kill, wiped themselves off and had sex to celebrate.[18] Afterward they carefully bagged all the bloody items and dressed in the clean clothes they had brought along.

In a town where people take great pride in having harmonious family lives, and where horrific crimes like this simply don't happen, one of the most harrowing parts of this story is comprehending the fear Skylar must have felt when her two best friends attacked her.

"Skylar must have been terrified," one mother said. "Can you imagine the pain she felt at knowing her two friends were trying to murder her? That poor little girl."

Skylar's story can bring the strongest person to tears, and many people have followed it and the associated rumors from the time they first heard her name.

Everyone now knows Rachel Shoaf eventually confessed, turned State's evidence, and pled guilty to second-degree murder in Skylar's death. For almost nine months after that, Shelia Eddy insisted she was innocent. In a stunning reversal, though, Shelia also pled guilty—to

---

[18] There is no evidence to support this, but Officer Jessica Colebank, the first investigator on the case, believes this is what occurred because planning and carrying out Skylar's murder provided them with excitement like nothing else in their lives could.

first-degree murder—on January 24, 2014. She was sentenced to life in prison and given mercy, making her eligible for parole in fifteen years.

People who followed the tragic story know Shelia's last-minute plea came about because Rachel confessed. Most of them don't know that before her confession, Rachel had a nervous breakdown and was committed to a psychiatric hospital. Some people also know bits and pieces of the puzzle: rumors of the affair between Shelia and Rachel, the growing discord between Skylar and her two friends, and the fact that Shelia and Rachel planned the murder as much as a year in advance.

Rachel's descent into despair began within hours of stabbing Skylar to death when she went home and talked to God in the pages of her diary. Rachel wrote that only He knew what had happened the night of July 6—and it was going to stay that way.

Rachel also wrote, in page upon page, how sorry she was about what had happened. In the days to come, Rachel kept writing about "all the lies and lies, the terrible lies," as she begged God to forgive her.[19]

However, because appearances were of the utmost importance to Rachel—and because she knew how horribly she had disgraced her family—she treated the entire UHS student body and the community of Morgantown, West Virginia, to the performance of her lifetime. She did so to keep people from learning what she had done.

For six tumultuous months, no one suspected the ugly truth. A budding actress and singer with no small amount of talent, Rachel convinced all her friends she was innocent and had nothing to do with Skylar's disappearance. Rachel performed the role of "typical teenager," living a life of pretense and lies that was emotionally exhausting. Unfortunately for Rachel, the one person she couldn't convince was herself.

---

[19] Personally related by Liz, Patricia Shoaf's closest friend.

———————
·

Skylar's disappearance tore through Mary and Dave Neese. It sapped their strength and left them drained. They lived a number of private and public hells after losing their only child. The police investigation seemed to yield little fruit. Every day Mary and Dave volleyed between hope and despair. Family and close friends rallied around at first, but that support eventually soured, dissolving into a whirlpool of accusations and innuendo. Skylar's absence quickly sparked fires at UHS, too, since the pretty teen trio had been a fixture there. Some teenagers believed Skylar had run away. Others speculated she had overdosed and her body had been dumped down a mine shaft. Rumors roared like forest fires as students claimed Rachel and Shelia were hiding something, while others defended them, insisting that neither girl had anything to hide.

In spite of Rachel's amazing performance, by the time she broke down and was transported to Chestnut Ridge, the local psychiatric hospital, many teenagers knew the truth: Skylar Neese, they said, had been killed the same night she disappeared.

eight

Vanished

When Skylar clocked out of Wendy's at the Glenmark Centre on July 5, 2012, she had every intention of returning to work the next day. Her shift ended at 10:00 P.M. and the drive across Morgantown to Star City took only ten minutes. When Skylar walked through the front door of her home, she found Mary and Dave sitting in front of the television, watching *CSI*.

After greeting her parents, Skylar headed to the kitchen for some of Mary's homemade sweet tea. She loved the stuff and drank it by the gallon.

"Honey, are you hungry?" Mary asked from her recliner. The Neese apartment is open and airy so from her vantage point Mary could see Skylar standing in the small kitchen-dining area. Even before Skylar answered, Mary knew what her daughter's dinner had consisted of: one of those little berry ice cream desserts Wendy's sold. She just loved those.

"No, Mom, I ate at work."

Skylar crossed the wood-laminate floor and came into the carpeted living room. There, she perched on the arm of the recliner and hugged Mary. "Love you, Mommy," Skylar said, kissing her mother on the cheek.

Then she jumped up, leaned over the couch, and kissed Dave in the same fashion. "Love you, Daddy," she said. "I'm really tired. I'm going to bed."

"Do you work tomorrow?" Mary asked.

"Yeah."

"Do you want me to wash your uniform?"

"Yes, it smells like French fries," Skylar said, wrinkling her nose. Because she hated the smell of grease on her uniform, she always made a beeline for the shower. Not a minute later, Skylar tossed her dirty clothes out the door for Mary to throw into the washing machine. It was the same mother-daughter routine every night after Skylar finished work.

Mary waited for the wash cycle to end, then loaded Skylar's uniform into the dryer. After switching it on, she said goodnight to Dave and went to bed. She didn't know it, but Skylar's slender arm peeking around the bathroom door as she tossed out her uniform was the last glimpse Mary Neese would ever have of her daughter.

Dave was more fortunate; while he was dozing on the couch, he received one last "Love you, Daddy," when Skylar reappeared from the bathroom, wrapped in a large bath towel. She got a drink from the kitchen, went into her bedroom, and locked her door like every other American teenager who has a secret.

Dave Neese received no response when he knocked on his daughter's bedroom door the next afternoon. "Hey, honey, get up. I want you to take me back to work so you can have my car."

Nothing.

He knocked again. "Sky?"

Again, no answer. Usually, she was up—bam—as soon as she heard the car was available. Dave knew he shouldn't be letting Skylar drive by herself; with just a learner's permit, the teen was supposed to have a licensed adult in the car. However, he also knew she'd drive just enough to take him to work and then go to her own job. She'd come straight home after her shift. That was their agreement. The Neeses saved on gas and Dave always checked the odometer to make sure she was sticking to the arrangement.

After getting no reply, Dave went to the hall closet and grabbed a coat hanger—the door locks in the apartment easily popped open. But when he peered inside Skylar's bedroom, she wasn't there. Her unmade bed looked like it had been slept in, so Dave first assumed she must have gone shopping with a friend. Then he remembered her door had been locked from the inside. He called his wife at work.

"Mary, did Skylar tell you where she was going?" Dave's voice rose as he spoke. He paced the small kitchen, feeling his worry build.

"Just calm down." Mary knew how close to the surface Dave's emotions ran. "Don't flip out. She probably went shopping with one of her friends or something. She never misses work."

"That's what I thought, but her door was locked."

"She probably just accidentally hit the button closing the door in a hurry. You know how she does."

"Okay, maybe. But I'm going to look for her."

Dave rushed back to Walmart, a few minutes away, and told a supervisor he had to take the rest of the day off. "Listen," he said, "I can't find Skylar. I don't know where she's at, but I gotta find my kid."

He decided to check at home once more to see if she'd returned while he was gone. Skylar was largely a responsible teenager, and although she might forget to let her parents know where she was going, she would usually remember at some point to check in. But she was also fearless and willful, and that concerned Dave.

Skylar still wasn't at the apartment when he returned. Dave walked through the kitchen and out onto the small balcony for a smoke. He wanted to think, to plan his next steps. That was when he noticed a small black bench sitting at the base of the back wall of the apartment complex, just around the corner from Skylar's first-floor room.

Dave flipped his cigarette into the round ceramic bowl he and Mary kept for cigarette butts and went back through the apartment, out and around to Skylar's window. The screen was leaning against the wall, her window open a finger's breadth. That was the moment he knew: *Oh, my God. She snuck out.*

nine

On the Verge

On that Friday afternoon when Dave came home to find Skylar gone, the Neeses discovered Skylar hadn't learned her lesson about sneaking out, like they had thought after her joyride with Floyd and friends.

Thinking about the bruises she used to sometimes see on Skylar's thighs, Mary realized she had missed some clues. At the time, she and Dave believed Skylar when she said she got them at work. Looking back, Mary said, "We fell for it. She really got them from sliding down the windowsill."

That terrible July 6 day was when her parents realized Skylar hadn't learned a thing. Just the opposite. In fact, as the Neeses would discover from one friend of hers, then another, in that first month after she disappeared, Skylar snuck out a lot.

When she recalled Skylar's lies, a shadow passed over Mary's heart, no doubt brought on by thoughts of what she and Dave should have done differently. Should have seen. All the red flags they'd missed.

Looking back, Mary couldn't help but criticize herself for not keeping a closer eye on Skylar. She was confronting the difficult realization almost all parents eventually face: children who have been open and truthful in the past can, as teenagers, become deceptive and intensely wrapped up in their own worlds. They have extremely private lives and keep secrets from their parents. Skylar's disappearance brought many of her secrets into the open.

After Mary and Dave learned over the next month that their missing daughter had been sneaking out frequently, Floyd Pancoast, the boy Star City police had caught joyriding with Skylar, came forward. He knew some of Skylar's secrets. "He was one of the suspects in the beginning," Mary said. "We pretty much harassed him. Dave and I went to him in person, and he told us, 'I loved Skylar. I miss her so bad.'"

Mary heard Pancoast was big into marijuana, which is why she asked him directly, "How could you guys drive around every night, getting high, and Skylar's getting up and going to school every day and has a 4.0 average?"

Pancoast told her, "We didn't get high every night. We'd just drive around. She listened to me."

Through the police investigation, the Neeses learned Skylar and Floyd were no more than good friends. He didn't have anything to do with her disappearance. "So I had to apologize to him," Mary said. "He still feels terrible about losing Skylar."

A compassionate woman, Mary's expressive eyes often reflect her own sadness as well as the sorrow she sees in others. She and Dave must have realized they were wrong when they saw the raw emotion on Floyd Pancoast's face. Afterward, they offered him comfort, as they did repeatedly with various teens who had been touched by Skylar's disappearance.

Almost immediately after people learned Skylar was missing, the rumor mill began churning out stories. One of the most persistent involved a boy. No one seems to know who this boy was, but every variation suggested he was instrumental in her disappearance. Pancoast was one of many such "boys" the police questioned: *Were you romantically connected to Skylar? Did you do drugs with her? Did you see her the night of July 5 or the early morning hours of July 6?*

Mary insisted Skylar and Pancoast were not romantically involved, and just "buddies." In truth Pancoast, who sported a buzz cut and tattoos, wasn't Skylar's type. Mary couldn't say exactly what her daughter's type was, though, because Skylar never had a boyfriend.

Everyone believed Skylar was focused on getting a good education so she could go to college. For the time being, she was not interested in romance. Occasionally, she giggled with her girlfriends over one cute guy or another or took part in drunk-girl kissing games, but she wasn't serious about dating or sex the way many teens are. Perhaps Skylar was on the verge of such stirrings.

***

The afternoon after she and Rachel killed Skylar, Shelia was headed back toward Blacksville. She probably wondered if Rachel was going to ruin everything. She had to be more careful. How could she have lost her phone? Rachel claimed she had looked everywhere and couldn't find it.

"It must have fallen out when…you know," she'd informed Shelia a couple of hours earlier. Shelia told her to shut up—not over the phone—but at least Rachel hadn't texted it. Their plan had been very clear: all communication about anything suspicious must be in person or on FaceTime. The police could get everything else—phone calls, tweets, texts—*everything*. FaceTime, an app that let the two girls place a video call, was the only safe way. On FaceTime, once a conversation was over it was gone forever.

As she drove toward the spot where they'd gone the night before, Shelia might have thought about what happened, glorying in the crime they had gotten away with.

Or maybe not. Shelia was proud of her ability to block out unwanted thoughts and emotions, and she was very, very good at it. She tweeted as much, quite often.

When she arrived, Shelia pulled over and got out. She tried sending a text to Rachel's phone and then listened carefully. She didn't hear anything. Again, she texted Rachel's cell. Shelia probably would have kept her eyes turned away from the newly gathered pile of leaves and branches. The search took several long minutes, as she sent text after text—until finally she heard Rachel's ringtone. There it was, a little ways off in the grass. Shelia slipped it in her pocket and headed back to her car.

No doubt Shelia saw the large dark stains in the road, but she was so elated over finding Rachel's phone she likely didn't give them a single thought.

ten

The Timeline

After Dave found Skylar's bench and realized she had snuck out, he immediately called Shelia. If anyone knew where his daughter was, Shelia would. That afternoon when Dave asked Shelia if she'd seen Skylar, the teen said no. But she did admit she had talked to Skylar around midnight the night before.

A few miles away, Mary was growing more concerned about Dave being worried, so she gathered up her purse and prepared to leave work early. The walk from the hospital to Mary's car took longer than the short drive home. When she arrived, Dave was still on his cell. Just as she'd expected, he'd worked himself into a distraught state.

Dave was missing two key phone numbers: for Skylar's friends Hayden McClead and Shania Ammons. He called Shelia again to ask for them. He wasn't sure Shelia would have Hayden's number, because she usually steered clear of Skylar when Shelia was around.

He knew Shania was an old friend of Shelia's from Blacksville. They had gone to middle school together. For social activities like making a McDonald's run or going to concerts and movies, Skylar, Shelia, and Shania were together as often as Skylar, Shelia, and Rachel were. When it came to teen secrets, Shelia often confided in

Shania—which is why Shania knew more about the Skylar-Shelia-Rachel trio than almost anyone.

As Dave expected, Shelia didn't have Hayden's phone number. She also reminded him Shania was at the beach.

Dave snapped shut the cell phone and turned to Mary. "Now what?"

Mary shrugged. "We could give it a little time, see if someone gets back to us."

"Mary, she's *missing*." His tone was exasperated and pleading at the same time.

"Okay, then call 911." As Mary walked toward her recliner, the house landline rang. Mary answered and learned from the Wendy's manager that Skylar hadn't shown up for work.

She hung up and faced Dave. "Call 911 *now*."

The house phone rang again. It was Shelia.

"I need to tell you the whole truth," she told Mary, "about what happened last night."

"What happened?" Mary's thoughts raced to images of Skylar at a party, Skylar drunk, Skylar drugged after a boy slipped her one of those date-rape drugs. She even envisioned Skylar deserted in a dark corner after passing out at a party.

"I did see Skylar. She snuck out about eleven. Rachel and I picked her up and we went joyriding for about forty-five minutes. She made me drop her off at the end of the road so we wouldn't wake you."

Mary was momentarily relieved. She was more concerned about the girls sneaking around than the thought of some random stranger snatching Skylar off the street. That kind of scenario seemed far-fetched in their tiny suburb of Morgantown.

"Why do you girls continue to sneak out when we've told you just come to us when you want to do something?" Mary scolded. "You don't need to do this sneaking stuff." Mary didn't know how upset she was until she realized she'd lit her cigarette inside the kitchen, a strict violation of their lease. She opened the sliding door and stepped out on the balcony. "We can't find Skylar anywhere."

"I heard. Do you know what happened yet?"

"We don't know."

Tara, Shelia's mother, then got on the line.

"Mary, what's going on?" Tara asked.

"I don't know. We can't find her. Wendy's called and she hasn't showed up at work." At that moment worry seized Mary Neese's heart. Somehow, by saying the words "we can't find her," Mary finally realized Skylar definitely was missing.

"Do you want us to come over?"

"Yes, I do."

When Shelia and Tara arrived, they accompanied Mary as she went door to door down one side of Crawford Avenue, asking if anyone had seen her daughter. Dave waited for the Star City police to respond to the 911 call. Officer Bob McCauley arrived at 4:41 P.M. and the two men covered the other side of Crawford. No one had seen a missing sixteen-year-old girl.

Contrary to the rumors saying otherwise, Shelia did not cry during this search. Dave described her face as impassive and expressionless, her walk slightly wooden. At the time, Mary thought it was because Shelia was upset and scared. Shelia's mother, Tara, had cried when she first got to the apartment, but Shelia hadn't.

After the search of the immediate neighborhood proved fruitless, the five of them walked back to the apartment. That's when Mary had an idea: *the surveillance video.* She was surprised the police hadn't already checked it. Security cameras had been installed around the small apartment building, primarily to capture shots of people trying to break in. Cameras were also trained on the inside hallways of both floors. Jim Gaston, the landlord, could access the security tapes. Dave called him, and Gaston said he'd be right over.

An unmarked door close to the Neeses' apartment led to Gaston's small video room, the size of a walk-in closet. The landlord sat at the computer controls and the others—Dave, Mary, Tara, Shelia, and Officer McCauley—gathered around to watch the large monitor. Jim chose the view from the side of the apartment where Skylar's room was located. The camera faced the complex's parking lot, a small side street, and another apartment building across the way. Jim rewound the tape and let it play forward at double speed.

"Wait, wait," Dave said when he thought he'd seen something. "Back it up."

Jim rewound the tape and the small group saw part of Skylar's head blur past. Then nothing for a few seconds, although Dave noticed the shadowy image of a car in the background of the video. The time signature on the video read 12:31.

He tapped the screen. "You picked her up at eleven, Shelia?"

Shelia studied the image. "Yes."

Suddenly Skylar's head emerged, and she was seen walking briskly toward a gray car. She opened the back door and climbed into the back seat. There was no sign of a struggle. No indication the people inside were strangers. No clue of any foul play whatsoever. Then the car drove off and the scene was empty again.

It was as if they watched Skylar vanish, right before their very eyes. It was all Mary and Dave could do to keep from reaching out and trying to pull their precious daughter back—back into the picture, back into their lives.

For several long seconds, silence filled the small room. Finally Jim spoke up. "I think that looks like an SUV," he said. On the video, the car had been blurry and indistinct. Officer McCauley said he wasn't sure it was. Shelia said nothing.

"Do you know if any of Skylar's friends have cars like this?"

"No," Shelia said, shaking her head back and forth.

After McCauley took Shelia's statement, her word became the official story. His handwritten notes were the first recorded in the case. Shelia told McCauley she and Rachel picked Skylar up at 11:00 P.M. and dropped her off at the end of the street about 11:45. By that account she and Rachel were home and in bed by midnight. It was possible, given the three teens lived so close together. Everyone there believed the vehicle they saw had to be someone else's. It couldn't be Shelia's, because she drove a sporty silver

Toyota Camry—the one her stepfather purchased for Tara before they got married.

That left only one logical explanation in Mary and Dave's minds—but it was the last one they wanted to consider. After her friends dropped her off, Skylar left again—in a second car. In a car whose driver parked in the lower parking lot near the Dumpster, which was captured in the surveillance video.

But who did Skylar leave with? And why?

Most people unwittingly believed this theory for months; it became the basis for a general timeline of Skylar's disappearance:

11:00 P.M.: Skylar sneaks out of the house to joyride with her friends.

11:45 P.M.: Skylar's friends drop her off at the end of Crawford Avenue, along University Avenue.

11:45 P.M.–12:30 A.M.: Skylar's activity is undetermined.

12:31 A.M.: Skylar is seen getting into the back seat of an unidentified vehicle.

For almost two years, people who have seen the video replayed online at various news sites have asked the same question: Why did no one recognize Shelia's car as the one in the video? More important, why did no one realize Skylar was never seen leaving the first time, when she snuck out with Shelia and Rachel? And why did it take trained law enforcement as long as it did to come to these same conclusions?

The answer is: it didn't. People believed that's how it happened, but it really isn't.

Initially the police didn't suspect anything was amiss because they knew the vehicle seen in the grainy video couldn't have been Shelia's—not when she told McCauley she and Rachel parked on Crawford Avenue in front of a different apartment building, next to the Neeses'. After picking up Skylar they then turned onto Fairfield Street, which intersected with Crawford just a few feet away from where Shelia said she parked that night.

It all made perfect sense: the vehicle in the video couldn't be Shelia's. It had to be someone else's. However, within two days law enforcement realized Shelia's story sounded phony.

That first night, though, no one had a reason to believe Skylar's best friend would lie about the exact time Skylar snuck out or where Shelia had parked. Especially not Mary and Dave. To them, Shelia was still simply a trusted teenager.

No one suspected the real liar she would turn out to be.

eleven

Long Weekend

Two of Skylar's closest friends learned about her disappearance while on vacation at the beach.

Compared to teens like Morgan and Daniel, Shania was a relatively new friend of Skylar's whom she met through Shelia.

"I was at the beach when I missed a call from Shelia," Shania said. "She left a message saying no one knows where Skylar is, so I called her right back. 'What do you mean no one knows?' I asked her."

Shelia told Shania how Skylar had snuck out with her and Rachel the previous night, but she said that after a small tiff, Skylar insisted they drop her off at the end of the road. Now, no one could find her. Shania was really concerned and had all kinds of questions, but Shelia didn't seem worried about Skylar at all.

"She was casual about it," Shania said. But she wasn't, and immediately texted and called Skylar, trying to reach her.

Over the next two days, Shania thought about nothing but Skylar. She recalled their last conversation, and how Skylar felt abandoned by her friends. Shelia was in Indiana visiting her maternal grandfather, Rachel was going away to church camp, and Hayden and Shania were both at the beach with their families.

"Skylar was staying at home and going to Wendy's to work," Shania said. "So...she did feel like, out of the circle."

Skylar hated feeling left out. Her diary said so.

"Skylar was less fortunate than we were," Shania explained. "Her parents never told her no [or] anything, but she didn't have the money Shelia and I did. And she wouldn't ask for things like we did, because she knew her parents wouldn't have the money. What she did have, it was like a big deal to her. So I can see where she would feel that."

The last time Shania remembers talking to Skylar was after midnight on July 4, and they made plans to hang out when Shania returned from the beach.

"Skylar said, 'Yeah, 'cause you're the only one who actually tries to hang out with me anymore,'" Shania said. "Nobody else likes me."

"That's not true."

"Well, you're the only one who puts effort into hanging out with me," Skylar replied.

Hayden wasn't just Skylar's coworker at Wendy's. She and Skylar had been friends since they were small children. So when Daniel texted saying Skylar was missing, Hayden knew something was wrong. At first she didn't believe him. So she asked her mother to call Mary and Dave. That's when Hayden learned it was true: Skylar was gone—and no one knew where. Or why.

Hayden knew Skylar was upset because she thought they would spend the weekend together. But Hayden had gone to Ocean City with her parents at the last minute, and called off work. So when Skylar got to Wendy's and realized she was the only girl in her social circle stuck at home, she felt abandoned.

Hayden worried about her childhood friend all the way home, and tried to reach out to Skylar, too. Naturally, Hayden didn't hear anything back.

Several teens reported receiving a text message or phone call from Shelia Eddy about Skylar's disappearance. All of them say the same thing: Shelia seemed nonchalant over the fact no one could find her best friend. However, there is one person Shelia did not reach out to with the news—Crissy Swanson.

That singular fact struck Crissy as very odd. "She knew I really liked Skylar," Crissy said. "She knew I was a huge fan of Skylar. I loved Skylar. I told her that all the time."

Skylar often visited Crissy's home with Shelia, where they would hang out, watching movies or sometimes drinking and playing cards. Crissy said she loved Skylar, in part because Skylar didn't feel the need to hide her activity from people. If she thought it, or did it, Skylar talked about it.

The tendency to be open often got her into trouble with Shelia, like the time Skylar told Crissy about Shelia losing her virginity to Dylan Conaway. Crissy said Shelia gave Skylar a dirty look to try and silence her, but it was too late. Crissy was glad Skylar spoke up— because she was like Shelia's big sister and was better able to give her advice about being sexually active.

When Crissy learned Skylar was missing three days later, on Monday, July 9, she was shocked Shelia had not told her. Crissy later related that day's events, saying she was stunned to learn about Skylar's disappearance from a Facebook friend in Virginia. At the time, Crissy wasn't in the same Facebook social circles as Mary and Dave, so she wouldn't have automatically seen the news online.

I heard Skylar's missing, just let me know if you hear anything, the friend messaged Crissy. *I just wanted to let you know…let me know what's going on.*

Where did you hear that? Since when? Crissy said she immediately replied.

She's been missing since Friday.

You're shitting me.

Crissy was at work, but she immediately texted Shelia, *What's going on? What's going on with Skylar?* Shelia said she didn't know. *I guess she's been missing since Friday. No one has heard from her,* she replied.

All through her shift, Crissy couldn't believe it. "I told my mom, 'Shelia didn't even tell me Skylar was missing. Did you know?'" Her mother told Crissy that she had found out earlier in the day.

Crissy also reached out to Tara, hoping she might have answers. Tara was really worried, too. "She was scared for Shelia, like this would alter her life—because Shelia's best friend had gone missing," Crissy said. "Like it would ruin her childhood. Like Shelia...would just be traumatized, basically."

The next day Crissy printed copies of the MISSING Skylar flyers, picked up Shelia and Shania, and the three of them headed to Fairview, where they plastered the flyers all over storefronts and utility poles. They had so many the three teens ran out of time long before they ran out of flyers.

Crissy stashed the extra copies in her car trunk. When she discovered them there months later, she didn't have the heart to remove them.

While Shelia was busy alerting her closest friends about Skylar's disappearance, that first weekend was a blur for Mary and Dave. Watching Skylar vanish on videotape had been harder than they realized. Worry, hope, fear, and despair filled the atmosphere of the apartment. They both felt the urge to do something, *anything,* to find their only daughter. At the same time, they felt too trapped and helpless to come up with an effective course of action. All they could do was cling to what the Star City police told every parent of a missing child. Trying to reassure Mary and Dave, the police said not to worry because Skylar had probably gone on some kind of crazy summer getaway.

Even though they knew Skylar would never be that irresponsible, Mary and Dave tried to talk themselves into believing she had. The alternatives were too grim. "They said teenagers do this," Mary said later, referring to what the Star City Police initially said, "and we should give it the weekend."

They almost convinced themselves Skylar would be home Sunday night. Almost. At the end of the weekend, she would magically appear. Her reckless, impromptu beach visit would be over, and their beloved daughter would be all apologies.

The weekend was torture for Mary and Dave. They sat. They waited. They wondered when they would hear Skylar's ornery laugh, see her mischievous smile. They barely noticed the endless parade of friends and relatives that weekend. Through it all, every time someone knocked, every time the door opened, Dave would think, *God! It's her. It's her. It's her.*

But it never was.

twelve

Rumor and Silence

From the moment they knew Skylar was gone, the nearby sound of police sirens set Mary and Dave's nerves on edge. Was an officer coming to tell them Skylar was home? Or were the sirens conveying something worse?

Actually, the shrill sounds had nothing to do with Skylar. One fire whistle that ripped through the night, waking them up, went off because a couch was in flames. Another West Virginia University student igniting another couch. As one popular T-shirt said, "WVU: Where greatness is learned and couches are burned."

Skylar had planned to attend WVU, Morgantown's great equalizer. Although many residents, like Mary and Dave, didn't have college degrees, others jumped at the chance for their child to receive an education and have a better life. West Virginia PROMISE Scholarships provided free tuition for bright, hardworking students like Skylar. The money helped them cross the line from blue-collar to white-collar status.

The population of greater Morgantown swells to almost 100,000 when class is in session, but shrinks by half when students leave for the summer. The town is well-to-do, but with coal mining on the wane in the outlying communities—with names like Core, Osage, and Blacksville—life can be hard. The university boasts faculty and students from around the world, a diverse population that the families who have lived in these mountains for generations mostly succeed in ignoring. The two cultures mix to some degree, but they often clash at the two largest high schools, Morgantown High and University High, where the children of university folks go to school with the children of townspeople.

Early on, before most adults even knew there was a missing girl named Skylar, UHS students were abuzz with speculation. While Mary and Dave and their immediate circle worried and searched around the clock, most of Morgantown remained in the dark.

Not so the town's teenagers. In fact, those teens were coming to conclusions the adult world wouldn't reach for months.

———

In the days following Skylar's disappearance, while the Neeses were filled with panic, Shelia and Rachel showed very little concern. This was odd, given how close they had been to Skylar. In fact, UHS students said the trio had been inseparable in their freshman and sophomore years. Where you saw one, you usually saw all three.

On Friday, July 6, while the Neeses were searching for their daughter, Rachel and her mother were sunning themselves at Cheat Lake, out in the suburbs. Patricia Shoaf, a full-time communications sales rep, had originally planned to go out onto the lake with her good friend, Kelly Kerns. But for some unexplained reason, Rachel asked to tag along. Patricia really thought Rachel should be home sleeping, since the dark circles under her eyes belied Rachel's claims that she hadn't been awake the entire night.

Rachel usually relished the chance to be home alone without her mother, and Patricia couldn't be sure, but something in Rachel's nervous demeanor suggested she didn't want to be alone that day. Patricia shrugged it off, happy to have her daughter along for the day trip since Rachel was leaving for Camp Tygart the next day.[20]

———

[20] The camp has since been renamed Camp Boscoe.

While Patricia and Kelly chatted and sunbathed, Rachel was glued to her mother's cell phone. Both women noticed the three-inch cut along Rachel's lower right leg, close to her ankle. "What did you do to your leg, Rach?" Kelly asked.

Rachel shrugged. "I must have scraped it on the boat motor when I climbed into the boat."

No doubt Patricia could tell the cut looked angry, like it would leave behind a nasty scar. "You need to be more careful, Rachel."

Rachel continued texting, without even looking up at her mother. "I sure do."

On Saturday, Shelia and her mother Tara helped the Neeses canvass door-to-door again. They walked the rail-trail down by the river, an old railroad track that had been converted into a hiking trail. Unlike the day before, Shelia was now as tearful as Tara, and they both hugged Mary repeatedly. Tara's heart went out to Mary and Dave; their only daughter was missing. She could not imagine how she'd feel if Shelia was gone. Mother and daughter promised they would be back the next day and every day thereafter for as long as it took.

The next time Shelia stopped by the Neeses', she was alone. She asked Mary if she could sit in Skylar's bedroom. Mary agreed, but several long minutes later, when she heard Shelia crying, she hurried down the hallway. Shelia was sitting on Skylar's bed, hugging a pillow to her chest and sobbing. Mary, feeling sorry for Shelia, sat down beside her and rubbed her arm, as if the girl was her own distraught daughter.

In the following days, Shelia appeared to grieve for her missing friend. She spent hours with the Neeses trying to help find Skylar. However, when Mary and Dave looked back on events, they saw her sadness as feigned. Shelia was the picture of sorrow in real time, but her activity in cyberspace revealed not all was as it seemed. Saturday night at 11:45 she tweeted, *tired of losing sleep over this*. The meaning of *this* was unclear. One can only guess Shelia's loss of sleep had to do with the disappearance of her best friend.

An hour and a half later, at 1:24, she posted another mystifying tweet: *when you text me and my stomach drops to my ass <*. The < symbol indicated she did not like what she felt. Was Shelia talking to someone with whom she shared some important knowledge, perhaps a secret discussed only in texts? And why were they talking at nearly 1:30 in the morning? Most of Rachel's tweets disappeared from the web in the spring of 2013, but it's likely she was the one who shared Shelia's secret.

The most intriguing aspect of Shelia's Twitter traffic that weekend was not what she said, but what she didn't say. Why wasn't Shelia reaching out to Skylar via Twitter? Why wasn't she sending out tweets begging Sky to come home? Shelia's silence was a huge departure from her usual blowing up[21] of her Twitter feed, and what she didn't know was some people were starting to notice. She didn't tweet *to* Skylar. She didn't tweet *about* Skylar. Nothing.

---

[21] "Blowing up" refers to sending a lot of digital messages rapidly, either on Facebook, Twitter, or cell phone text messages.

thirteen

Nagging Doubts

Officer Colebank never thought of Skylar as a runaway. In fact, Shelia's story "sounded hinky" the minute Colebank heard it. The only problem was, she couldn't tell the Neeses.

Jessica, as Mary and Dave referred to her, was the Star City Police Department's lead investigator into Skylar's disappearance. Initially, Bob McCauley had handled the case, but though he had spent many years as a deputy sheriff, he now worked only part time for Star City. Since this case involved a missing teenager, it required a full-time investigator like Colebank. As soon as Colebank came back to work after two days off, McCauley handed the case over to her. Included in the file were Skylar's phone records. Due to the fact Skylar could have been in immediate danger, McCauley had filed the appropriate paperwork with the phone company the same day he responded to the 911 call, citing exigent circumstances.

Colebank found the records very telling: most of the calls and texts going to and from Skylar's phone were among her, Shelia, and Rachel. In fact, Skylar had called Shelia six times just before midnight—and the last call Skylar received was from Rachel.

Around the station, Colebank was considered the department's unofficial "detective" because she liked to dig deep when working her cases. Six years as a 911 dispatcher had helped motivate her to become a cop—every time a call came in, she longed to be on the other side of the radio.

Difficult cases were her lifeblood. Colebank was the type of cop every small-town police chief loves: intelligent, dedicated, and hardworking. She also has an investigator's keen instinct for sniffing out falsehood and an innate ability for reading suspects' behavior. Liars pissed her off, and she had no qualms about telling them.

When Colebank inherited Skylar's case, she'd only been in law enforcement four years. She had already become a thorough and aggressive investigator—partly because her father, on the force for thirty-five years, had helped train her when they worked together as Fairmont, West Virginia city cops. The Star City Police Department dealt with four or five missing-juvenile cases a month; Colebank handled the majority of them. Most had been runaways; up to this point, Skylar was the only missing juvenile on Colebank's watch who had never made it home.

Officer McCauley entered Skylar's name and other vital data into the FBI's National Crime Information Center database July 6, the same night law enforcement first learned of her disappearance. Important details about missing juveniles go into this central crime database, the country's largest, which the FBI makes available to facilitate the flow of information among police agencies. That's how local FBI agents learned Skylar was missing, and why they called the Star City Police Department to offer their help.

Chief Propst also called State Police headquarters in Charleston twice, asking the agency to issue an AMBER Alert. But the alerts are issued only for abductions—a status determined solely by state officials. Since the surveillance tape clearly showed Skylar getting into a car voluntarily, both requests were denied. Instead, Skylar was classified as a runaway—not an abducted teen.

Dave Neese had solid reasons to insist Skylar hadn't run away. She left her contact lens container and lens solution behind, just as she did the charger for her TracFone. She left her window open and carefully placed her vanity bench outside to help her climb back inside when she returned.

Most importantly, Skylar left Lilu—her dog and real best friend—behind. In elementary school, Skylar had begged her parents to let her have the tiny white ball of fluff after seeing one of her friends' Bichons. Against their better judgment, Mary and Dave agreed, and the Bichon had become Skylar's baby. Dave said again and again Skylar would never have left home for good without taking "that damned dog."

Lilu, Skylar's dog and best friend.

The FBI didn't see Skylar as a runaway, either. In fact the federal agency gets involved in cases of missing juveniles when sexual assault, physical abuse, abduction, or internet crime is suspected. Since the FBI was working on an ongoing investigation an hour south of Morgantown, they wondered if the two cases could be connected. Aliayah Lunsford, three, vanished from her Lewis County home in 2011, a year before Skylar disappeared. The massive search for Aliayah lasted for weeks, but FBI agents continued working the case long after searchers went home. Sadly, the toddler has never been found. When they heard about Skylar, the FBI worried they might have a serial killer on their hands.

In the beginning, only a few people helped Dave and Mary look for Skylar. Shelia and Tara came immediately. A friend of Mary's from work brought copies of the MISSING flyers that were being posted on Facebook. More support began pouring in as the situation turned into a crisis. Shania Ammons and her grandmother, Linda Barr, offered their assistance. Dave's aunt, Joanne Nagy, organized volunteers to cook meals for Dave and Mary.

Ultimately, Aunt Joanne proved to be a one-woman army. She fortified the shattered parents with emotional support and canvassed the rail-trail behind Sabraton, a suburb on the eastern side of Morgantown where sightings of Skylar had been reported.

Joanne also organized numerous search teams that met in the Sabraton McDonald's parking lot. The first search on July 10 drew such a huge crowd Joanne was sure she'd picked the wrong place to meet—the parking lot was overflowing. When she went inside the restaurant, she discovered most of the people were there to look for Skylar.

One week after Skylar disappeared, more people volunteered from all over the region, and complete strangers became close friends after hopping into cars together, bound by a common purpose: finding Joanne's missing niece, Mary and Dave's missing daughter. They split into teams of four and plastered flyers everywhere they could. The searchers drove up and down the winding country roads, dirt lanes, and interstates that led away from Morgantown, looking for Skylar night after night.

At first, Shelia was arguably the most persistent searcher of all. She stopped by daily, usually with Tara. Her questions were always the same: "Did the police tell you anything new? What have they found out? What are they telling you?" To Mary and Dave, she seemed like a concerned ally, by turns energetic and distraught. Naturally, they shared everything they learned.

In retrospect, Mary and Dave remembered Rachel never offered to help. Mary wondered about her absence and asked Shelia about it. Shelia said Rachel had been away at camp since the previous

Saturday morning, the day after Skylar vanished. A couple of weeks later, Mary realized she still hadn't seen Rachel, but with hundreds of thoughts preoccupying her, she was too distracted to dwell on it. Still, it felt strange they had heard nothing from Skylar's other best friend.

On July 9, the first Monday after Skylar disappeared, when Shelia and Tara helped the Neeses search, mother and daughter both knew the police investigation was well underway. They were also aware the FBI was involved. Officer Colebank had already been to Shelia's house earlier that day with Special Agent Morgan Spurlock. During the visit Colebank noticed something strange.

"I will never forget this," Colebank said, recalling her first encounter with the animated, watchful teenager. Everyone—Shelia, Tara, Shelia's stepdad Jim Clendenen, Shania, and Crissy Swanson, a distant cousin—was gathered at Shelia's house, "in the garage just hanging out, sitting on chairs, just chillin'. I'm, like, okay.... 'Your supposed best friend is missing. Why are you sitting here having a good old time?'"

In actuality, the family had gathered at the Clendenen home to watch the first televised newscast about Skylar's disappearance. The atmosphere still seemed less somber than Colebank thought it should be. Shelia told Colebank she just hoped Skylar would come home.

Colebank decided to tackle the social media first. "I have some questions about Skylar's Twitter. Do you know what Skylar meant when she tweeted 'you doing shit like that is why I will NEVER completely trust you'?"

"No," Shelia said.

"Do you know who she was tweeting?"

"No, not really."

"What about her last tweet, 'All I do is hope'?"

Shelia just stared at Colebank. "Probably some boy."

"Any boy in particular?"

"Not that I can think of. She and Eric Finch were close, and she had this other friend, Floyd Pancoast. Then there was Dylan Conaway. You might ask him."

Colebank scribbled in her notebook. "Have you tried calling Skylar?"

"It just makes me so sad to hear her voicemail, to hear her voice," Shelia said, looking like she might cry any second. "I can't call her number."

Colebank checked out Shelia's bedroom. It was pretty typical, except most teenager's bedrooms didn't have a cardboard toilet paper roll sitting on the desk, with some dryer sheets right beside it. Colebank recognized the homemade tool for what it was: a bounce blower. Some young people thought exhaling pot smoke through the dryer sheet kept the scent down. It didn't, really. She had suspected Shelia's parents were pretty permissive with Shelia, but this was proof.

Next Colebank asked to see Shelia's car. In fact, she wanted to see Shania and Crissy's vehicles, too. Neither one of theirs resembled the one in the grainy video, but as Colebank walked around the silver Toyota Camry she couldn't help thinking: *This could be it. It really looks like that type of car.*

Colebank glanced at Shelia periodically as she circled the little car, but the teen "didn't even bat an eyelash," the officer later said.

She also heard Shelia's firsthand account about her and Rachel dropping Skylar off. Colebank didn't buy it. Why drop Skylar off almost four blocks away for fear of waking Mary and Dave when they had picked her up nearby the apartment complex earlier that night? When she asked Shelia, the teen said Skylar had been mad and insisted on being let out there.

Something sounded wrong to Colebank's trained ear, so she had Shelia go over the entire evening again. This is what Shelia told her: She and Rachel parked on Crawford Avenue; Skylar came out her window, ran up the slight incline to where they were parked, and got in; and they turned onto Fairfield Street, where they pretty much stayed, cruising and smoking weed on the side streets of Star City. She and Rachel were both dressed in shorts and sweatshirts, and the three girls talked about Rachel's boyfriend, Skylar's money problems, and how her shift at Wendy's that day had been boring. Skylar wasn't on her phone much, but she seemed upset and began acting weird, which is when she insisted they drop her off away from her home. When Shelia asked why, Skylar refused to say. According to Shelia's second written statement, they were with her "for at the most thirty minutes."

Colebank thought that sounded plausible, so she decided to let it rest. Instead, she tried another line of questioning. "Why haven't you done more online to try to locate her?"

"I've been too upset."

"That's bullshit, and I don't believe it for a second. If that was my friend, I'd be blowing up their Facebook page. I'd be blowing their Twitter account up if I didn't know where they were. You know where she's at. So tell me."

"I told you, we dropped her off," Shelia said.

The story didn't make any sense to Colebank, and she immediately suspected Shelia was lying. She just wasn't sure why.

The key takeaway from the visit was Shelia's attitude. "I did not like Shelia from the get-go," Colebank said. "Her demeanor was wrong. Arrogant. Narcissistic. But I had nothing, no actual evidence for me to go on. It was just a gut feeling." The young officer also sensed Shelia was a very capable manipulator.

Colebank was sure of it when Shelia started crying and mumbled something about missing her best friend—and Tara shut the interview down.

―――――――――

When Colebank returned to the station she watched the video again, playing it back and forth. She realized there were a few dead spots in the surveillance coverage—which is why she couldn't see Skylar leave her bedroom window. Nor did the video show any traffic from Crawford Avenue.

Colebank did, however, see headlights from nearby cars. That fit with Shelia's statements to police, so Colebank reasoned the teen's story was plausible. Which meant the car captured by the video couldn't be Shelia's. It had to be someone else's.

The dead spots would also explain why the video didn't show Skylar going back inside—but perhaps she had crouched down beside her apartment building, hiding and waiting, and then gotten into the second car after it arrived.

Still, Colebank's gut told her it wasn't. She didn't know what it *was*, though.

A few hours later Colebank was still pondering the question of the unknown car when two retweets went out from Shelia's phone. A UHS girl had tweeted a pic of Skylar's MISSING poster, and Shelia sent it out for all her network to see. Another student had tweeted the same MISSING flyer and the message, *Hey guys this girl goes to UHS please retweet.* Shelia did.

fourteen

A Wild Child Runaway

On July 9, WBOY, one of three area TV stations, told viewers a local girl was missing. That same day, WAJR, a radio station with a popular call-in show, tweeted *Police looking for a missing Star City teen.*

One day later, *The Dominion Post* ran its own story. "Police, Family Seek Missing 16-year-old," read the headline in the July 10 edition. The story described the teenager and the clothing she was last seen wearing. It also quoted Dave, who said Skylar's cell phone was "shut off or out of power."

The article ended on a poignant note, relaying the distraught father's message for his missing daughter: *Just come home, baby.*

As the media geared up to cover the story, the Star City Police Department received good news: Skylar had been spotted in Carolina Beach, North Carolina. She was reportedly seen hanging around a boardwalk with an unidentified red-haired girl. A local woman with West Virginia connections had learned about Skylar on Facebook and called in the tip.

Colebank was skeptical. She had read Skylar's Twitter feed, and those of Shelia and Rachel. She saw the constant online arguing between them. But it was the June 9 tweets that really captured the young officer's attention. Skylar had been angry at someone but she wasn't willing to name them publicly, so she subtweeted, *youre just as bad as the bitches you complain about, and a liar,* and *well now im too fucking annoyed to sleep.*

As she read them again, looking for any clue, Colebank realized Skylar's tweets were growing angrier by the second: *fuucckk yoouu..,* then *and no I do not type like that,* which made it sound like perhaps Skylar was texting someone—or receiving texts at the same time she was tweeting. If so, it was a really good way to hide a private conversation, while blaring your anger about that person through tweets. Then there was Skylar's final tweet from the argument—and it sounded like she got the last word: *just know I know.*

Colebank leaned forward in her chair, eagerly staring at Skylar's Twitter feed. "Know what, Skylar? What did you know?" she mused, talking to the computer.

Colebank did not believe Skylar was a runaway so she doubted the teenager would surface in North Carolina. She'd been wrong before, though, and she fervently hoped she was wrong this time.

While Carolina Beach police tried to track down the lead, Colebank phoned the Neeses. Dave answered.

"Who has red hair, Dave?" Not having met her, Colebank didn't know about Rachel Shoaf's trademark tresses.

"That'd be Rachel. Why?"

"We may have something. I'll call you back."

Next, Colebank called church camp officials. It was possible Rachel had left camp, and she and Skylar had taken a mini-vacation. Maybe they were skipping out on their responsibilities and worrying their parents, acting like typical teenagers. She hoped so.

Colebank lost her optimism when camp officials put Rachel on the line. Skylar's other best friend claimed she didn't know the teen was missing. Colebank found that odd. Even if Rachel was out of touch at camp, she could have learned the news almost any time Friday before she left Morgantown. Rachel suggested Colebank call

Shelia, saying she wasn't as close to Skylar as Shelia was. Colebank said she would. Before hanging up, the young officer asked Rachel to stop by the department when she returned to Morgantown.

"I will," Rachel promised.

She never did.

Despite the absence of an AMBER Alert in Skylar's case and the lack of widespread media coverage, the news was spreading. Momentum was building on social media, especially on Facebook. More and more people were sharing Skylar's MISSING poster. On Thursday, July 12, Joanne's daughter, Rikki Woodall, posted the following:

Hey family—I'm Al & Nina's granddaughter—my cousin Skylar Neese (on my other side of the family) went missing last week. . . . She's a wild one, so we're hoping it's an extended teenage party break, but the thought of it being something else is terrifying. Would you mind please sharing this? I normally don't share things like this, but she's local in Morgantown area, and she's my family. I appreciate the help!!

In truth, Rikki did not know her cousin at all. Mary and Dave said they had never met. Despite her concern, Rikki was hardly an insider and her knowledge of the teen was based primarily on what was broadcast through social media.

Oftentimes, social media communication conceals as much as it reveals. It's not necessarily about conveying the full truth so much as sustaining a public image and managing that image. By all accounts, Skylar wanted to be *seen* as a wild child, but she wasn't, not really. Not to say she didn't occasionally get drunk or smoke weed, because she did. Accounts of her drug use vary—some teens maintain it was confined to marijuana and alcohol, while others said Skylar used other substances. In truth, the wild child image Rikki Woodall disseminated appears to have been largely manufactured by Skylar herself.

Skylar looked up to Shelia—even though she had a questionable reputation. As a result of their association with Shelia, many teens thought both Skylar and Rachel were hanging with the wrong crowd—and even tried to tell them. It did little good, since both girls loved the excitement they felt whenever they were with Shelia.

At various parties she attended, Skylar was often seen sitting on a couch by herself, playing with her phone or her iPod. Rachel was often absent from the party scene; her mother almost always refused to let her go with the other two girls. So while Shelia and her crowd were all drinking, drugging, and making out, Skylar was on Twitter.

Like so many teenagers, she wanted to be perceived as "cool." Her tweets and Facebook posts reveal a girl who just wanted to have fun. At the same time, they concealed Skylar's true nature. They obscured the girl who was insightful, had exceptional writing skills, and planned to be a criminal lawyer. This was the real Skylar, the one whose peers said was by far the smartest person in her social circle, the Skylar who was a rock for the friends who depended on her.

Not long after Skylar disappeared, Carol Michaud went to the beauty salon to have her hair done. She learned Shelia went there, too, and that's when the beautician told Skylar's aunt an odd story.

"She said she hung one of the MISSING posters in her shop, but someone took it down," Carol said.

The shop owner later said she remembered the day she hung it near the front entrance, "with tape on all four corners, so clients would see it as they were leaving."

One day when the owner went to the foyer, the MISSING poster was "just gone. I stood and stared for full two minutes," she said.

She knew the poster had been there earlier, and said she was confused about why it was gone. The poster couldn't have fallen down. Then she remembered: Shelia and her mom were there earlier, when Shelia had her hair highlighted.

Looking back, Carol had to wonder whether Shelia took it down to keep people from connecting the dots to her and Rachel. But the salon owner has another theory: she believes Tara could have removed it, "because she didn't want Shelia upset over seeing it there."

It wasn't the first time someone noticed Skylar's MISSING posters were being removed. Many volunteers who spent hours every day hanging up posters began to wonder what was happening to them. They kept disappearing. Was someone following behind and taking them down as fast as the volunteers were putting them up? The MISSING posters had been removed at more than one local grocery store. Dave's aunt Joanne said it had happened repeatedly in Sabraton, too.

It turned into another mystery, since no one could say who was behind it.

fifteen

Gone

On July 13, the day after Rikki's Facebook post, Mary and Dave loaded their bags into Carol's car and prepared to drive down to North Carolina. Skylar had bonded with her mother's sister at birth. Carol and Skylar had spent so much time together since then that Carol looked at Skylar like the daughter she never had. Skylar was also like a little sister to Carol's son, Kyle, who was two years older. Carol would do whatever it took to bring Skylar home.

Mary and Dave's car wasn't in the best shape. They had already put a ton of money into the beater to keep it on the road just so they could get to work each day. Taking it on a road trip was another matter. Dave was afraid it would break down and leave them stranded. God knows they already had enough stress; the last thing they needed was more.

They had to check on this latest Skylar sighting, though, to see for themselves if the girl spotted on the boardwalk was their daughter. For all they knew, it *was* her. In just a few hours, they believed, they might see their baby again. Carol's offer of her own car had been an answer to their prayers.

The same day Mary and Dave were getting ready to drive to North Carolina, someone who called herself "Pisces_Sun" posted on

Websleuths, one of the largest online crime discussion sites, saying she had barely seen or read anything about the story. Pisces_Sun's post highlighted a disturbing reality: *Me and my husband drove through Star City on our way to the store just now...I'm shocked that there aren't missing posters for this girl up anywhere on the main drag!...Haven't heard anyone mention it around town, either.*

Even though Skylar had been missing for one week, few people outside of Mary and Dave's immediate circles seemed to know about it. Skylar's story illustrated a sad truth: traditional media can't raise awareness as quickly as necessary in the case of a missing juvenile. Thus the need for AMBER Alerts. The program was a testament to Amber Hagerman, the 9-year-old who was riding her bicycle when she was kidnapped and brutally murdered in 1996. It was the brainchild of Dallas-Fort Worth broadcasters and local police who wanted a fast, efficient way to warn communities when children are abducted.

However, the AMBER system didn't consider Skylar to be in danger. As far as Mary and Dave were concerned, the AMBER Alert system was broken and needed to be fixed.

Once national news programs did pick up the story, the networks requested sound bites from the parents. Ultimately, all of them came from Dave because Mary couldn't look into a camera without crying uncontrollably. With his close-cropped, gray-flecked hair, knitted eyebrows, and a tight skepticism pulling at the left corner of his mouth, Dave reminded people of the actor John Goodman. In spite of his obvious concern and frustration, every news clip portrayed a man who was bearing all the disappointments with an admirable, soft-spoken dignity.

As the online momentum intensified, more people learned about Skylar's disappearance. The mainstream media struggled to catch up to all the social media sites that had been covering the story since it began. By the time the Neeses were ready to leave for what they hoped would be a joyful reunion with Skylar, Colebank got word from the Carolina Beach police. The girl who had been seen was indeed a runaway. She just wasn't Skylar.

Mary and Dave could barely find the energy to unpack Carol's car.

On Sunday, July 15, a week and a half after Skylar came up missing, Mary Neese awoke to the certainty she'd never see Skylar again. Her maternal instincts told her as much. Across town, her sister Carol had the same feeling. Carol dressed quickly and drove to Mary's.

On the way, Skylar memories kept playing inside her mind as if on a loop. Carol had been there the day Skylar was born. She had driven Mary and Skylar home when Mary called her, insistent she leave the hospital a day early. Mary, angry at Dave over some spat or another, refused to ask him for a ride. Carol never forgot how the car containing her, Mary, and their two only children spun around on black ice in the middle of a busy road. Carol held it together long enough for her husband Steve to come and rescue them. The minute she got home, though, she burst into tears.

Like Mary, Carol cries easily. She does so even as she relates stories about Skylar: the time Skylar borrowed her earrings to wear to a middle-school dance, all the times Skylar insisted she had to come clean Carol's house when Carol was sick, and every time her favorite niece gave her another teapot.

Carol entered the Neeses' apartment without knocking. In north-central West Virginia, people leave their doors unlocked when they are home—and often when they're not. It's common for relatives and close friends to simply enter, especially if they are expected. Mary was on the couch, her eyes rimmed with red.

"Carol, she's not coming back," Mary said. "If she was coming back, she'd be back. I'm telling you now."

"I know. I can feel it, too. Skylar wouldn't do this." Carol sank onto the couch beside her sister.

"You know what else?" Mary said. "Her period was going to start, and you know how she gets."

Carol nodded. "Cramps so bad she has to go to bed for the entire first day. And she always has to have Goody with her." Carol suddenly realized something. "Mary! Where's Goody?"

Mary shook her head. "In Skylar's nightstand, same as always."

"If Skylar had run away, she'd have taken Goody with her," Carol insisted. The women were referring to a fuchsia piece of cloth cut from Mary's nightgown that Skylar had kept since she was a toddler. Any time she was sick or in pain, Skylar wanted Goody nearby.

With that shared realization, Mary and Carol cried together, long and hard on the small balcony outside the dining room. They talked and wept for much of the afternoon.

When Dave got home after his shift, Mary and Carol were on the deck.

"What's wrong?" he asked, his brows knitted together with worry.

Mary spoke quietly. "Skylar's gone."

"What?" He felt suddenly panicked. "How do you know that?"

"We just know."

Dave didn't want to hear that. The family was just pulling out of a rocky patch. Skylar had sensed the change and was once more becoming the amiable and happy kid she had always been. He couldn't bear to think Skylar was never coming home.

sixteen

Digging a Hole

One week after Officer Colebank first spoke with Shelia, the Blacksville branch of the Huntington National Bank was robbed. It was just after 10:00 A.M. on Monday, July 16, when a sturdy man in black wearing a full-face mask entered the branch carrying a backpack. He didn't say a word—the large gun in his right hand said it all. The lone teller triggered the silent alarm. The thief either didn't notice or didn't care. He walked to the counter and handed the backpack to the female teller. Fingers trembling, she filled it with the contents of the cash drawer. The robber fled through the back door. From start to finish, the crime took less than thirty seconds.

Corporal Ronnie Gaskins and Senior Trooper Chris Berry from the WVSP arrived first on the scene. Trooper Berry knew the bank well. He had been transferred to Morgantown to help solve a rash of recent bank robberies. Berry's family was from the Blacksville area, so he was happy to spend time working in his hometown. His grandfather, a Monongalia County deputy sheriff, had been shot in the neck at the same bank Berry was assigned to investigate. Luckily, the shot had grazed him and only required a few stitches.

Senior Trooper Chris Berry. (Photo courtesy Dana Berry.)

Berry immediately liked Gaskins, his new partner, who was also second-generation law enforcement. At one time Gaskins and his father were the only father-son state trooper team working the same West Virginia detachment. While their personalities were like day and night—Berry, talkative and excitable; Gaskins, reserved and thoughtful—both men were driven. Their shared family tradition made for a good working relationship.

This was Gaskins and Berry's second visit to the bank, because it had been robbed over five weeks earlier, one month to the day before Skylar disappeared. Neither trooper yet knew the bank robberies would draw them into the most complex case of their careers.

————

Colebank sensed they were being watched.

She'd gotten that sensation as soon as she pulled her Star City Police cruiser into the Shoafs' driveway a few moments earlier. Sure enough, within seconds, a blonde woman appeared at the entrance of the house next door. Once she made eye contact with Colebank, the woman bustled down her walkway.

Still behind the wheel, Colebank grabbed her notebook and motioned to her male passenger. "Let's do this," she said, opening the car door. FBI Special Agent Morgan Spurlock followed her lead. In a suit and tie, Spurlock looked like a classic FBI agent—until he hoisted his ever-present backpack over his shoulder. Instead of brief-cases, today's federal agents carry backpacks.

Once outside the car, Colebank turned toward the blonde woman she thought might be Rachel's mother.

"We're here to see Rachel," Colebank said.

"Oh, I'm not Patricia," the woman said. "I'm a neighbor, Kim Keener. Her mom's not here. Can I help you?"

It was July 19, almost two weeks since Colebank had spoken with Rachel at church camp. Colebank was eager to talk to her again, but the teen had never showed up at the station as she'd promised. The officer wondered if her first face-to-face with Rachel would make her as uneasy as when she'd met Shelia.

"Yes, Star City Police." Kim had already pulled out her cell phone and was talking to someone. "It's about Skylar, I guess. They wanna ask Rachel some questions about her disappearance. You need to talk to them or come home. Okay?" Kim nodded, eyeing the officer and the agent.

She held the phone out to Spurlock. "Patricia wants to talk to you."

"Thank you, ma'am," the FBI agent said, taking the phone.

Colebank listened as he introduced himself and gave Rachel's mom the names of their respective agencies. She heard Patricia's reply, too: "Ask her whatever you want. We're trying to help here."

Patricia was two hours away when her cell phone rang. She couldn't understand why the police wanted to talk to Rachel. She had been at church camp when Skylar went missing. The police must have their facts wrong. They should be talking to Shelia; those two girls were always together.

Patricia had long ago heard what other teens said about the Eddy girl. She didn't want her daughter with Shelia or Skylar, if the two were together. So she rarely let Rachel spend any time with them.

Liz said Patricia didn't realize how serious the situation was or she would have turned around and come straight home. By the time she reached her destination, Patricia learned the full story: the FBI needed to question her daughter because Rachel was one of the last two people to see Skylar the night she disappeared. Patricia was mortified when she learned hours later Shelia was the other one.

Patricia was stunned by the realization Rachel had snuck out that night, and had been with Skylar before she went missing.

In the back of Colebank's mind was a single nagging doubt: the car has to be Shelia's. She and Spurlock had requested more security video from a couple of Star City businesses. The recordings they had already requested from corporate headquarters wouldn't arrive for at least a few days, but in the meantime they planned to scout the area for any vehicles resembling the one captured on the landlord's surveillance video.

Colebank remembered what it was like to be a teenager; high school girls are usually confused about something, and if they were high, it would be easy for their times to be off. Maybe they picked Skylar up later than they said, but they didn't realize it.

That's why Colebank wanted to talk to Rachel. She also knew the girl was religious and thought she might be easier to get information from than Shelia.

The officer hadn't conducted many interviews so she was eager to pick up a few techniques from Spurlock. He was whip-smart and Colebank hoped to learn a great deal from working with him. Even though Spurlock appeared to be in his early twenties, she knew he had extensive training in criminology and accounting, so he had to be older. She didn't realize Spurlock had only been out in the field a couple of months.

————————

By the time Spurlock returned Kim's cell phone, she had already grabbed Patricia's hidden house key. Kim unlocked the front door of the Shoaf home and yelled up the stairs. "Hey, Rach! Star City Police are here to see you!"

In the dim light, Colebank could just make out the figures of two other people who hung back, watching as Rachel walked over to the officer and the agent. Colebank didn't know Kelly Kerns, but learned Patricia had left Kelly in charge of Rachel for the weekend. Colebank immediately recognized the guy's name. He was Mikinzy Boggs, Rachel's boyfriend.

————————

Rachel and Mikinzy had recently started dating—again. The two had first gotten together at the end of the previous October, drawn together by a mutual love of the stage. Rachel sang, played guitar, and was a rising star in UHS drama circles. Mikinzy wrote songs, played guitar, and sang lead in a band christened "Call Us Next Tuesday," a name presumably chosen for its shocking acronym.

His band mostly played house parties. Slender, with a prominent nose and teeth, some people say Mikinzy looks like Napoleon Dynamite. Even so, he was the front man in a band, and as anyone who's attended high school in America knows: That. Trumps. Everything.

Their school friends knew Rachel and Mikinzy's relationship was rocky. They were always on again, off again. Some students said it was because Rachel used weed; Mikinzy was said to be an outspoken critic of drugs. Others said it was because he tried to control Rachel. Either way, by the time they were firmly committed to the relationship, Mikinzy's stance on drugs had softened considerably. Perhaps it was because Rachel frequently enjoyed getting high with Shelia and Skylar.

The day the FBI dropped in to see Rachel, she and Mikinzy were newly reunited and their bond seemed stronger, almost unbreakable. Almost.

Several minutes into the interview, Colebank felt she was getting nowhere. "So when you dropped her off—I'm sorry, Rachel, I just want to make sure we have this right. Tell me again, where did you drop her off?"

The three of them, Rachel, Colebank, and Spurlock, were talking in the upstairs living room of the Shoafs' split-level house. Rachel and Colebank faced each other on the couch. Spurlock sat alone in a chair. Kim, Kelly, and Mikinzy were downstairs in the family room.

"I told you, at the end there," Rachel whined, as if she was annoyed at having to answer the same questions again. She would glance away or doodle with her pencil on a nearby notepad. "University Avenue. Skylar got angry and told us she didn't want us to take her all the way to her apartment."

"You dropped her off," Spurlock asked, "after riding around smoking marijuana?"

Colebank broke in. "Look, Rachel, we don't care about the weed. We care about where Skylar's at. Where did you guys drive around?"

Rachel looked thoughtful, and then shrugged nonchalantly. "I'm not really sure where we drove around exactly. I was pretty messed up. I think we drove down Patteson Drive."

Patteson was the main artery leading up to the WVU Coliseum, where it formed a T intersection with Beechurst Avenue at the top of the hill. A right takes one past the State Police Detachment to Star City and a left leads along the river, into downtown Morgantown.

"Thanks." Colebank looked over at Spurlock, nodding her head. "There should be cameras."

Many businesses along Patteson had video cameras, but most focused inside the establishments, on the doors, and on parts of the parking lots. None really showed a clear view of traffic but Colebank suspected Rachel wouldn't know that.

"Yes, check the cameras," Rachel said, "but I don't know if you'll see much. We stayed on side streets as much as we could."

"Do you know the names of any of the side streets?" Colebank asked, masking a grin. She knew it was impossible to drive along Patteson *and* the side streets at the same time. She also knew people who are lying often stall by repeating the question.

"The names of the streets? How am I supposed to know that?" Rachel sighed. "They were just streets. With houses. Like a regular neighborhood. I wasn't driving. Ask Shelia."

"We have." Colebank let the silence draw out as she intently focused on Rachel. At the same time, Rachel's neighbor Kim was pacing—visiting the kitchen, perching on the steps, going up and down the stairs—as if unsure of what to do with herself. Colebank fought an urge to tell Kim to take a seat and stay there.

Eventually, Kim went downstairs with Mikinzy and Kelly. "I want to help find her, I really do," Rachel said, "but I was really loaded."

Colebank felt herself getting frustrated, but she managed to keep her voice calm. "You can't drive on Patteson Drive *and* stay on side streets, Rachel."

Colebank and Spurlock decided to focus on the contradictions in Rachel's story. With her missteps as leverage, Rachel might be convinced to explain what had really happened. From the start, Colebank had been certain something bad had gone down—an accident, an overdose, something. She was equally sure Shelia and Rachel knew what it was.

"Just tell us exactly what happened and we'll take it from there," Spurlock said. He pulled a map of Star City from his backpack and opened it up. "Maybe this will help. After you dropped your friend Skylar off—at eleven-thirty, right?—after that..."

Downstairs, Kim was talking to Mikinzy.

He was lying on the carpet, hands over his eyes. "The story was always she was home by 11:45," he kept repeating.

"Let me tell you something, Mikinzy Boggs," Kim's voice was so loud snatches of her conversation carried up the stairwell. "You don't sneak out and get back home at 11:45. Okay? I snuck out plenty. You don't sneak home at 11:45. You sneak *out* at 11:45."

"She told me she didn't," Mikinzy kept repeating. He seemed confused.

Kim and Kelly exchanged a long glance. "You know what, I'm— that doesn't even make sense on any level." Kim stomped back up the steps.

To observers, it seemed like Mikinzy[22] was doubting his girl-friend for the first time.

---

[22] Mikinzy said his comments were in reference to Rachel smoking weed.

seventeen

Business in Blacksville

The same day Colebank was interviewing Rachel, Gaskins and Berry were paying their first visit to the Conaway place. It was one of many homes in Blacksville they were visiting in their search to find out more about the bank robberies. When they pulled up to the house, they saw a man digging in the backyard. As they walked toward the front door, the man came around the corner carrying a shovel. The officers recognized him from his police mug shot.

Darek Conaway held the shovel out from his body by the tip of the handle, the muddy blade waist high. Bare-chested, Darek was clean-shaven, his hair sweat-caked to his skull. The man was ripped, all corded muscle. He glared at the two troopers. Neither trooper was easily spooked, but they tensed when they saw Darek.

"Hello, Darek," Gaskins said. "I'm Corporal Gaskins and this is Trooper Berry. We're here to chat with you a few minutes."

Darek's shovel blade lowered a little and he shrugged. "Okay."

Neither trooper wanted to square off against an angry man with a shovel, so Gaskins and Berry tried to defuse the tension.

"What are you digging back there, Darek?" Gaskins asked lightly.

"Oh, I ain't digging anything," Darek said.

"You ain't digging? You trying to hide a dead body or something?" Gaskins meant it as a joke, but that's not how Darek took it. He drew himself up, his eyes large, and Berry and Gaskins could see his heart hammering inside his chest.

The two troopers exchanged a look.

"I'm just joking with you, Darek," Gaskins said.

Just then an elderly woman poked her head around the open front door. She stepped slowly out of the shadows and onto the porch.

"Hey Grandma, it's okay," Darek said.

She walked down the steps to the front yard, clearly suspicious. "What do you want?"

Gaskins spoke up. "We're just out talking to people about those robberies. If people saw anything, heard anything.... We'd like to come in to talk with you all for a few minutes."

"I guess that would be okay," she said, turning toward the house.

Berry didn't move. "Before we go inside, ma'am, just to make me feel safe, I need to ask you a question. There any guns here at the house?"

Grandma chuckled. "Heh, this is Blacksville. There's guns in all the houses around here."

"Yeah, I know," Berry said. "I grew up over on Jake's Run. I just like to ask. I'm not saying you're going to blow me away or anything, but where's the closest one you got?"

"In my daughter's bedroom."

Berry grinned. "Oh, really. What kind you got?"

"Revolver," she said, heading back up the steps.

"I love revolvers!" Berry glanced at Gaskins like a kid with a new toy. The gun used in the bank robbery was a revolver, a type of gun that was increasingly rare. "Can I see it?"

"Sure, come on in."

Berry went inside with Grandma while Gaskins waited in the yard with Darek. A few moments later, Berry came back holding a black revolver. The weapon looked just like the one from the bank security video.

Within a few hours, Gaskins and Berry returned to the Conaways with a search warrant. They wanted to confiscate the gun before Darek had a chance to ditch it. They brought along a State Police Special Response Team, a tactical team, in case Darek got squirrelly. He didn't.

Hours later, the thirty-member team had confiscated not only the revolver but several other firearms and items of clothing they believed matched those worn by the bank robber. Even if the search turned up nothing more, Gaskins and Berry were convinced they had unfinished business with Darek Conaway.

eighteen

The Wall Is Built

Jessica Colebank knew Rachel was lying long before the Shoafs' front door closed behind her. She and Spurlock had talked with the teen for an hour and a half but they knew little more than when they arrived. The interview told her Rachel was stonewalling as much as Shelia.

Colebank couldn't figure out why or what they had to lie about. Nonetheless, their behavior and attitudes turned her initial frustration into anger. She was mad Skylar was still missing, angry she wasn't getting answers, and pissed Rachel's and Shelia's parents seemed more concerned about their precious daughters than about finding Skylar. They were clueless.

She was also sure they knew more than they were saying. After Colebank had combed through the Twitter feeds of all three girls, she was more convinced than ever Skylar was angry with both girls on June 9, when she tweeted: *just know I know*. The only problem was, she had no proof.

Then there was Skylar's next-to-last tweet, *you doing shit like that is why I will NEVER completely trust you*. From everything Skylar's friends—Daniel, Hayden, Shania, among others—said, it looked like Skylar was upset because Shelia and Rachel had been leaving her behind lately. So maybe the night she snuck out, Skylar realized her two best friends were going to a party without her. She could have called another friend and asked for a ride so she could join in the fun, too. If so, they needed to find that car.

Colebank realized the teens' cell phone records would help clear up the mystery. She would need warrants, and she was going to start by searching Shelia's and Rachel's cell phone records. If she needed to, she could branch out from there, getting warrants for other teens' phones. Maybe if she could piece together the tweets with the texts, as well as see who called whom that night, she would be able to come up with answers.

The process was time intensive. There was no telling how long it would take the phone companies to respond—but it needed to be done. Colebank could not escape the feeling those girls were hiding something.

It also bothered her that Shelia seemed to be asking more questions than anyone in her situation should be. "Anytime I talked to Shelia," Colebank later recalled, "she'd say, 'What have you figured out? What do you know?'"

Shelia didn't call Colebank or seek her out, but whenever the officer called to set up an interview, Shelia immediately wanted to know how the investigation was going. She didn't seem intimidated by the constant questioning. In fact, Colebank thought the teen brash for even asking, and she didn't like it that Shelia seemed amused.

Colebank's concern over Shelia's behavior turned to alarm when she learned Shelia was asking Mary and Dave the same questions. She urged them to stop telling Shelia or Rachel anything. *At all.*

"They're wanting to know where we're at in the case," Colebank warned.

Mary and Dave waved her concern away, defending the teens as good friends who were simply worried about Skylar. The Neeses had known Shelia for many years and were confident if the teen knew anything useful, she would say so. They didn't know Rachel well, but they automatically felt protective toward her, as they did with all of Skylar's friends. They were afraid cutting off communication with Shelia was the worst approach. After the tragedy of Skylar's disappearance, the Neeses also felt like they needed the teens as much as the teens needed them.

Colebank disagreed. She was certain Shelia's "concern" was nothing of the kind, and suspected Shelia was doing something she'd seen other people do—trying to insert herself into the investigation. Shelia could be doing it for the thrill of being on the "inside," but Colebank was afraid that wasn't it at all. Whatever Shelia's real reason, the young investigator was determined to find out.

At the same time, Colebank also wondered what Rachel was hiding. Whereas Shelia probed for information, Rachel was wide-eyed and solicitous. Plus, the teen actress kept claiming she had been too drunk and stoned to remember anything.

Looking back, Colebank realized how different the two teens' demeanors were. Shelia was crafty, but Rachel came across as wanting to say the right thing. "It was a little more sincere, I guess you could say. You could sense shame or...a lot of it was fear. We got fear."

nineteen

A Spy in the House?

Officer Colebank wasn't the only person who was angry. Mary Neese was growing more annoyed by the day and Dave wasn't far behind. By the time Wednesday, July 25, rolled around, Skylar's parents were addled and exhausted from worry, fear, and the slowly dimming hope their daughter was still alive. It had been almost three weeks since that horrible first weekend and they found themselves reacting like robots to one strange event after another. A rumor here. A sighting there. Along the way, they continued to help hang more posters, walk the rail-trail yet one more time, and search continuously for any sign of their missing daughter.

They still tried to go to work, even though they couldn't always manage it. The constant, overwhelming sorrow made it difficult to get out of bed in the morning, or to go to sleep in the evening. Their days had become nothing more than a string of minutes and hours, allocated to whatever needed to be done next. Maybe Dave needed to give another interview or Mary felt compelled to chase down another Facebook lead. Sometimes they had to meet with police. Before long, they weren't even sure what day of the week it was.

One day Star City cops again told Mary and Dave they had received word of several Skylar sightings—this time in Sabraton. The

Morgantown City Police, a much larger force, had been monitoring the tips, but Dave felt the need to do something. Anything.

So he staked out a supposed "drug house" in Sabraton for several days. It was in a rundown part of the neighborhood known as an easy place to get drugs. Many of the rumors Dave had heard connected Skylar's disappearance to drugs. Because Dave had once been addicted to prescription painkillers following a work-related injury, he knew what to look for. He knew which people to watch on the street, what their reddened eyes would reveal, how the desperation on their faces could betray them.

For days on end, Dave faithfully watched the house. Whenever he saw someone who had all the signs of an addict, Dave got out of his car to investigate. Sometimes they mistook him for a dealer, and asked what he was selling. Other times he was mistaken for a buyer, and they offered to sell him something. They occasionally believed he was an undercover cop—and then they usually turned and ran. Except for the time he saw a woman so ravaged by her addiction she couldn't stop shaking. She and the man she was with looked at Dave with eyes full of fear when he approached them.

"Listen, I'm not a cop. I'm just a father looking for my daughter," Dave said as he held up Skylar's photo. "Have you seen her? Please, I have to know."

During the times people believed he was a junkie, it was almost tempting to take what they offered, but Dave refused to return to that life. Despite knowing drugs would envelop his conscious thoughts in a wad of cotton so thick he would no longer feel the pain, Dave still couldn't do it. He'd made a promise to Skylar and he intended to keep it. He was going to be clean for the day when she finally came home.

It was hard work. The toll it took was even greater. No matter how many times Dave handed out Skylar's picture or begged the junkies to tell him if they had seen her, they never could. They didn't even know her and they certainly hadn't seen her. Not in Sabraton.

Still Dave kept waiting and watching—but finding nothing.

It's ironic: as much as people say they hate crime, they love to talk about it. This explains why crime discussion sites see some of the heaviest traffic on the internet.

Websleuths is one of the largest, with hundreds of threads. The discussions range from high-profile cases like the JonBenet Ramsey murder to obscure unsolved crimes. Anyone can start a thread on any topic.

Someone named "kmartin96" introduced a Websleuths thread about Skylar one week after the teen disappeared: *WV - Skylar Neese, 16, Star City, 6 July 2012.* He included a brief description of Skylar and a link to one of the MISSING posters. The earliest participants on the thread tried to expand on what little information was available.

On July 25, "Sheromom" voiced her aggravation: *I don't understand why some cases are followed so closely that I can't keep up and yet here is this beautiful young lady that no one seems to care about?*

Wherever Skylar's name was mentioned on social media, you could find people like Sheromom. Their written posts revealed a common complaint: they were angry over law enforcement's perceived failure to do anything. They were annoyed by the lack of information about the case. The boiling point was finally reached on Facebook. Scalding criticism poured out of Becky Bailey, an old high school friend of Dave's. Her online rant would eventually grow into landmark legislation, becoming law less than one year after Skylar disappeared.

Across town on Wednesday, July 25, Shelia was hating the day. Since she seemed so disturbed by Skylar's disappearance, Tara packed her daughter off to visit family in Florida. That morning she tweeted, *seriously not looking forward to this 17 hour car ride.*

By Saturday, Shelia's visit with her Florida family was well under-way. Her attitude remained sour though, as seen by a tweet to Shania: *getting up this early and going to the beach isn't even enjoyable.*

That same afternoon, Shania and her grandmother, Linda, visited the Neeses, as they had every day since Shania returned from the beach. Mary noticed Shania was often texting while she talked about the police investigation. It was as if the teen was more interested in her phone than what was going on around her. Mary suddenly realized: once Shelia left for the beach, *Shania* had begun asking questions about the investigation. Her sudden interest caught Mary's attention.

"You're always playing with your phone," Mary said. "Who are you texting all the damn time?"

"Shelia. She wants to know how it's going."

"I'll bet she does." Mary remembered Colebank's warning about talking to Shelia, and she was instantly suspicious of Shelia's motives. Moreover, she was furious.

"She's just scared for Skylar," Shania said.

"Right." Mary's sarcasm was palpable.

With all the commotion, Shania didn't hear her cell phone ring-ing. When it suddenly began vibrating like crazy, Shania looked down at her phone. She had a missed call from Shelia. When she didn't get the call, Shelia had blown up Shania's phone with several text messages, begging Shania to call her back.

Shania called Shelia while Mary continued to vent to Linda, loudly, about her suspicions that both girls were up to no good.

"Mary found out I was texting you," Shania said. After a brief pause, she added, "She thinks I'm passing info to you."

"This was supposed to be about Skylar," Mary said, still angry, "but you two are acting like it's all about you."

"Is she mad at me?" Shelia asked Shania.

"Oh, yeah. She's pissed. I don't think she believes you."

"About what?"

"She thinks you're not telling her something. But you are, right?"

"Mary doesn't believe me?"

"I don't think so," Shania said. "Look, Shelia, you can't lie. Just tell Mary anything you know. Now."

Shelia completely lost it, sobbing into the phone she wasn't lying and Mary had to believe her. She *had to*.

Shania held the phone away from her ear and everyone heard Shelia: "I've got to talk to her. She has to know I'm not lying."

"She wants to talk to you." Shania reached toward Mary, who snatched the phone.

"I know when you're lying. I helped cover for you too much, remember?" Mary said, referring to all the times she had tried to save Shelia from punishment.

Shelia continued to sob.

"Remember? I know when you're lying," Mary repeated.

"Please, Mary! Please!" Shelia pleaded through sobs. "You have got to believe me!"

"Why should I?" Mary was beyond disgust. "Would *you* believe you?"

There was a pause, then Shelia sniffed and murmured a word Mary thought sounded like, "No."

twenty

Facebook Friction

Across town, someone else was growing suspicious, too. The boy with the blond curls was one of Skylar's closest confidants—and vice versa. Although it's true Skylar didn't share much with anyone, if she did have something important to reveal, Daniel was one of the few people she would confide in.

Soft-spoken, with a pleasant and easy manner, Daniel really *sees* the people around him. He is wary with strangers but reveals an impish side once he feels comfortable.

Daniel knew he could trust Skylar with his deepest secrets so he came out as gay to her before he told anyone else. All his fears about revealing such a personal detail in a small town vanished when Skylar responded with love and unconditional acceptance.

In February of their sophomore year, Skylar had gotten Daniel a job at Wendy's. He tended to goof off at work, snapping photos and clowning around, while Skylar was all business. She was more committed in her academic life as well, but Daniel didn't mind. At that point he wasn't serious about much of anything.

That all changed after Skylar disappeared. Daniel became obsessed with one tremendously important matter—figuring out what had happened to his dear friend. Daniel began to reason that since Shelia and Rachel were the last two people to see Skylar, they had to know something. Skylar had said something, done something, texted someone, while she was joyriding with them. Daniel wasn't sure what they knew, but he planned to find out.

When he looked back on all their time together, Daniel began to remember small details he had noticed in the months leading up to Skylar's disappearance—tidbits about the three girls' behavior strange enough to get stuck inside his mind. These details haunted him and his close proximity to Rachel provided his suspicions with an easy target.

Having a goal for the first time in his life gave Daniel focus and drive. He vowed he would not give up until Rachel Shoaf came clean.

By the time Skylar had been gone a month, the rumors were out of control, both in real time and online. Some Morgantown teenagers believed Skylar was off partying and would be back soon. Many adults thought this, too. But the peers who knew her best were highly doubtful—such cavalier behavior wasn't characteristic of the Skylar they knew. Another theory suggested Skylar had met up with a boy and run off. Again, her inner circle thought that unlikely. Other, darker rumors had begun to circulate as well. Some wondered if Skylar had hooked up with an internet predator or had been abducted by a pedophile. After all, teens heard about these kinds of scenarios in the news all too often.

Less malevolent but equally disturbing rumors were floated on Facebook and discussion sites: Skylar went to a party and got drunk, fell, hit her head, and died. Skylar overdosed on drugs and died. On some boards the speculation turned lurid: Skylar was using hard drugs and running with the wrong people. Skylar was trading sex for drugs and was then killed when she fell in with a nasty crowd. Of course these rumors wounded Mary and Dave, who could only watch helplessly as the gossip grew. They knew the awful lies were baseless, but they were powerless to stop them. Besides, they had no concrete leads, either.

However, the teenagers who knew Skylar best had begun to believe one particular rumor. As it turned out, area students believed what Officer Colebank and Special Agent Spurlock suspected: Shelia and Rachel were lying.

By then Colebank and Spurlock had questioned Shelia and Rachel a number of times. They had their own opinions about each girl. Colebank believed from the very beginning the two teens knew something: "[Rachel] stuck with the story Shelia first gave. Their story was exactly—verbatim—the same. It was word for word."

Until it wasn't, and Rachel's version veered away from Shelia's.

Without access to the results of the psychological tests performed on Shelia, it's hard to say if her next actions were those of a scheming sociopath playing a game, a psychopath carrying out a devious plan, or simply those of a teenage girl living in denial about her part in a hideous crime. In hindsight they appear dark no matter how they're construed.

On August 6, one month to the day after Skylar disappeared, Shelia entered Skylar's inner circle of family and friends with her first post on the "TeamSkylar<3" page. She posted a photo showing her and Skylar from happier days. The picture showed Shelia smiling, head turned slightly, eyes closed, wearing a red tank top with white print flowers. Skylar is next to her, her right hand on Shelia's bare shoulder, her face pressed to Shelia's hair as if she's about to whisper something, her eyes peeking impishly toward the camera.

Shelia had been the photographer, taking a "selfie" of the pair. Underneath it she wrote, *want my bestfriend back <3*. Shelia's words—and the symbol </3—told the world her heart was broken.

Within minutes, eighty-two people signaled their approval by clicking Like. A little later Dave weighed in: *Love you Shelia, I want her back too.* In spite of his own pain, Dave wanted to be there for his daughter's friend.

A small cascade of approval followed with comments from: *Skylar your family and friends miss you* to *So glad to see something like this!* That evening, Shelia reciprocated: *thanks guys. love you too Dave.*

Her post was a hit.

TeamSkylar<3 soon became *the* place to post about all things Skylar. Anyone who wanted to learn more about the missing girl, offer assistance, leave a warm thought, or even discuss the case could do so. All they had to do was join the group, which was designated as open to the public. In short, everything the group did could be seen by the outside world—and it was. In a very big way.

Skylar's distant cousin, Hayden Hunt, started the group in July after he learned about her disappearance. Hayden lived with his mother, Jennifer, in Maryland and may have created the group because she asked him to. Jennifer had only met her distant cousin Dave once; Dave doesn't remember ever meeting Hayden. Nonetheless, the Hunts seemed to want to help. They even added links to their Facebook page so people could click, download, and print MISSING posters of Skylar.

Over the next few months, the TeamSkylar<3 group would evolve into a nasty source for gossip and innuendo—and a considerable source of stress for Mary and Dave. However, when it first began, neither of Skylar's parents knew much about social media or how to use it. TeamSkylar<3 soon became the easiest place for the Neeses to find an outpouring of support and sympathy. The page was also the first online group where their friends and the general public could show how much they cared about Skylar and her distraught parents.

One teen after another joined the group to leave messages for Skylar, hoping she would see them. The kids tried to get her attention. They urged her to let them know she was safe. Some teens reminded her school would resume in a week. Surely she would return to pick up where she'd left off, as a junior. School was what Skylar lived for. One teen's simple hope was heartbreaking: *Skylar, please come home, we miss you and just want you home safely. Your parents...just want to know your alright. You can even call me....I won't tell anyone where your at or what your doing. 304-555-9157 come home Skylar we love you.*

Four days after her first post, Shelia spoke up on the group page again. Her comment was equal parts longing for Skylar's return and something else entirely, something no other member of the group knew or particularly cared about:

all i want is for my bestfriend to come home. i wish i knew something to give the police a lead or so she can come home but i don't know ANYTHING....i wish i knew something like everybody thinks i do. come home skylar, it's been five weeks too long. i miss and love you.

With her post, Shelia revealed she clearly knew law enforcement was watching. She also knew exactly who they had their eyes on: her.

Meanwhile, on August 7, the unthinkable happened, giving police and the public even more to worry about. A local NBC affiliate station, WBOY, ran a brief story about a second missing teenage girl in Star City. The townspeople were horrified, afraid a serial killer was in their midst.

"The Star City Police Department is looking for another missing teenage girl. Police said Elise Nix, 16, was last seen at her home on Saturday and was reported missing on Monday...It was just one month ago that Skylar Neese, 16, was reported missing after she was last seen at her home in Star City. Neese is still missing. If you have any information, call the Star City police at (304) 555-4707."

Blind terror swept over Mary and Dave. Friends and residents throughout the region had similar reactions. Their worst fears could be true; Star City might have a predator loose. If so, he was targeting teenage girls.

Elise Nix was found the next day. She was merely staying with a friend, she told authorities. Her case turned out to be typical of the runaways Colebank searched for: gone a few hours or overnight, later found at a party or staying at a friend's house.

Mary and Dave's reaction to the news of Nix's disappearance illustrated just one effect losing Skylar had on them. Now Mary and Dave keenly felt the pain of any parents whose child vanished.

twenty-one

Social Problems

When Dave read Shelia's August 10, 2012, post, he swallowed the lump in his throat, placed his large hands on the keyboard, and began to type: *Hang tough babe. Do not let things get you down!*

Despite Mary's growing suspicion that Shelia was lying, Dave didn't let it stop him from weighing in with his support. It was, after all, what Skylar herself would have done if the tables were turned and Shelia was missing. Skylar had a big heart, and was always doing things for other people—especially if they didn't have anyone else to come to their aid. Dave and Mary repeatedly said Shelia was like a daughter to them—before and after Skylar's death. They joked about it with the girls themselves, when Skylar was still alive. They continued saying it when she no longer was—repeatedly, online, and in front of the TV cameras.

After a while, Shelia replied to Dave's paternal post: *it's hard but im trying, love you!*

Looking back, the Lawrences all agreed: eighth grade was the turning point in Skylar's life. Morgan said Skylar seemed to change right before high school: "Skylar as a seventh grader, I don't think I ever could have seen her doing the things she did as a sophomore. She was always very goody, very innocent in everything. Then we got to freshman year, and Shelia showed up and things started changing."

Morgan tried to advise her friend against hanging out with the new crowd, but Skylar wouldn't be dissuaded.

Shelia wasn't the only one Morgan worried about, although she admitted Shelia was sneaky. That new crowd was composed of girls who were experimenting with drugs and sex, and who ran around with older boys—even college-age ones. Boys Morgan didn't know—and didn't want to know.

Ever so slowly, Morgan's friendship with Skylar slipped away. Even though the three girls—Morgan, Skylar, and Shelia—had freshman history together, Skylar was pulling away from Morgan and vice versa.

"It happened gradually over that year," Morgan recalled. "I had friends other than just Skylar, and Shelia only had Skylar because Shelia had only been at that school for three months...More and more, every time you had to pick a partner, it was them. Every time you had a conversation, it was just them."

Still, Morgan wasn't overly concerned when she first heard Skylar was missing. She thought Skylar was mad at "Miss Mary." Morgan knew Skylar would be back as soon as she cooled off.

But when Skylar was still gone a week later, Morgan's thoughts turned dark. "She's not coming back," Morgan told her mother, Cheryl.

———————

Skylar wasn't just leaving long-time friends like Morgan Lawrence behind. As with most teenagers, Skylar had begun drawing away from her parents. She still loved Mary and Dave and spoke highly of them—even to her peers. However, independence was coming too quickly and Skylar was forging ahead in her own world.

When Skylar's relationship with Shelia intensified, the entire social foundation Skylar had built over the years began to shift. Many of Skylar's other friends drew away because of how they felt about Shelia. They preferred not to be around her. A few even described Shelia as "bad news" long before the murder.

Even though Skylar was aware her friends were uneasy about Shelia, it didn't matter. When Skylar wanted something she couldn't be denied, and her obsession with Shelia was consuming. By nature Skylar was caring and responsible, but right then, more than anything, she wanted to have fun and be cool, and Skylar equated Shelia with both.

Even Officer Colebank agreed. "Shelia carries herself well in front of other people. She's pretty. She has pretty hair." In short, Shelia's looks perfectly fit the standard for teenage beauty. Colebank believes Skylar compared herself to Shelia and wanted to do all the things Shelia could do and get away with.

Skylar also met people through Shelia—Crissy Swanson, Shania Ammons, Eric Finch, Dylan Conaway, and even Rachel Shoaf—people she might never have met on her own. During her freshman year, while hanging out with this edgier crowd and experiencing the world in a new, adventurous way, Skylar began habitually sneaking out of the house at night.

As teenage mischief goes, Skylar's was fairly benign at first. She mostly snuck out on weekends during the school year and typically rode around with her friends. They smoked pot sometimes, but that doesn't seem to be the primary reason Skylar snuck out. Skylar left mostly to socialize. At night, in the dark and in secret, Skylar was becoming her own person.

———

Mary believes Skylar's problems began when Shelia moved to town: "They were always together at school, always together [after school]. That is when Skylar seemed to start getting in trouble. Her attitude changed. She was nastier, more argumentative."

One huge regret for Mary and Dave is not paying more attention to the changes in Skylar's behavior. Even more, they regret not realizing where those changes were coming from—since they now know Skylar's behavior was tied to her friendship with both girls. Shelia especially seemed to be a bad influence.

Mary remembers the time she and Skylar got into a screaming fight while Skylar was on the phone with Shelia. As Skylar accused Dave and Mary of trying to control her, she used language her parents rarely heard from her. Looking back, Mary realized Skylar sounded like Shelia's clone. She called Mary disrespectful names, like the ones Shelia called her mother.

In hindsight, Mary now believes Skylar was putting on a performance for Shelia to gain her friend's approval. Skylar wanted Shelia to see that she was cool.

Mary wishes with all her heart she had recognized what was really happening to her daughter.

twenty-two

Roll Call

Everyone had a message for Skylar. People from around the world posted greetings and other words of comfort on the TeamSkylar<3 page the week before school resumed. Mostly they wrote they hoped the pretty teen was safe. They also wished she could read their messages. And they prayed Skylar would return home so she could start school with the classmates who missed her.

Shania Ammons' poignant message told Skylar no problem was too big to prevent her friend's return: *come home babe. that's all we ask. our junior year starts this week and you need to be here.... whatever is bothering you we can work through it.... <3*

Long-time friend and fellow Wendy's employee, Hayden McClead, added a moving message: *Skylar, it's been wayyy to long since we last talked. schools starting in 4 days and I don't know what I'll do without you there. I miss having you there when I need advice on something.... I hate going everyday and you not being there....*

Even Shelia's mother, Tara, had a message: *Hello Skylar. I hope that you are reading this post. You need to come home. Shelia is really missing you.... Your friends need you to be in school Thursday morning. I love you and hope that you come home soon.*

While words of love and encouragement were pouring in, fissures were forming in TeamSkylar<3. Among the more than 3,000 members, sniping and insinuations were becoming the norm. To make matters worse, the Hunts took away Mary and Dave's administrative rights. While Skylar's parents wanted to control the sniping by denying access to "haters," the mother-son administrative team refused to monitor what people said in their posts. Censorship was not part of the group's plan. Jennifer Hunt claimed the decision to remove the Neeses as administrators was made for "legal reasons." Without any sort of boundaries, TeamSkylar<3 was rapidly becoming a place to bicker. More and more, it was attracting mean-spirited people.

Mary and Dave could only watch in growing pain and horror as one person after another made false accusations. They had seen suggestions that they had caused Skylar to run away, that Dave was abusing Skylar, even that Dave had gotten Skylar pregnant. Wild speculation was rampant. The site that began as a tool to help find Skylar slowly turned into one that blamed her own parents of being responsible for her disappearance. Heartbroken and disgusted, Dave and Mary finally turned off their computer.

Stressed and alone in their Star City apartment, Skylar's parents couldn't even look at each other, much less speak. They were afraid the poison spilling over onto the TeamSkylar<3 page would somehow find its way into their home. They vowed not to let that happen. When Skylar walked through their apartment door, they didn't want her to see them snapping and screaming at each other.

One day, after having a cigarette on the back deck, Mary went to their bedroom and wept. Dave tapped up the volume on the remote until the TV was so loud he couldn't hear his own thoughts. Hours later, with a little help from the sleeping pills their doctor had prescribed, Mary and Dave finally found a bit of respite. Exhausted by worry, they slept for hours.

The next day Mary and Dave took control of the situation: they started their own Facebook group. Weariness with the growing discord had overtaken a number of TeamSkylar<3 members. Skylar's parents weren't the only ones who were fed up. Another member took the step of deleting herself—but not before trying to reach out to the rest of the group. She asked, in part, for all family members and friends and *the good people who are trying to help us find* [Skylar]…*please leave this group and come to the TEAMSKYLAR 2012 group this group has denied administration rights to the parents of skylar.… We don't think this is right.*

With that, the fracture was complete. TEAMSKYLAR 2012, a closed group, was up and running. Now there were two main Facebook groups—plus a dozen smaller groups or tribute pages—but the two main groups were at war.

Meanwhile, Skylar's absence left a hole in the hearts of her classmates when school resumed. Many of her good friends thought she might actually show up for the first day back, but on August 16, 2012, Skylar was no less gone than she had been on July 6, when Dave Neese found his daughter's bedroom empty.

Everyone who knew Skylar almost expected to see the famous trio stationed in their usual place at one of the four pillars in the UHS cafeteria. Logic told them Skylar had been gone since July, but something in their brains anticipated seeing her there, still hanging out with her two best friends.

"It was always Skylar, Shelia, and Rachel," several students recalled.

But not that day. As other students filed in, Shelia and Rachel stood alone. Their heads bent close, they talked only to each other. Their voices were hushed in the din of arriving students. Seeing the two together only made Skylar's absence more pronounced and it was jarring for many teens who passed by.

By this time the teens knew about Skylar's disappearance. The students knew about Shelia and Rachel's involvement, too—or thought they did. They had seen the various rumors texted, tweeted, and posted all over each other's cell phones and social media sites. They had heard the gossip as it spread through town—at coffee shops, fast-food restaurants, and all the other places where teens hang out. Of course, few students then blamed Shelia and Rachel for Skylar's disappearance.

At least one person was sure of it, however: Daniel Hovatter. He knew Skylar wouldn't be at school, but he wanted to believe she would be. He had even worn his brand-new gray and orange pullover with a pair of black-and-white plaid shorts and Nike sandals just to hear her tease him. The two shared a trust that let them rib each other, and both teens enjoyed it.

Daniel and another friend talked about how strange it was to have someone from their school missing as they continued along the familiar route the first day back to school for the fall semester 2012. Daniel recalled the last time he and Skylar had been together on the bus.

"I don't want to sit with some creep!" Skylar had said when reminding him to save her a seat on the morning bus, not that Daniel needed reminding. He always saved her a seat even though he had to protect it from students who got on before she did.

Skylar was his rock. Throughout that spring she had repeatedly helped him. Daniel's parents argued constantly and he often had to hide in his room or go out for long walks. With Skylar, he could vent.

"Life with my parents is shitty," he told her.

Skylar was optimistic and assured him the situation would improve. "Try to talk to them about what they're fighting about," she said. "See if you can help make it better."

That was Skylar's way: roll up your sleeves and dive in.

For Daniel, riding bus 257 would never seem the same again. Not without Skylar sharing his seat.

———

After getting off the bus, Daniel entered UHS through the back door of the school cafeteria. He stood with the rest of the student body, corralled there until the main doors opened, texting on his cell phone while waiting for the buzzer to signal the start of the new school year.

Jordan Carter saw Daniel when she arrived. She had been worried about Skylar since Jordan's mom first texted her about a missing UHS student. Jordan's mom was a big fan of Facebook and had seen the news there.

Omg! Jordan texted back. *That's Skylar, my friend from Kaleidoscope!* She recalled the summer program where she and Skylar had met years before. Skylar had been the only girl who would get ice cream at the swimming pool with her. Because Jordan was two years older than Skylar, their only other interaction was brief. They were in the band together for a year in middle school. Skylar had played flute, Jordan the cymbals.

Since Jordan dated one of Mikinzy Boggs' bandmates, she knew Mikinzy and Rachel were an item, so she was eager to see her school friends. She hoped they had good news about Skylar. More than anything else Jordan wanted her childhood buddy to show up.

So did Daniel, which is why he kept watching the pillar where Rachel's red head bent close to Shelia's darker one. By the time the bell rang and students scurried off to class, Skylar still hadn't turned up.

Daniel was afraid she never would.

University High School in winter. Photo courtesy Meredith Marsh.

When Skylar didn't appear in her scheduled classes, it signaled a finality: Skylar wasn't coming back. Many students knew about Skylar's disappearance and had followed the unfolding events online. But there were many teachers who had not. In at least three classes—chemistry, algebra, and AP English—teachers called Skylar's name during roll call. The silence afterward in one class was deafening.

"Skylar?" said Mr. Fisher. "Skylar Neese?"

The deep voice of a male student spoke up. "Uh, she's not here."

"Our first absence, then," the teacher said, bending down to make a mark next to Skylar's name.

"No, she's missing," a small female voice said.

That student said Mr. Fisher glanced up and saw everyone looking at him. "Oh, I'm so sorry. I didn't know."

She looked around, and realized she wasn't the only one crying.

———————

A few miles away in Star City, Mary Neese had taken the day off work—just in case. Because Skylar loved school, her parents thought she might return for the new school year. Mary had put in a request with her supervisor for time off, hoping for a miracle.

But it never happened. When the *Dominion Post* interviewed Dave, he said it was a crushing blow. What he didn't say was he and Mary both felt like they had a hole in their hearts.

twenty-three

Two's Company . . .

"Leave me alone, Daniel," Rachel hissed across the aisle in drama class. Daniel laughed, even though the situation wasn't funny at all. Ever since Skylar disappeared, he had learned laughing was easier than crying or screaming. School had been back in session for only one day, but Daniel was already tired of Rachel saying she didn't know anything else. She refused to say much about Skylar or her disappearance, but he was positive she had crucial information. After all, Rachel and Shelia had been the last known people to see Skylar before she got into the strange car. Daniel knew what she and Shelia had told police—because Mary and Dave told him.

"Right, like you just drove around for, like, an hour, then dropped her off. The most boring joyride ever." Daniel was disgusted. Rachel kept telling him the same story, like her voice was a looped recording. When he first heard Skylar had run away, Daniel didn't believe it for a second. He and Skylar worked together at Wendy's that day. She would have told him if something was wrong. No way Skylar would have run away without telling Daniel.

"Shut up, Daniel," Rachel said a little too loudly. Rachel had a flair for the dramatic.

From the front of the classroom, Mr. Kyer stopped talking and glared at them.

Daniel saw the glower and chalked it up to Rachel being one of Richard Kyer's favorite students. Whenever anyone said that, Mr. Kyer insisted he didn't have favorites. He said he treated all students fairly, but pushed the talented students harder than the rest. Many students agreed with him, since numerous teens thought the drama teacher was the closest thing to a saint they could imagine.

Daniel was leaving class when Mr. Kyer stopped him. "Daniel, you can't be accusing Rachel of doing something wrong without proof. This is America and people are innocent until proven guilty. If you have other evidence, then you need to tell the police."

That was the problem: Daniel didn't have any evidence. He just had a gut feeling based on how the girls were acting.

Daniel decided to back off, but only for the moment. He had been missing his buddy Skylar for almost six weeks, but now that he had access to Rachel, he was going to get answers. He had no plans to question Shelia. He never cared much for her. In fact, Daniel only hung out with Shelia because of Skylar. But Rachel, she would tell him the truth. Or else.

———————

But what if that truth—whatever *it* was—made Skylar look bad?

Ken Lanning says truth is complex. "Society wants simple answers to problems. They don't want complicated" ones that involve looking at multiple layers that lead to a murder like this one.

The long-time criminal profiler is now retired but he taught in the FBI's Behavioral Analysis Unit (BAU) at Quantico for more than two decades. Lanning has investigated many high-profile murder cases and says when it comes to crimes like this one, people often want a simplistic answer. They want it to be black and white, or good versus evil. Unfortunately, it's rarely that easy.

For instance, Skylar could be "the representation of all the things that [a killer] sees is wrong with her life," Lanning said. Or it could be Skylar unknowingly acted in a way that made Shelia and Rachel feel the need to kill her.

———————

As word of Skylar's disappearance spread, the world outside the high school walls began to feel the effects of her loss. Area parents couldn't comprehend the torment the Neeses must have been enduring. It was all too easy to imagine the horror of losing one's own child someday. But how terrible it would be if a daughter or son actually disappeared.

Communities grieve in their own ways. The grief must find a place to go, a way to find expression. A number of charity events were held around the greater Morgantown area the first few months after Skylar vanished. The Walmart in University Town Centre, where Dave worked, staged a candlelight vigil in August. T-shirts with Skylar's name and picture were sold at the event and $3,100 was raised for a "reward fund" established in Skylar's name. People donated because they wanted to help and needed to do something—anything.

A few weeks later the nearby town of Mannington hosted "Sky Ride," a community gathering held in Skylar's honor. Mary had grown up in Mannington, an old coal-mining town, along with her fourteen siblings. Practically the entire town turned out in a show of support. People jumped onto their ATVs and rode for hours around the local hills. Everyone brought a covered dish and after a long day in the sun, they broke bread together. Even more money was raised for the reward fund through an auction and a drawing. "Bring Skylar home!" was the day's theme, and against all logic some attendees hoped the missing teen might somehow show up. The weight of a missing child was a heavy burden for the small community.

According to WBOY TV, one woman in attendance, a friend of the Neeses, wistfully recalled, "I remember Skylar from when she was a little girl, four or five years old, and she was always running around with curls bouncing. She was the cutest little thing. When I heard that it was her who was missing, it just broke my heart."

Fortunately, the hometown show of support gave Mary and Dave a respite of sorts. They smiled and laughed with friends and family and actually felt lighter for a few hours. Even so, Skylar was never far from their minds. As dusk drew near and people began heading home, Mary and Dave returned to reality with heavy, aching hearts.

The truth is, just as Daniel suspected, that friction had begun to develop among Skylar, Shelia, and Rachel during their sophomore year. For a brief period, Skylar and Rachel were close, then they seemed to drift apart. It was her fading friendship with Shelia that Skylar bemoaned the most. Skylar even wrote about this in an essay for English class. There, she talked about how much Shelia changed after getting involved with a boy. Skylar wrote that the widening gulf between herself and her friend made her very sad.

On February 2, 2012, Skylar reflected on how this happened:

"I used to be extremely close with a girl who I loved dearly. She had such a fun personality and didn't have a care in the world about what people thought of her. That all changed dramaticilly [sic] when she got a new boyfriend. She transformed from an independent, free spirit into a needy doormat. Her boyfriend became all she cared about and began losing self-respect. I hated watching my dear friend change before my eyes. Sadly we're no longer close, but even if we were she's not be [sic] person I became friends with."

In truth, Skylar and Rachel were never as close as Shelia was with either girl. Skylar and Shelia's bond went back almost a decade, but in some ways Skylar was losing her rank. She was becoming the third member—the odd girl out—of the trio. This may have been because Skylar was maturing more slowly than Shelia and Rachel—not mentally or emotionally, but physically. In some ways, Skylar was still a girl, but Shelia and Rachel—both sexually active—were young women. Skylar was turning into the "little sister" of the trio.

"Skylar and Shelia were real close," Amorette said. "And then Rachel came along. That happened with me and my best friend. We started letting another girl hang out with us, and then before I knew it, she kinda took my place."

Like so many of Skylar's close friends, Amorette didn't believe the rumors going around that first week of school.

"If she ran away, she would *definitely* tell me," Amorette asserted. "I even told her [on Facebook and in texts] if you went to a party and messed up, it's going to be okay. We'll help you figure it out. I never heard back, and I knew something must be wrong."

twenty-four

Behind the Scenes

If Morgantown residents thought they had heard every conceivable tale surrounding Skylar's disappearance, they were wrong. A brand new cycle started when school resumed in August 2012.

The story of what happened to Skylar wasn't just hallway fodder at the two most competitive high schools in town, UHS and Morgantown High School. It was also a topic of water fountain discussion at Clay-Battelle High School, where the Cee Bees were buzzing like crazy about Skylar. Those teens wondered whether she could be hiding out in their end of the county.

All through the first full week of class, rumors flew at warp speed through the county's three high schools through talk, texts, and tweets. The students had even begun to talk about other scenarios. Someone started a rumor Skylar had been invited by a boy to a big drug party in Blacksville, where something bad had happened. A boy had called her the night she snuck out to tell her about the party, and Shelia and Rachel had driven her there. Some variations of the story had the two teens abandoning Skylar after she got drunk. Other versions placed them at the party when Skylar overdosed and either left with a boy or was raped and murdered. Some teens said Skylar had hooked up with one boy in particular: Dylan Conaway.

Another theory started to make the rounds but only a few teens discussed it. Dylan's older brother Darek was the young man Gaskins and Berry had questioned after the Blacksville bank robbery. Theirs was the house that had been raided by a SWAT team. Police were rumored to be looking at him for the bank robberies in the region. Darek had also been indicted on five counts of third-degree sexual assault in September. That made law enforcement more suspicious of him.[23]

Not only had Darek been at parties with Dylan and his friends, but at times Darek had even given Shelia, Shania, and Skylar a ride there. Some students wondered if her close association meant Skylar had discovered a solid connection between Darek and the bank robberies. Maybe Darek and Dylan had killed the teen to keep her quiet. The Conaway boys were under an umbrella of suspicion—and they knew it.

While armchair psychologists chatted online about their theories, Colebank and Spurlock were working day and night to discover what really happened to Skylar. In fact, on August 24, the same day the Neeses were preparing to come to the Star City Police Department, Colebank was applying for search warrants for Shelia's and Rachel's phone records. Filling out the initial paperwork didn't take long and neither did running down to the magistrate's court to get the warrants, but she might wait a week or two for a response from the phone company. However, it needed to be done. Those girls were hiding something.

As far as the Neeses knew, however, the police were doing nothing—and they certainly weren't looking for their missing daughter. Consequently, eight days after Mary missed work in case Skylar came home, she exploded.

---

[23] Darek later pled guilty to one count, and the other four were dismissed. He is now serving out his sentence under home confinement.

Dave had never seen Mary as angry as she was on August 24—with good reason, he thought. Skylar's parents were convinced from the beginning that Chief Vic Propst considered Skylar a runaway. That was her classification in the AMBER Alert system, after all.

In actuality, Propst says he never viewed Skylar as a runaway and he had personally called WVSP headquarters to ask for an AMBER alert to be issued.

On July 8, the veteran law enforcement officer had given Officer Colebank his blessing to pursue all leads and follow any hunches she had with regard to Skylar Neese's disappearance. After over six weeks of hearing nothing, Mary and Dave were so frustrated they went to see him. All the grieving parents had to go on were terrifying rumors. Colebank had assured them all leads were being explored, but she could offer them little in the way of substance. The case was incredibly challenging; to date, no solid information had been uncovered. The Star City Police Department—primarily Colebank, but other officers as well—had logged several hundred hours on the case in the previous six weeks. Still, for all their efforts, the cops had learned little.

Colebank couldn't discuss case details with Mary and Dave because it was an ongoing investigation. She had her own suspicions but didn't feel she could share what she knew with the public. That included Skylar's parents.

Colebank didn't want anyone doing anything rash, either. She and Dave had had a few long Saturday morning talks and she was concerned about him. The dedicated officer still had no idea what had happened to Skylar, but she was certain Shelia and Rachel were key to the puzzle. The last thing Colebank wanted was for Dave to go off on a vigilante hunt—especially when there was no evidence to support her hunches.

Being kept in the dark wasn't even Mary and Dave's primary gripe. The bigger problem was Jennifer Woodall Hunt—and the things she had been saying on Facebook. She seemed to know details about the investigation she should not have known.

As they prepared to visit the chief, Dave could tell by the fire in his wife's eyes that Mary was furious. For a minute, he thought of Skylar and how wound up she could get when discussing a topic she was passionate about. She inherited that from Mary. More than anything else, Dave wanted one more chance to debate with his daughter. It could be about WVU football or greenhouse gases or even (God forbid) gay rights. The topic didn't matter. He just wanted to see Skylar's eyes flash like her mother's again. One more time.

That thought got Dave back on track, got him thinking about the thumb drive he had been given by someone at work, which he had later passed on to Skylar for school. When he found the drive in Skylar's room, he turned it over to Colebank. At the time he thought it might have information to help the police locate his daughter. Dave had forgotten the drive contained survivalist literature, with advice about how to disappear if one wanted to.

Somehow, Jennifer Hunt knew this and she had been posting it on Facebook. Her posts insinuated Skylar had used the information on the thumb drive to run away. She implied Skylar was in hiding because she was afraid to come home. Or maybe Skylar was off partying with friends.

Mary and Dave couldn't understand how Hunt would have known about the specific material on the drive, unless there was an informant. They just needed answers.

Once inside the tiny police station they were determined to learn the truth, and the confrontation rapidly escalated. In response to their questions about which police agencies were involved, Propst told Mary and Dave he had called the State Police at the outset of the investigation.

"What about Jennifer posting on Facebook the authorities think we're hiding something?" Mary demanded, her voice getting louder.

"Yeah, why would you tell anyone that?" Dave said. "We've even agreed to take a lie detector test if you want us to."

"Look, Dave, Mary, I understand why you're upset," Chief Propst began. But Mary cut him off.

"You don't know anything! It's not your daughter who's missing!"

"No, ma'am, it isn't. But I know how hard these cases are on the parents, and how stressful they are for everyone involved, including the police."

Suddenly the emotional strain of the previous six weeks became too much, and the dam that contained all Mary's emotions burst. All of her grief, frustration, and anger came flooding out. Accounts differ as to who started shouting first, but before long Mary and Propst had both raised their voices. Dave could only stand by helplessly and watch. Propst told Mary if she didn't calm down, he would have to ask her to leave.

Mary didn't calm down, so Chief Propst did ask her to leave. By then, with the pressure from the previous six weeks suddenly unleashed, Mary couldn't have stopped even if she wanted to.

One important accomplishment came from the confrontation, though. The minute Mary and Dave marched out of the police station, Mary reached a decision. Her next action was fueled by anger, adrenaline, and fear for her daughter. Back at their apartment, a sobbing Mary began punching numbers on the home phone.

"West Virginia State Police," came the dispatcher's voice.

"Hello, I'd like to know if you're investigating my daughter's disappearance," Mary said. "This is Mary Neese. Do you know anything about my daughter, Skylar?"

The dispatcher put Mary on hold, then a Sergeant Kennedy got on the line. "I can't say for sure if Chief Propst called us," Kennedy told Mary. He then did something that may have saved Mary's sanity. Kennedy assured the distraught mother his troopers would immediately look into it.

On Saturday Mary and Dave told the world they had been kicked out of the police station by Chief Propst. Jennifer Hunt insisted they were lying and had not been kicked out. Hunt also posted, *It seems as though* [Skylar] *may have left for good reasons.... Many are questioning Dave and Mary's intentions at this point (for good cause).... For me this triggered suspicion immediately* and *The police are positive she is not dead and partying with friends.*

The minute Hunt's comments appeared on the TeamSkylar<3 group page, people were abuzz over the news and its meaning. Once again, Mary and Dave felt like their private life was being turned into a public spectacle.

No one seemed to know where Hunt got her information.[24] In addition, the negative public comments created discord among Mary and Dave's supporters. Intentional or not, they led to more lies, innuendo, and misinformation.

———————

A mile away, WVSP Corporal Ronnie Gaskins and Senior Trooper Chris Berry were chatting in their office at the Morgantown Detachment. They discussed various theories about the recent bank robberies.

"You remember how Darek acted when I said that thing about burying bodies?" Gaskins said.

Berry nodded. "He got all worked up."

"We didn't know this at the time, but you know that girl who went missing? Star City girl. Been thinking about her." He began shuffling through a pile of papers, searching.

"Neese, I think." Berry had kept an eye on the case for the last month. "Skylar maybe?"

Gaskins held up a photo. "Here's her picture," he said, handing it to Berry. "Maybe Darek *was* burying a body."

Awareness grew on Berry's face. He remembered how scared and, well, a little crazy Darek had suddenly appeared after Gaskins teased him. "You think they had to shut her up?"

"I talked to Colebank. She's been going at it pretty hard but she's got nothing. Now get this—Spurlock's working her case."

Berry cocked his head. "Really?"

Bank robbery is a federal crime, so naturally Spurlock was working the robberies. Berry wasn't surprised to learn about the FBI's

———

[24] Jennifer Hunt declined to be interviewed.

interest in Skylar. He knew the FBI doesn't officially investigate missing juveniles unless they have evidence of a sexual assault or kidnapping. He wondered if the FBI believed Skylar's disappearance might be connected to that of Aliayah Lunsford's a year earlier. Or maybe Spurlock was thinking the same thing as Gaskins.

"Are you thinking this girl's in on the robberies?" Berry asked.

"No idea. Maybe Skylar helped, but she's tied in somehow. You want to ride over and have a talk with Skylar's parents?"

The two troopers arrived at the Neeses' address a little before 10:00 A.M. The vinyl-sided, two-story apartment building had a small parking lot on three sides. Inside they found the Neeses weren't home.

"Guess it's gonna be Blacksville after all," Berry said as they headed back toward their cruiser.

When Mary pulled into the apartment parking lot after dropping Dave off for his shift, the first thing she noticed was the patrol car. Then she saw the two troopers. Her heart clenched. All of a sudden Mary could barely breathe. She knew they were there for one of two reasons: either Skylar's body had been found or they were finally getting off their asses. Mary thought maybe her phone call had done the trick. She parked her car and got out to meet the troopers.

"Mary Neese?" Gaskins asked.

"That's me," Mary said. "You're here about Skylar."

"Yes, ma'am. Can we talk with you inside?"

She gave them a long, even look, her eyes wary. "You're not bringing me bad news, are you?"

"No, ma'am. Nothing like that. I'm Corporal Gaskins, and this is Trooper Berry. We just need a few minutes of your time. Could we look through her room, some of her things?"

"Come on in," Mary said, leading the way to the apartment. "If it's going to find my daughter, you can go through and take whatever you want."

By the time Gaskins and Berry left the Neese home two hours later, both troopers were determined to do whatever it took to bring Skylar home. Mary had shown them Skylar's room, and even though Star City officers had already searched it, the troopers looked around again, hoping for any clue at all.

What they found was Skylar's diary. "Do you mind if we take this with us?" Gaskins said. "It might tell us something important."

Mary said they could, so the two troopers left with it. Berry began reading as soon as they were inside the cruiser. He couldn't stop. Seeing Skylar's own words made her come alive in his mind. He could tell how much she cared about people.

But would a girl like that get mixed up with the Conaway boys? Dylan was only a couple of years older than Skylar so he could have known her. Even so, Gaskins and Berry were equally certain Skylar Neese was no armed bank robber.

The troopers eventually made their way to the Star City police station to learn more about the case. During that visit, Colebank brought them up to speed on the information she and Spurlock had gathered. Gaskins and Berry turned and gave each other a long, hard look at Colebank's next words: Shelia Eddy had been linked romantically to Dylan Conaway.

Back at the detachment, Gaskins and Berry looked at the bare bones of the case.

"Skylar never comes home," Gaskins said. "She was last with Shelia and Rachel." The teens said they picked her up at 11:00 and had dropped her off at about 11:45. The security video showed Skylar getting in a car, but the video was too blurry to identify it. The timestamp was 12:31.

One possibility was Shelia and Rachel had picked her up at 12:31, and that was Shelia's car in the video. That would mean the teens were lying. Maybe they had taken Skylar to a party, something had happened, and they were scared to tell. Maybe Skylar actually *had* run away, and they were trying to cover it up.

Another possibility was they were telling the truth and the car was someone else's. Perhaps she went with a boy—or an adult male. Possibly Dylan or Darek Conaway. Or maybe that was just the car that took her to a party.

Either way, they needed to get more information. Colebank told them she had called Sheetz about video surveillance but learned it was of Sheetz property only. But maybe a visit would prove more fruitful. It had been a long day, but Gaskins said to Berry, "Let's just go to Sheetz and check for ourselves."

At Sheetz, the manager took the two troopers into the back room and showed them how to access the videotape archives of the store. Gaskins and Berry cued up the video and took it back to the late evening of July 5. Gaskins progressed the video in short spurts, tapping on a key for each jump.

"I'm 'tap-tap-tap,'" Gaskins said. "I'm slow because I don't want to miss something. Then I see this car and the rims stick out to me. It's like a silver car, and I'm thinking, 'Okay, well, I know a silver car picked up Skylar.'"

The time was after midnight, and the car was headed toward town. The two men kept watching the video, and with each tap the timestamp moved toward 12:30.

"Tap-tap-tap," Gaskins said, "and at 12:39, I see this same car go toward the interstate."

The times lined up perfectly. They'd found more footage of the car that picked up Skylar, and it was definitely headed north, toward the interstate or Blacksville. They thanked the manager and put in a request for a copy of the footage.

"You guys are lucky," the manager said. "After fifty-four days, they permanently delete those files. That footage would have been gone in two days."

twenty-five

About a Boy

Skylar disappeared because of a boy. That's what everyone said. What no one seemed to know, though, was whether it was a teen boy or a random adult pedophile.

Rumors like these are easy to believe when romance is at the heart of so many teenage upheavals and males commit most crimes. In addition, people still believe the biggest threat to children comes from a strange man lurking in a trench coat, so-called stranger danger. The truth is, most missing children who aren't runaways are snatched by people they know—including their own family members. If Skylar's disappearance had to do with a boy, it was likely someone she knew.

The problem was, Skylar couldn't be linked to very many boys, and none of the anecdotal reports had romantic overtones. So while rumor had it a boy was involved, the facts showed otherwise.

The only known story about Skylar and a boy illustrated how little experience Skylar had with the opposite sex. Amorette Hughes remembered Tommy,[25] the "really cute" boy in dance class all the girls fawned over.

---

[25] Not his real name.

"He was kinda, like, skaterish," Amorette said, referring to a look modeled after skateboarder subculture. "He wore T-shirts, and liked skinny jeans. We would never talk to him. We were scared."

When Skylar did talk to Tommy, she became so nervous she stammered. The most she could do was watch him from afar and giggle with Amorette.

Not so with one of Skylar's friends. That girl chatted easily with Skater Boy.

"Shelia," Amorette said. "I think they might have gone out on a couple of dates. I remember Skylar telling me about it. I know Shelia said Tommy was awkward."

Skylar couldn't have been happier for her friend. "She was like, 'I'm living my life vicariously through Shelia! I'm not there, but it feels like I am!'" Amorette said.

Accounts connecting Skylar to romance with boys were non-existent, suggesting only that she wasn't ready for dating. In fact, Skylar's lack of interest in boys may have been part of what drove some teenagers to speculate Skylar was a lesbian. (*I heard she doesn't like boys . . . and those other two girls she always hung around with, weren't they seen kissing at some party?*)

Gaskins and Berry had also heard Skylar's disappearance was con-nected to a boy, although in those versions it wasn't necessarily a roman-tic relationship. One name they kept coming across was Eric Finch, a sophomore at Clay-Battelle. Eric, who looks like he could pass for a teenage Dave Neese, lived on a farm ten miles south of Blacksville.

Because Skylar was a Daddy's girl, and because of Eric's dark hair and stocky looks, people might have thought he was Skylar's type. But that wasn't true, either. Eric and Skylar met through Shelia years earlier. They went to the same parties and also attended a Snoop Dogg concert at the WVU Coliseum with Shelia and Shania. Skylar had even been to one of Eric's birthday parties. Since becoming teens their friendship existed primarily through text messages. In fact, they were texting right before Skylar snuck out for the final time.

Police found out Eric was the last person who received a text message from Skylar. His final text to Skylar was at 12:11 A.M.; she replied one minute later. At 12:12 Eric said Skylar simply texted, *Goodnight.*

While Eric denied having had a crush on Skylar, other people say he did. His tweets on March 13, 2013, when Skylar's remains were conclusively identified, seem to suggest sincere feelings: *Easy, the hardest day of my life. Its something that only few understand. Pure brightness turned into darkness. Rest in peace, love you babe* and *Lord, I ask for strength! You, above all, know I need it.* Of course, it's also possible Eric was another in a long line of teens who saw in Skylar the perfect confidante—and nothing more. In any event, the police never considered him a likely suspect.

Shelia was Eric's first girlfriend, something he said came about largely because their last names, Eddy and Finch, meant they stood next to each other in the hot-lunch line in middle school. Eric was also a friend of—or at least acquainted with—Dylan Conaway.

The parties at the Conaway house were rumored to get a little wild; some people claim alcohol and drugs flowed freely. Gaskins and Berry learned Shelia had taken Rachel to parties there. In addition, it was common knowledge around Blacksville that Dylan Conaway once had a sexual relationship with Shelia—and she and Skylar went to Blacksville a lot.

The more closely Skylar was connected to the Conaway brothers, State Police thought, the more likely her disappearance was linked to the bank robberies. They were equally convinced Darek Conaway was somehow connected to those felonies.

Before they made any more moves on Darek, the two troopers decided to ride out to the western end of the county. They wanted to have a little chat with Eric Finch before they paid another visit to the Conaway house.

Just talk. It's easy.

After typing the text into his phone, Daniel hit *send.* Then he leaned back in his chair and tried to listen to Mr. Snyder. It wasn't easy. This year Daniel had two math classes—precalculus and trigo-nometry. Usually math came easily to Daniel, but the way Mr. Snyder went over and over points in trig class made it almost impossible for Daniel to tune in. The fact Daniel thought the teacher was cocky didn't help. Daniel believed the only way he could handle his bore-dom was to go to class stoned.

Daniel imagined Rachel receiving his last text. He'd sent her texts regularly in the two weeks they'd been back to school and he knew he was annoying her. Personally, he thought Rachel was beautiful, had an incredible voice, and was a great person—even if she was a little over the top. After all, Daniel knew he was, too. Plus, they'd spent hours and hours together, in and out of class, working under Mr. Kyer's direction or driving around town getting high with Skylar and Shelia.

This school year wasn't turning out to be as much fun as Daniel thought it would be. Of course after Skylar disappeared, everything had changed. Lately Daniel was having trouble remembering the things he liked about Rachel. He kept thinking it wasn't fair, the way Rachel and Shelia were being all quiet and sneaky. They seemed to be keeping to themselves a lot more than they used to.

As if that wasn't enough, Rachel's attitude was really beginning to annoy him. Daniel had seen the pair several times—in the cafeteria, at Shelia's locker, even just walking down the hallway. Their heads were always close, they were always whispering. There was some-thing so secretive about them now.

If he could get Rachel to talk about it—whatever it was—she could tell him and it wouldn't go any further. He was going to keep pressuring her until she did. He didn't even try bugging Shelia; once that girl had her mind made up, she didn't change it. Instead, Daniel completely ignored her.

He keyed his phone again:

Hey Rachel. We really need to talk in 4th period. You know what about too.

Daniel hit *send*.

Dave's aunt, Joanne Nagy, and her daughter Rikki talked every day. They were very close, so it was only natural much of their conversation centered on Joanne's missing niece and Rikki's missing cousin, Skylar. Where she could be, why she had left, what they could do to help find her.

Joanne had never met the brunette teen, since she and Dave's uncle had parted ways years earlier. It was a contentious divorce, and Joanne cut herself off from her ex-husband's family. She only saw Dave for the first time in more than twenty years when his mom died, and they reconnected at the funeral home. Joanne was so happy to see Dave and his brother, Mike, again, and looked forward to catching up on their lost years.

One year later Joanne was devastated when she learned Dave's daughter was missing. So Joanne did what she does best: she went into action, taking charge like an efficient military commander. She had MISSING Skylar posters made, organized search teams, and then sent those teams of complete strangers out to various areas of the region. She also scheduled people to take food to Dave and Mary, and she even scoped out various locations around the region where Skylar had supposedly been sighted.

Along the way, Joanne joined TeamSkylar<3, the Facebook group created by Dave's cousin, Jennifer Hunt-Woodall. So did Rikki, who was also Jennifer's cousin and her closest friend.

After dissension broke out, Joanne left TeamSkylar<3, totally breaking away from it. Rikki stayed on, and a few months later tensions were so high Joanne issued an edict: "We're not going to talk about Skylar. That topic is off limits." She hated telling Rikki that, but mother and daughter had taken sides—and the result was not pretty. Joanne loved her daughter and she knew Rikki loved her, but when it came to Skylar they couldn't see eye to eye.

So when Rikki called her mom one night, and told her to stop looking for Skylar, Joanne was at a loss. Why on earth should she stop looking? Then Rikki told her mom Jennifer had learned through someone at the FBI where Skylar was, and Mary even knew about it, so Joanne should stop wasting her fuel and her time.

"Where is she?" Joanne asked.

"She's in a home for unwed mothers up in Bobtown," Rikki said.

Joanne didn't realize the small Pennsylvania town had a home for unwed mothers, so she Googled the place—and was surprised to find not one, but two such homes. The next day, instead of taking Rikki's advice, Joanne loaded up her team and they crossed the state line, making a beeline directly for Bobtown. Once there, they did a reconnaissance mission, parking across the street at each location and watching anyone who came or went. Finally, they decided to take a poster into the homes and simply ask the receptionist: "Have you seen this girl?"

Of course, neither place had.

twenty-six

You're Either With Us . . .

It was time to change tactics.

Gaskins and Berry brought new intensity to the search for Skylar but they were running into too many dead ends. They had scoured Blacksville and surrounding areas for small silver cars. A number of knock-and-talks at residences had turned up nothing. No one had heard word of any party out that way in early July. They had talked to Eric Finch and Dylan Conaway again—nothing. Berry was convinced Eric was hiding something, but the evidence proved otherwise.

They'd had several conversations with Colebank and Spurlock, going over and over the little information they did have. They still couldn't be sure whose car it was, where it was taking Skylar, or why. Colebank and Spurlock both believed Shelia and Rachel were lying about something, stonewalling for some undetermined reason. Colebank was insistent they look harder at the two teens.

But no one had any idea why the girls would lie. Mary and Dave assured police they wouldn't. But the investigators had several conversations about *why* the teens might be lying—and always came back to square one. They were the same possibilities enshrined in so many rumors: Skylar got drunk and hit her head when she fell, she overdosed, or she ran away with a boy. Maybe it was speculation—but maybe the rumors were a version of the truth.

Asking the question, "What if that was Shelia's car?" led the conversations right back to the same set of fruitless speculations.

Finally, Colebank filed for warrants, asking a local magistrate to find probable cause to search the persons and homes of both teens. She took them down to the magistrate on September 6 and he signed them immediately. The warrants included the power to seize any and all devices used to transmit vocal or electronic signals.

Later that same morning, Colebank received Shelia's cell records from the phone company. In particular, they revealed Shelia made or received 5,215 phone calls or texts during six days, from July 4 to 10. As Colebank glanced through the pages and did the math, she noticed that was the average number of calls and texts going in and coming out of Shelia's phone throughout the entire summer. Colebank couldn't believe how much that girl was on her phone. She couldn't wait to begin digging through the hundreds of pages of records, and had a gut feeling they would lead her straight to Skylar.

She hadn't requested Rachel's records yet because all the teens she interviewed said Skylar was really close to Shelia, but not so much Rachel.

On Friday, September 7, the first warrants on individuals in the case were served on Shelia and Rachel. The girls weren't suspects, but law enforcement wanted to find out what they were hiding.

Gaskins and Berry were in one car; Colebank and Spurlock were in another. The four officers entered UHS, went to the office, and introduced themselves. Together they should have presented a formidable front to anyone there since they represented all three levels of law enforcement: city, state, and federal.

However, even after Assistant Principal Cheesebrough, arguably the primary student liaison at UHS and the "face" of the administration, learned why the investigators were there, he was skeptical. "Those girls are good. Their skirts are too short sometimes, but they don't do anything wrong," he said.

Colebank wasn't impressed. Neither, it turned out, were the other three officers. Gaskins said it was odd, the cold welcome they received at the high school. The sense of being unwelcome extended beyond the administration, they later discovered. "It felt like we were a nuisance to the teachers," he later said.

The officers asked to talk to both girls. Cheesebrough pulled Rachel and Shelia out of class and led them back to the office. Gaskins remembered the moment well.

"They just had a big smile on their face like they had not a single worry in the world, life was good," he said, "then they see us, and their faces fell. Like, 'Ugh, we have to deal with you guys again?'"

Gaskins and Spurlock escorted Rachel to one room while Berry and Colebank took Shelia to a separate room. Each girl was shown the warrant, and a phone and a bag of marijuana were discovered in Shelia's purse.

"Shelia immediately began crying, wanting us to throw it away," Berry said. "'Throw away the marijuana! Get rid of it!'"

Since recreational drug use was hardly a priority at that moment, Colebank turned it over to Cheesebrough.

"Here's your little angel's weed," she said, tossing him the bag. "You deal with it."

They also confiscated Rachel's cell phone, after she agreed to give them the password. It was apparent she didn't want to relinquish her phone. Gaskins knew a bad attitude when he saw one.

"Look Rachel," he said quietly, "You're either with us or you're against us.'"

Rachel grew silent and didn't say another word.

Back outside, Berry was the first to speak. "I'd bet a pizza their cell phones are golden."

The four officers would continue their search for the girls' secrets at their homes.

"Chris and I will take Rachel's place," a somber Gaskins said. Of the four, Gaskins was the most reserved. "We know how much you want to search Shelia's home, Jessie."

When Colebank saw the small smile on Gaskins' face, her own split into a wide grin. Colebank had grown to especially dislike Shelia. She and Spurlock got into her cruiser.

"It's go time!" Berry said as Gaskins pulled away from the curb. He couldn't wait to see what they would find at the Shoaf house.

Patricia Shoaf's modest residence sits in a tidy upscale housing development in the Pierpont area. The property is almost bereft of trees, and an open expanse of lawn stretches behind the home Rachel shares with her mother. It's a house many teens would love to live in.

Rachel wasn't one of them. Ever since her parents' divorce, Rachel wanted just one thing: to live with her father. Her relationship with her mother was filled with conflict and everyone knew it. A self-proclaimed Daddy's girl, Rachel was not beyond acting out to spite her mother, which only made the situation worse. Word from observers was that Patricia could be equally difficult.

Many teens observed the mother-daughter trouble firsthand, both before and after Skylar disappeared. Like the night in late spring 2012, when Rachel was in a car with three other teens and her cell phone rang. "Hi, Mom, I'll be home—" Her words were cut off by her mother's screams at the other end of the line. Everyone in the car could hear Patricia. "Mom, calm down! I told you, we're almost there," Rachel said, ending the call as quickly as she could.

"Psycho bitch!" she seethed, cramming her cell phone deep into her purse. "I so want to move in with my dad."

"We actually felt sorry for Rachel," one girl said later.

Liz said Patricia's version of that night is somewhat different. Rachel claimed to have been at one of her Young Life meetings. The popular religious group known for its teen ministry has a branch in Morgantown, and Rachel was a devoted attendee.

The girls in the car only heard Rachel's side of the story; Liz said Patricia was livid because Rachel wasn't where she was supposed to be that night, and Patricia found out about it.

Either way, a little before eight that evening, right after Gaskins and Berry hauled away her electronic gadgets, Rachel tweeted that she was jealous of Shelia's relationship with her mother, Tara. She sent the tweet from her mother's computer, which the police left behind because Patricia needed it to work from home.

"Why are you doing this? Why are you picking on my daughter?" Tara asked Colebank and Spurlock when they showed up with the warrant. "She doesn't know anything."

According to Colebank, no sooner had the girls' cell phones been seized at the high school than Tara bought her daughter another one. "Shelia had a new cell phone five minutes after we took hers," Colebank said, "because she couldn't live without one."

Rachel thought that was terrific. She tweeted, *sooo jealous of the relationship @_sheliiaa and her mom have*. At the same time, it let Rachel get in a little dig at her own mother. Just four minutes later, Shelia retweeted, adding *we're buds :)*.

In fact, all three girls—Skylar, Rachel, and Shelia—liked going to Shelia's house best. Tara was laid back and permissive; she simply let the girls do whatever they wanted.

Before Tara married Jim, she never could have afforded such an indulgence as a new cell phone. With finances tight, Tara had to choose luxuries carefully. Life in Blacksville had been hard for mother and daughter until Jim came into the picture, bringing marriage and a move to Morgantown. Although Shelia also wanted to move to be near her best friend Skylar, going from financial insecurity in a rural area to relative luxury in an urban setting was a big change for them.

Soon after the searches, both girls began a pattern of skipping school and getting into various kinds of trouble. Their behavior forced school officials to repeatedly call the girls' parents. No doubt

Cheesebrough then wondered what had happened to cause those behavioral changes. It's difficult to know if he attributed them to Skylar's disappearance, or just "normal" teenage angst, because UHS administration has had a gag order in place almost since school resumed in 2012.

twenty-seven

And Tara Makes Three . . .

One Saturday in September Colebank stopped by the Monongalia County Sheriff's Department to say hello to her fiancé when she ran into another deputy.

"What're you up to, Tim?" Colebank said.

Deputy Hunn, known for his solid, stocky physique, had just finished his workout in the department's gym and said he was heading home. "How about you, Jess?"

"Still trying to find Skylar. Only problem is, she hasn't come back on the radar. Phone records told us nothing except she hasn't been using her phone," Colebank said. "I keep hoping someone will see her, but so far we've got squat."

Hunn suggested she focus more on his end of the county, out in Blacksville. That was all the encouragement Colebank needed.

"You're right," she said. "Screw it. Let's get some four-wheelers."

On their next day off, Hunn and Colebank teamed up with Trooper Berry. Having grown up in the Blacksville area, he had gone to school with Hunn. The trio turned onto Route 7 and headed west. When they got to Blacksville, the three off-duty officers got on their four-wheelers and took off. Together they covered every path and trail they could find. They rode all over the one-lane back roads and even on the golf course behind Clay-Battelle High School, until it was too dark to see. They continued searching throughout the month of September, riding for hours on end. Still they had nothing. They knew it was hopeless.

Skylar was the type of friend who kept in touch with the people she loved, people like Daniel, Shelia, and Rachel. She also posted or tweeted nonstop, so no way was she going to cut off all her social media ties. Even if she'd run away because she was angry at her parents—and there was no evidence to support that idea—Colebank knew Skylar would have reached out to someone.

Except she didn't. No one had heard one word from the missing girl.

"Skylar would've called someone," Colebank said later. "She wouldn't let all these people who love her worry about her. That's who she was." Although none of the law enforcement officers ever met her, they felt like they knew her. Through the pages of her diary the appealing teen had made an impact. Across all departments—from the young FBI agent to the troopers to the detectives and veteran cops—every officer working the case felt that Skylar had touched his, or her, heart.

Even though they suspected Skylar was dead, they weren't giving up. They would keep searching until they found her, even if it was only her remains. The officers promised Mary and Dave—and each another—they wouldn't stop looking until they brought Skylar home.

Behind the scenes, both girls were finding it more difficult to keep up pretenses. In September, Rachel moved in with Rusty to give mother and daughter a much needed break.

Given the way Rachel was behaving, Patricia felt like she was running out of options. Not long after Rachel went to stay with her father, Liz picked her up from Rusty's place. Rachel didn't know her mother had staged the lunch date because she was so worried about Rachel.

"I think she knows something about that night, about Skylar, but she won't tell me," Patricia told Liz. "You're so close to her and she thinks the world of you. See if she'll open up."

Liz chose Rachel's favorite restaurant and while they nibbled on nacho chips, she tried to get Rachel to talk. At first it was difficult. Rachel wouldn't say a word. Then Rachel mentioned Tara. "I had to check with Tara—"

Liz cut her off. "What do you mean you had to check with Tara? She's not your mother, Rachel. You don't need to check with her, or in with her, about anything!" Rachel glanced away, silent.

"Why won't you tell me what's wrong? What really happened that night? What are you not saying?"

Liz could not stop thinking about Skylar. She was terrified of what had befallen the missing teen. She didn't think Rachel would deliberately harm Skylar, but she knew the girls—especially Shelia and Skylar—had been arguing a lot. Patricia had told her about the screaming that had gone on the previous August, and how angry the two girls had been.

Rachel took a sip of her soda.

Liz pressed further. "Did you girls get in a fight?"

Rachel nodded.

"I'm sure when you picked her up, you were in the front seat. Let me guess. Skylar was pissed she had to get in the back seat, and you got to sit with Shelia, right?"

Rachel, silent, nodded again.

"She was jealous of you, wasn't she?"

Rachel only nodded.

Liz sensed Rachel was weakening. "That's why she and Shelia were constantly at each other, isn't it?"

Rachel's head bobbed faster.

To Liz it felt like Rachel wanted her to guess what happened. "Did something go wrong?"

This time Rachel's head went even faster, her nod an emphatic *yes.*

"You girls were out in Blacksville, weren't you?"

That's when Rachel shut down. She looked like she might cry. Liz tried to get Rachel to tell her what went wrong the night Skylar disappeared, not taking her eyes off of Rachel's for a second. She knew if Rachel's eyes darted around she was lying.

"Look, I know you were in Blacksville that night," Liz felt her temper rising. "Why? Why are you lying to me? What happened to Skylar?"

"We got into a fight and she ran...Skylar ran away...into the woods."

It wasn't the whole story, but it was more than the police had heard. When Liz and Rachel left the restaurant two hours later, both their faces were red and splotchy, and wet with newly shed tears. Liz was convinced Rachel knew what happened to Skylar—she was just too terrified to say.

After Liz recounted her conversation with Rachel, she and Patricia brainstormed, trying to come up with answers. They wanted to understand why Shelia and her mother had so much control over Rachel. So many times since July, Rachel had openly defied Patricia to be with Shelia, often with Tara's assistance. Patricia didn't get it, and the more she and Liz thought about it, the less they liked it.

The two women would have been even angrier if they knew what Crissy Swanson knew. Crissy's parents live in Core, a little community just outside of Morgantown on the way to Blacksville. There is a medical clinic and a post office, but not much else.

While Liz and Patricia were busy wondering about Tara that September, so were the Swansons. Crissy's mother was Tara's best friend as well as a distant relative. After Skylar disappeared, Tara seemed to take solace in her visits to the Swanson house. Crissy said it seemed like she needed someone to confide in, and Tara would often tell Crissy's mom details about the case, who in turn would tell Crissy.

What Crissy remembers most is how Tara seemed to be helping the girls coordinate their stories whenever they had a police interview. "Rachel would call Shelia," Crissy said, "and tell her the new story or they would get together and then they would go and tell Tara the new story."

Crissy said it was weird, and overhearing Tara help the girls this way made her really uncomfortable.

By late September law enforcement was widening their net in the search for Skylar. On September 24, Colebank applied to the phone company for Rachel's cell records and the records of the cell towers. When that material arrived, the investigators would learn for certain the girls were lying: the records showed that at the time they'd said they were with Skylar, they were actually calling and texting each other.

Shelia and Rachel weren't even in the same place.

twenty-eight

Facebook Follies

As October approached and the leaves began turning vibrant autumn colors, everyone following Skylar's story on Facebook wanted to weigh in on the role Mary and Dave had played in their daughter's disappearance. While the real-world drama was moving from a slow simmer to a fast boil at UHS, the virtual world was being whipped into a firestorm. Tension, innuendo, and outright accusations only increased on Facebook and Twitter. As if Skylar's parents hadn't already endured enough, Mary and Dave felt like some people were determined to see them suffer even more.

What began as a small schism in a public Facebook group grew into a big and very ugly family battle. In numerous private emails and public postings during August and September, Jennifer Hunt insinuated her cousin Dave and his wife were hiding something. She said their story had changed several times and implied that, as a result, the police were no longer sharing any information with the Neeses. In fact, Jennifer said, police had begun investigating Mary and Dave. One August 30 she wrote, *When her parents became suspicious early on, info wasn't being shared with them anymore. They are part of the investigation now.*

Even though Dave tried to keep from looking in on TeamSkylar<3, sometimes he just couldn't help himself. Other times he didn't need to, since many members were very loyal to the Neeses and would alert them to such nonsense. So Dave could do nothing but watch as some of the 3,000 people from TeamSkylar<3 took the rumors at face value and ran with them.

Other people weren't as rash; they just accused Mary and Dave of being evasive. They claimed the couple was withholding information from TeamSkylar<3 members in preference to their own, closed group, TEAMSKYLAR 2012. Some said Mary and Dave weren't open with law enforcement. While their countless questions went mostly unanswered, the group seemed to believe it had a right to know anything and everything. After all, hadn't members been posting, sharing, and praying for this missing girl for months? Hadn't Skylar become their child, too? Didn't that mean they owned a stake in the story, and that her parents owed them an explanation?

Mary and Dave somehow found the strength to respond to as many Facebook messages as they could, in an attempt to control the damage. But inside the privacy of their own home, they both teetered near the edge of collapse. The Facebook drama piled on the trauma of Skylar's disappearance was almost more than they could bear.

One night Dave grew so angry when he saw another post from Hunt that he wanted to hurl the computer through the living room window. Mary urged him to calm down, have a smoke, or take Lilu for a walk. She told him to do anything to get his mind off the cousin he'd never even met, as well as all the people on Facebook they'd once considered their friends.

In truth, Mary realized she didn't even know most of the TeamSkylar<3 members. They were just as much strangers as Hunt and her son. Mary knew only one thing: those "friends" were making it harder and harder for her to get through another day at work.

Joanne Nagy knew what Dave and Mary were facing and felt compelled to intervene. On September 23, Dave's aunt Joanne told TeamSkylar<3 members she wanted *to clear up a few things*. She wrote:

Just because Dave and Mary do not report their every move on FB doesn't mean they are not doing anything. People really need to accept this fact. Dave and Mary are not holding up good at all right now. But they get up every morning and somehow keep going. God knows how.... They cry every day. Their health is suffering.... They barely have the strength in them to eat.

She reminded the Facebook group that the Neeses' lives had become a public spectacle. Neither Mary nor Dave had the energy to answer the hundreds of questions posed to them, especially the *really far-fetched* ones.

Anyone reading her poignant note had to sense the pain Nagy felt for her family. When she begged every one of the 3,000 TeamSkylar<3 members to *please stop the bickering and fussing [and] to refocus [on] the reason we are here,* you could see Joanne, a very religious woman, down on both knees praying that her words would help convince people to back off.

Aunt Joanne's words did seem to provide a respite of sorts. For a while, at least, the level of drama in the Facebook sphere dissipated. Until Hunt's story changed: in the blink of an eye, she claimed in a private email that Skylar was safe and sound. Hunt promised to share the truth with the public very soon. But Hunt's promise was as empty as Rachel telling Colebank she would stop by the police station after camp.

Mary and Dave were furious. Who was this woman? What right did she think she had?

About the same time the adults on Facebook began backing off, Twitter, at the time a more popular venue for teens, exploded. Tweets from real people and from those who were hiding their identities tumbled headfirst into the Skylar drama.

The constant stream of tweets intensified public pressure as Rachel and Shelia tried to get through each school day. At first most of the tweets were relatively harmless. Some made light of the growing suspicions that were beginning to surface. There were days when Shelia and Rachel would be walking down the hallway between classes and someone would blurt out, "Uh-oh! Better step back! Murderer alert!"

Twitter wasn't the only problem. The pressure was two parts Twitter, one part Daniel Hovatter. He kept haranguing Rachel, demanding information. He wasn't alone. Students throughout UHS wanted Shelia and Rachel to come clean, too. Very quickly, a relentless Twitter campaign came from the direction of two new anonymous Twitter accounts: @Snyder28Josie and @MiaBarr8. The newcomers seemed to have one goal: to harass Shelia and Rachel until they buckled.

To onlookers, it seemed like a game, the only players being @Snyder28Josie and @MiaBarr8. For example, @Snyder28Josie subtweeted *besties dont like having to answer questions of their guilt!!* to @MiaBarr8. Shelia and Rachel were clearly the targets of this "shame game"—and there was no way they could win.

The jokes and accusations against the two girls morphed into something uglier, as some tweets and comments could be classified as threats. Two factors seemed to trigger the onslaught of negative tweets: investigators concluded Skylar was dead, and rumors started circulating that Shelia and Rachel were culpable. The result was tweet after harsh tweet, aimed directly at the two teens.

Shelia's friend Shania Ammons was fed up with the accusations. Shania was also disgusted that people she didn't know were directing their rage at her simply because she was Shelia's friend. So on September 30, Ammons came to Shelia's defense, tweeting, *no matter what I will always have @_sheliiaa back. that girl is my bestfriend #loveyou #staystrong.*

Indeed, Shania's battle cry did fortify her friend. Two days later, Shelia lashed out in typical fashion by tweeting @MiaBarr8: *and a fake twitter account...you don't know shit so do us a favor and shut your fuckin mouth.*

Shelia's cousin Crissy had also seen enough. Not only was she being harassed at work, but everyone seemed to believe she had something to do with Skylar's disappearance. That could be due to her family connection; Crissy was distantly related to Shelia through marriage. Crissy believed people's accusations were ridiculous and amounted to nothing more than guilt by association. She was angry.

The petite blonde took to Facebook rather than Twitter. There, on the TeamSkylar<3 page, Crissy posted her heartfelt defense: *Pardon me for being so blunt & know that I feel SO much for Mary&Dave & their situation,* she typed. *I can't imagine the things they're going through at the moment.*

Then Crissy got to the point, with as much tact as Joanne Nagy had employed two weeks earlier. Crissy spoke eloquently, encouraging people to think before they typed words that could ruin more lives—namely Shelia's and Rachel's:

BUT for those of you trying to place blame on any of Skylar's friends. . . all you are doing is taking away the innocence and life of another's child. Placing blame on someone DOES NOT automatically bring Skylar home. . . . We are all here to help Mary&Dave through their struggle & bring back their beautiful little girl NOT ruin someone else's life. . . .

Gradually, battle lines were being drawn. Three alliances had formed, but at the heart of their skirmishes there was only one big question they all wanted answered: What were Rachel and Shelia hiding?

Beyond that, they also kept trying to figure out whose car the surveillance tape showed Skylar getting into. It was a question for which there seemed no answer.

The first group, which included the girls' UHS classmates, believed that Shelia and Rachel were, at best, not sharing information they had known from the beginning. Some people, including law enforcement, felt certain that the car in the video was Shelia's.

Few of these people still believed Shelia and Rachel's story about dropping Skylar off at the end of her street.

Another faction, filled with the friends of both girls, took their word as gospel. This group believed in Shelia and Rachel's innocence. Its members stood up for the girls in a show of solidarity and support and often directly asked—or even told—anyone who disagreed to back off.

A third camp, represented by Hunt and her TeamSkylar<3 followers, also believed Shelia and Rachel had been telling the truth since the day Skylar disappeared. They believed Skylar had been dropped off before midnight, just like the two girls said. They thought the surveillance video showed Skylar getting into a *different* car. This third group, however, was growing defensive and its members were openly ugly when publicly expressing their staunch beliefs.

But the importance of those beliefs to the search for Skylar was, by then, irrelevant. Regardless of whose car she'd gotten into, Skylar still had not been found—which meant the search was, by then, not for a missing girl but for her remains.

twenty-nine

Opening Night Approaches

Rachel whined into the phone: "Mom! Make them stop!"

She was complaining to Patricia about the harassment coming from Gaskins and Berry and Spurlock and *everyone* at school. Several students overheard conversations like this more than once.

Rachel huffily pushed away the plate full of lettuce she'd been picking at. She was sitting at the cafeteria table she and Shelia shared. Shelia sat across from her, looking down. She was texting.

"Mother!" Rachel held the phone away from her ear as Patricia's voice burst from it. She looked at Shelia. "I don't believe this shit," she said, rolling her eyes. Shelia still didn't look up from her phone. When the phone grew quiet Rachel put it back to her ear.

"They won't leave me alone." Rachel waited a second for her mother to finish, then shouted, "I want you to do something!" into the cell. Heads around the cafeteria turned as more people took notice. Rachel gripped the phone tightly, her eyes widening. Then her eyes got watery. She burst into sobs.

"I don't know how much longer I can take this!" Rachel's voice collapsed under the weight of her sobs. Shelia glanced up with a disgusted expression; Rachel kept right on crying.

The more Daniel pressured Rachel, the more she stonewalled. Most often the teen claimed she had been so wasted she couldn't remember that night very well. All she could remember was dropping Skylar off at the end of the road.

"You know how she gets," Rachel had said. Daniel did know how Skylar "got." Skylar could be pigheaded when she'd made up her mind, and there was no talking her out of her position. Sometimes she'd get angry if people kept pushing.

But the story made no sense to Daniel. Skylar had snuck out with Shelia and Rachel dozens of times and he'd never, ever heard of Skylar insisting on being dropped off like that.

By then he'd been hounding Rachel for almost six weeks. That fall UHS was staging *A Midsummer Night's Dream*, the Shakespearean comedy. She and Daniel were at play rehearsal for several hours each night, since both teens had big roles in the production.

One day in October, Rachel finally cracked.

The argument took place in the auditorium during studio acting, one of the classes taught by Mr. Kyer. Small groups were scattered around the auditorium, performing various exercises. Kyer circulated, checking each group's progress.

As usual, Daniel had been picking on Rachel the whole class, and as they fought their voices grew louder.

"You need to quit telling everyone I know stuff," Rachel said, her voice quivering.

"You do!" Daniel answered. "You need to tell what it is."

"You don't know anything." Rachel tried to walk away but Dan kept at her.

"I know you're hiding something!"

"I don't know shit about Skylar!" she yelled. "I don't know anything!"

"Rachel, just go freaking confess. Go tell them what you know."

Rachel burst into tears and ran out of the room with Kyer following close behind.

When he returned a few minutes later, the drama teacher drew Daniel aside.

"You need to give her a break, Daniel. False accusations can lead to serious problems."

"They're not false. I'm only trying to get her to talk."

"It's hard for her," Mr. Kyer said. "She's going through a lot since Skylar disappeared. People keep asking her what she—"

"That's because she's lying! She knows something and the police need to know what it is so they can find Skylar."

"She's not lying. I've talked to her. She doesn't know anything more than she's told the police."

"That's bullshit."

"That's enough, Daniel. Leave Rachel alone."

Daniel knew better than to argue with him. Kyer couldn't see that Rachel was lying, but pissing his drama teacher off wouldn't help. Daniel shrugged.

"I did upbraid her and fall out with her," Daniel said.

Mr. Kyer smiled. He recognized one of Daniel's lines from the play. "That's it. Focus on the play. We only have two weeks."

With all the tension in the air, all over school—not to mention in drama class and during rehearsals—Daniel wasn't so sure they could pull it off. Opening night was two weeks away, and he didn't have a lot of confidence in Rachel. She was acting pretty weird.

Meanwhile, "Josie Snyder" and "Mia Barr" kept tweeting to Shelia and Rachel. By then their tweets were also for the public's benefit. Josie Snyder's tweets were often taunting and judgmental. Her October 26 tweet tied Shelia and Rachel to one of their favorite TV shows: *bring pretty little liars down together . . . #promisetoneverleaveyoucold.*

Pretty Little Liars was a mystery-thriller, as much soap opera as mystery. The premiere shows five teenage girls at a slumber party. They get drunk and the next morning one of them is missing. By the end of the episode, the other girls discover she was murdered and one of her pretty, popular friends had killed her—but which one?

Josie Snyder's reference to Shelia and Rachel as "pretty little liars" was the first time the two teens were linked to the TV show publicly, but law enforcement had privately been referring to the pair that way since Skylar disappeared.

The next day, Josie Snyder's tweet incorporated lyrics from a Merle Haggard song entitled "Mama Tried": *Turned 21 in prison doing life w/o parole #loveoldiesmusic*.

A few days later, she tweeted again. This time it was a lyric from the theme song of the TV show *Cops*: *Whatcha gonna doo whatcha gonna doo when they come for you.*

Whoever Josie Snyder was, her unceasing pressure on Shelia and Rachel was taking its toll—especially on Rachel. Numerous people said Rachel was having a difficult time with the play. Daniel's relentless push for answers hadn't stopped after Mr. Kyer called him out; it only became more subtle. Daniel began texting Rachel more and speaking to her less. And Rachel's on-stage behavior in the run-up to the play was outrageous: As opening night approached, her tears, outbursts, and tantrums threatened to turn the comedy into a tragedy.

thirty

Becky's Rant

On the opening night of UHS' production of *A Midsummer Night's Dream*, a cast and crew of about forty teens rushed around taking care of last-minute preparations. A few parents, school personnel, and other adults drifted through the chaos. Thirty minutes before show time, most of the actors were in costume. A few were still sitting for their stage makeup. In the auditorium, people had begun to arrive and select their seats for the show.

Daniel paced back and forth reciting his lines in the hallway behind the auditorium. With glitter on his face and his hair teased large, he couldn't wait to play the role of Oberon, the Fairy King. Down the hall, Daniel spotted Rachel in costume for her role as Helena, speaking to her mother. Rachel appeared to have been crying. Daniel heard Rachel's and Patricia's voices rising. He gestured to one of the girls who had applied Rachel's makeup to go rescue her. Mother and daughter were obviously in the middle of another fight. *Great timing*, Daniel thought.

Just then Daniel thought he saw Patricia's hand smack Rachel across the cheek. The smack was followed by, "Get your shit together, Rachel!"

While Daniel said he had no idea what provoked Patricia, her best friend, Liz, insists there is "no way" Patricia slapped her daughter.

"Patricia never believed in corporal punishment," Liz said, "so she wouldn't lay a hand on that girl."

Liz witnessed the exchange between Rachel and her mom that night. Patricia had just learned Rachel didn't show up for the previous night's performance because she was off somewhere with Shelia.

Patricia was furious with Rachel. The police had warned her to keep Rachel away from the other girl, and not only had Rachel lied to Patricia, but she also skipped out on a performance. Patricia had gone to great pains to try to follow their instructions, but every time she turned around Rachel was being defiant and flaunting her friendship with Shelia.

When Mr. Kyer told Patricia that Rachel's understudy had to go on instead, Liz said Patricia was enraged. She confronted Rachel and when the teen realized she had been discovered, her eyes widened and she burst into tears.

―――――――――

While all of the backstage drama was going on, no one suspected anything was amiss because Rachel's Twitter traffic during that time was upbeat, reflecting her excitement and love of the stage. She sent a shout-out to Mikinzy for showing his support by being in the audience and bringing her flowers. Her enthusiasm peaked on November 3, the last day of the play. Rachel tweeted: *round three boys and girls, let's kill it tonight!*

Rachel's good mood didn't last long. Several area teens received subpoenas to appear before a federal grand jury in Clarksburg, about forty-five minutes from Morgantown. Grand jury subpoenas are supposed to remain secret, but Shelia and Rachel learned that Eric Finch, Crissy Swanson, and a teen named Aaron Roupe—all of whom had known Skylar through Shelia Eddy—were called to provide information.

Law enforcement was unaware Shelia and Rachel knew about the grand jury, but they did. The girls were upset and it showed in their tweets. Rachel's *sick of being let down* and Shelia's simple *F M FREAKING L* ("FML" is textspeak for "fuck my life") were easy to decipher.

Later that day, Shelia's tweets revealed sadness—although the remorse might have been feigned (*i would do anything to go back to the beginning of 2010 literally anything*). Could her tweets have been a reference to the fact that in 2010 Shelia still lived in Blacksville and Skylar was still alive?

Shelia's sadness was short-lived. The next day she was back to her old form and feeling cocky: *no one on this earth can handle me and rachel if you think you can you're wrong*. This may have been meant as a warning, possibly for the police working the case.

The official transcript of the grand jury proceedings remains sealed; however, it appears to have been a fishing expedition. The fact that a federal grand jury was convened in the first place helps explain the FBI's presence, since the FBI always works cases brought into federal court. Given all of this, the precise nature of the investigation remains obscure.

Was the grand jury looking for evidence of the bank robberies? Was Skylar's disappearance connected to those bank robberies? Afterward, the subpoenaed teens said it seemed the grand jury was more about Blacksville drug traffic than either the bank robberies or Skylar's disappearance.

But Shelia and Rachel clearly believed the grand jury was all about a girl—Skylar. For instance, Shelia tried to alleviate Rachel's worry in a November 6 text: *Mark said it was ALL gunna be about drugs.*

By "Mark," Shelia may have meant Mike Benninger, her attorney. Both girls' parents had retained attorneys for their daughters sometime in September, not long after police began questioning the two teens.

Rachel texted back: *okay how does he know that's all this is about? im sure its more for me.*

Shelia replied, *because thats what the us attorney said their gunna follow the drugs to get to skylar.*

If Rachel was worried about the federal grand jury, that was nothing compared to what came next: the two girls learned that authorities wanted them to take a lie detector test. Neither teen was happy. It felt like the heat had been dialed up another notch.

Meanwhile, their Twitter enemies couldn't wait to bring on even more: *Pretty little liars keep on lying!!* Josie Snyder tweeted. Then, *Ever seen the show I (almost) got away with it… They ALWAYS get caught may take a little but criminals end up behind bars :).*

By the time the federal grand jury met, social media users around the state, and to some degree around the nation, were fully engrossed in Skylar's story. Becky Bailey's late-night Facebook rants had become especially famous; many members on the TEAMSKYLAR 2012 site loved reading them. The rants began after Bailey saw one of the first Facebook posts about Skylar right after she disappeared. It didn't take long for Bailey to learn the pretty teen was Dave Neese's daughter. She and Dave had gone to high school together.

Bailey poured out her frustration on Facebook, talking about the terrible dangers facing today's children. One of the many topics Bailey vented about was the fact that no AMBER Alert was announced for Skylar. Dave's former classmate promised the Facebook group she would continue to post until "Skylar is returned home safe and sound."

Bailey was infuriated that AMBER Alerts could only be issued once law enforcement determined a missing child had been abducted. (AMBER is actually an acronym: "America's Missing: Broadcast Emergency Response.") She believed missing teenagers—even those who left of their own free will—were still in danger. Bailey wanted every case of a missing teen to be scrutinized as though under the lens of a microscope.

Becky went to work, trying to fix the AMBER Alert problem. On December 4, she posted her plan in an online petition. After providing some background on Skylar's case, Bailey stressed that the first forty-eight hours after a child disappears are critical—whether the teen ran away or was abducted. She closed with a powerful appeal:

This petition matters to everyone who has a child, grandchild, niece, nephew, brother, sister, this could have been anyone's child, it could be yours, it could be mine....I never in a million years thought this could happen to someone I knew but it did, so please no one think you are immune. Changes in this law may be, God forbid, too late to help Skylar but please sign this petition so someone else may have a better chance.

"I did this for Skylar, so she would have a lasting legacy. I did it for Dave and Mary," Bailey said, "and the zillions of kids who slide through the cracks on a daily basis."

Bailey's plea struck a chord in the heart of every reader who's ever been a parent—and perhaps some who haven't. Within a few short months, more than 23,000 people signed her petition.

Dylan Conaway was starting to sweat. He'd been the focus of a police investigation into Skylar's murder—and the target of local gossip for months.

"I obviously knew I wasn't guilty," Dylan said, "but everybody, literally, *everybody* I knew and grew up with thought I was a murderer. Even the people I thought were my friends. That's a horrible feeling."

Dylan was one of the many people in Morgantown and Blacksville who were wrongly accused of Skylar's murder. Not only did law enforcement have their eyes on him, but his name repeatedly came up on websites that discussed the case.

Of course Dylan wasn't alone. Crissy, Shania, and Shelia's first cousin, Lexy Eddy, were all similarly targeted. Lexy and Crissy were both related to Shelia. Unwilling to believe she had done anything wrong, they defended her throughout that fall. So did her loyal friend, Shania. After Rachel confessed, the girls' pictures were circulated online as gossips tried to implicate them in Skylar's murder. The accusations were baseless but all three girls suffered.

At work, Crissy's coworkers talked about her, speculating about her involvement in the crime and even taking their concerns to their boss. At nearby North Marion High, Lexy was hounded by fellow students until she left school that semester.

Even though Shelia and Rachel eventually pled guilty to Skylar's murder, none of these people feel free from all the accusations.

In the autumn after Skylar's murder, social media gossip speculated that Skylar had a crush on Dylan Conaway, or that he had a crush on her. Neither idea seems likely.

"Skylar was cool. Quiet sometimes," he said. "Nothing to really dislike about her. Even if she was as old as Shelia, she looked a lot younger. She seemed so innocent. Shelia seemed more mature, rambunctious. Skylar was more shy. It definitely seemed like she looked up to me, in a big brother way. Like she wanted to be like me."

Dylan admitted he's done hard drugs many times and said Shelia and Rachel had become involved with harder drugs through their sophomore and junior years. Skylar only smoked weed, so far as he knew.

Dylan had been with Shelia the first time she smoked pot. It was in the back of a Ford Explorer after a Clay-Battelle football game during their freshman year. Dylan was driving and his cousin, Kevin, was in the passenger seat. In the back seat was another friend of his, along with Crissy and Shania.

"Shelia and Skylar were in the very back in the hatch," Dylan recalled. "We were parked on a back road. Football season, 2010. After Shelia had moved to Morgantown."

Shania, who admits she smoked weed long before either girl, said she thought it odd because neither Shelia nor Skylar wanted anything to do with weed and then, suddenly, they did. It appears Shelia smoked weed to impress Dylan, who she thought was cool.

Shania said Skylar did the same thing one week later. Skylar wanted to impress Shelia, and be cool, too.

Most of Dylan's interactions with Skylar, Shelia, and Rachel were when they were freshmen and sophomores. He was Shelia's first[26] lover, and they remained party friends. Now, after all that's happened, people ask him if he ever saw any hint of what was to come.

"If I had, I would have gotten out of it way sooner," he said.

On discussion boards and in local gossip, the Conaway house has been portrayed as a sort of party central. Dylan's mother, Debby Conaway, denies this, saying she was at home whenever Dylan invited friends over.

So does Dylan. He says the "parties" at his house mostly consisted of a few kids sitting around getting high. He confirmed that Skylar was often playing on her iPhone during these gatherings.

One night Kevin came over when Shelia, Rachel, and Skylar were there. "I had some vodka and they got pretty drunk," Dylan said. "I definitely let them drink a little too much. I looked at [Skylar] and I was, like, 'Skylar if you gotta puke, just go to the bathroom, make yourself throw up, whatever, just don't puke on my bed, please.'"

Skylar insisted she was fine, but moments later, when she tried to stand, she said, "I'm fine"—and threw up all over his bed.

After she finished, "she seemed like she came back a little, but she was, like, 'Oh, boy, what did I just do?' She definitely felt bad."

Dylan was not happy, so Kevin offered to give the girls a ride to Shelia's dad's house.

"By the time he got home," Dylan said. "I was outside burning my entire bed."

---

[26] Dylan has repeatedly stated this in interviews.

thirty-one

Hiding Out

That November, Crissy Swanson fidgeted anxiously in a federal courtroom of the Northern District of West Virginia. She'd been subpoenaed to testify before a grand jury, and she had no idea what they planned on asking her.

Crissy had been terrified of this day ever since she'd met Berry and Spurlock at the Dollar General store in Blacksville. She remembered the meeting well. It began with a phone call from her mom: "Um, there are two state troopers out here looking for you."

"Can you ask them why?" Crissy said. "'Cause I know I haven't done anything."

"They wanna ask you about the Blacksville bank robbery."

"I don't know crap about the Blacksville bank robbery. So send them my way."

The two plainclothes officers arrived at the Dollar Store, walked up to Crissy, and introduced themselves. She remembers them as Berry and Spurlock, who told her that if she lied, "it's gonna get you seven years in federal prison."

"Okay," she said, slapping her leg with her hand, and suddenly feeling quite warm. "I wasn't gonna lie to you before, but now I'm really not. What do you want to know?"

Once she got down from the witness stand at the grand jury hearing, Crissy felt waves of relief roll over her. She knew she had been honest and forthright, which was all that mattered, all the United States District Attorney was looking for. She even thought her testimony had helped alleviate suspicions about Shelia, after the DA asked Crissy if Shelia would take a polygraph.

"Oh, Shelia will take a lie detector test," Crissy said. "Why wouldn't she? She has nothing to hide."

When Crissy arrived back home in Fairview, she dialed Tara's number.

"We called to let her know we were out of grand jury," Crissy said, adding that she wanted to reassure Tara and Shelia that none of the questions had been too troubling. That was when Tara said something that made Crissy question the loyalty she felt for her cousin.

"I know I shouldn't say this over the phone. I know they can hear me," Tara said, reflecting her belief that the phone was tapped. "Shelia came out and said they were out in Brave that night." The town of Brave is about 3.5 miles west of Blacksville, just over the border in Pennsylvania.

"You've got to be kidding me!" Crissy said. Her anxiety instantly turned to anger. She knew exactly where that was—it was one of the darkest, loneliest stretches of road around. If the girls were out that way and Shelia had lied about it all along.... Crissy stopped the track her thoughts were taking. If Shelia had lied about that one thing, what else did she lie about? "You heard this from Shelia?"

"Benninger. He said Shelia had admitted that to him."

They hung up not long after and that's when it hit her: Crissy realized Shelia wasn't the only one stonewalling. She remembered back in September when Tara said, "If Shelia had a passport, we'd be gone." Then there were all those times Crissy's mother told her Tara seemed to know details about the crime before anyone else did. Crissy also found it troubling that Tara was giving Shelia alcohol and weed to calm her down, saying she was uptight because the police were harassing her.

Crissy worked at an assisted-living home in Fairmont, about twenty miles southeast of Morgantown. She decided to call Shelia on the way to work, because she had told her she would let her know how the grand jury went. "Then I'm not going to talk to her about it anymore," Crissy told her mom. "I'm not going to ask any more questions."

"Good," Crissy said her mom said. "Because whatever's going on, you don't want that on you. Shelia's lied once. You better just leave it alone."

Crissy called as she promised. Shelia had only been out of school for about a half hour. "Okay, I have you on speakerphone," Shelia said. "Rachel's here with me."

"Grand jury went fine," Crissy said. "I really don't think anything's weird. You know, they just asked me about the boys." Crissy had gone back and forth about the question—was the grand jury really convened to look for drugs or Skylar? From the tone of the questions, it sounded like they were looking for drugs. Which is exactly what she told Shelia.

"Oh, okay. Whatever."

"Shelia, don't you tell your mom I called you right now, okay? Don't say anything to her, but I want you to understand that you're ruining your life."

Dead silence came from the other end of the line. Finally, Crissy spoke up; the rumors and innuendo had eroded her faith in her cousin.

"This is going to destroy you if you're lying."

"I'm not lying."

"Even if you have nothing to do with this, you're going to go to jail if you lie. You can't lie."

"I said I'm not lying."

Crissy couldn't tell if Shelia was angry, but she still wanted to help her—if she could. "Good, because why would you do that? Why wouldn't you help Skylar come home?"

"I promise that's all I know," Shelia said. "I promise. I would tell you if there was something else. I promise I would."

With that, Crissy felt like Shelia was leaving her no choice. "Okay, and if there's anything else, I don't want to know. I want you to tell the FBI."

———

On December 1, Gaskins knew he had the girls. Now it was only a matter of time.

The day before, Rachel had changed her tune. During an interview, she told Gaskins they dropped Skylar off at the Conaway house—not at the end of her street like they had been saying since early July.

Since Shelia had an interview scheduled the same day, Gaskins couldn't wait to hear what she said. Shelia, though, apparently wasn't up to speed with Rachel. Her story remained the same. No one tried to contradict her or ask her any questions that might tip her off. They just jotted down her information.

The very next day, Shelia called Benninger and told him she wanted to tell him the truth. Benninger called the U.S. Attorney's Office to report what his client told him: "They did drop Skylar off at a house in Blacksville."

Gaskins was elated when he heard the news, because Shelia's story was identical to Rachel's. That's when he knew: Rachel changed her story, but forgot to tell Shelia in time. When Shelia found out, she had no choice but to change hers. The wall of lies was wobbling.

———

Two days later Tara was leaving a local grocery store with Shelia and Rachel, who each had another appointment with the police. A Fairmont woman[27] who recognized the two teens from their photos

———

[27] She wishes to remain anonymous.

says that as they were getting into Tara's car, she overheard them telling Tara what happened to Skylar.

"Skylar got mad," Rachel started.

Shelia finished. "And ran away—"

The woman says Tara broke in before the two teens could finish the story. "That's it, right?' She ran away and you didn't see her again? Right, girls?" Tara said, as if telling them not to say anything else.

The girls spoke in unison. "Right."

———

Not long after, Shelia and Rachel changed their story again. "We went out to the Brave bridge to smoke pot and Skylar ran off in the woods. We looked for her for hours. We couldn't find her and had to leave."

That's when the girls became official suspects. At the time, investigators believed the two teenage girls were probably terrified to tell the adults the truth: Skylar had died from an accidental overdose.

They had no idea the truth involved murder.

State and federal officers agreed: it was time for a polygraph. The test would help convince one of the girls to reveal the truth. Berry and Gaskins thought it would be Rachel.

———

Crissy wasn't the only one thinking about the FBI. So were Jessica Colebank and Chris Berry. It happened the same day Rachel skipped out on her polygraph exam. Both girls were scheduled to take their exams at the WVSP detachment in mid-December.

Tara drove Shelia to the detachment for her exam and Shelia's lawyer, Mike Benninger, met them there. He and John Angotti, Rachel's attorney, had already talked with their teenage clients and their parents. Both men felt the girls were well prepared. Even if the questions strayed away from drugs and toward Skylar's disappearance, Shelia and Rachel had maintained essentially the same story for five months now. Neither attorney was worried.

Shelia's lawyer wasn't the first person to talk with her about the polygraph. She and Rachel had repeatedly texted each other, discussing the procedure. Shelia also had a text conversation with Rachel in early November. At the time, Rachel had asked Shelia where she would take the exam.

SHELIA: *police station probably gonna fail cause of nerves no big fucking deal*

RACHEL: *As long as you don't fail cause you're lying. You can ask to take it again because you were nervous the first time*

SHELIA: *oh well im definitely not scared about lying but its not like theyd know the difference lol*

She should have been scared. Shelia did "fail" the polygraph. Twice. At least inasmuch as anyone can fail. The test is really scored on a question-by-question basis. The outcome is ambiguous in several ways—that's why it's not usually used as evidence in court. Still, Shelia failed hers.

Rachel was another story. She was nervous and jittery while getting ready at her father's South Park home, a little place near downtown Morgantown. Rusty tried to reassure his daughter as they got into the car. But it did no good. As they drove across the Pleasant Street bridge, Rachel jumped from the moving car—one block away from Angotti's office. She ran in the opposite direction, down Spruce. Stunned and trapped in traffic, Rusty was powerless to stop her. He watched his daughter run until Rachel disappeared down Spruce Street.

Somehow undetected, Rachel made her way upriver about a mile, to a location where she would find safe haven from her parents and the police. The one place they would never look for her.

Tara's office. Rachel knew she would be safe there.

When Berry and Gaskins heard what happened, they suspected Rachel's actions were those of someone with a guilty conscience.

They began making calls and looking at all the places they thought she might be. They desperately wanted to go after her and were trying to determine if she met the status of a runaway.

Colebank told Berry that Tara was coming to see her after work to get Shelia's electronics back, so she wouldn't be able to sit in on Rachel's polygraph exam at the detachment like she planned.

Instead Colebank went home to get her son from the bus after her shift ended at four, and then returned to the station to wait for Tara. She didn't learn until Berry showed up that Rachel skipped out on her polygraph.

"Yeah, Rachel didn't show," Berry said when he dropped by. "Maybe Tara can tell us where she is."

"Good, let's see what Tara knows," Colebank said.

The city officer had all of Shelia's electronics ready when Tara arrived, but she was determined to get as much information as she could before she released them. "By the way, you know Rachel's missing, right?"

"No she's not. Rachel's down in the car with Shelia," Tara said.

"What's she doing with her?" Colebank said. Her eyes met Berry's. "She's supposed to take her polygraph."

"Well, she's hanging out with Shelia now."

"We need to take her over to the State Police detachment before they list her as a runaway."

"Her dad knows she's with me."

Colebank was pissed. So was Berry. They both believed the more the two teens were together, the less chance they had of finding Skylar. They also knew they couldn't question either girl without their attorney present.

That's when Colebank realized: *Tara doesn't have an attorney. I can question her.*

"Tara, why are you helping them lie?"

"I have nothing to do with what these girls are doing," Tara said.

"Christmas is coming up. How would you feel if your child was missing at Christmas? You need to end this."

"Me? I told you they don't know anything."

"You need to try and appeal to them as a mother. Step up and if they did something, we can deal with it." As a mother herself, Colebank thought this approach was worth a try. "I want Skylar brought home. So does everybody else."

"We do too!" Tara said. Colebank believed her distress was genuine. The strain showed on her face as it increasingly had for the last few months. She wasn't yet sure why Tara was so worn down. Was it from the pressure to learn something—or to hide something?

"How can you do this?" Tara continued. "You guys are ruining their lives. They're getting harassed and picked on at school. All their friends are accusing them. The whole town's accusing them. They don't know anything."

That's when Colebank snapped. She was tired of how Tara coddled Shelia. She had seen enough of Shelia's arrogance and Tara's constant defensiveness and accusations. Whenever she or Spurlock got close to something, either Tara or Benninger would shut down the interview.

"You are her tool and she is using you to hide from us," Colebank said. "These girls know *exactly* where Skylar is. You are an idiot if you have not seen that by now, after all the evidence you know we have."

While Colebank was dealing with Tara, Berry texted Gaskins, asking if they could hold Rachel and take her to the detachment. He was waiting for a reply when the confrontation occurred.

As Shelia's parent, Tara had been present for many of the interviews and had spoken to Colebank and Spurlock. They pointed out inconsistencies and small changes in the story. Tara refused to listen, refused to see the obvious.

"I just can't believe it," Tara said.

"Well, you need to open your eyes and *believe it* because those girls did something to her and know *exactly* where she is. She is *dead*," Colebank said. "Wherever she is, she is dead, and they know where she's at. You need to end this for Dave and Mary's family."

Tara began crying and left the building.

"Like daughter, like mother," Colebank said to Berry.

They wanted nothing more than to follow Tara out and yank Rachel from the car. Make the truant teen wait there until her parents showed up to take her home. But they couldn't. The minute Tara told Colebank and Berry that Rusty knew Rachel was with her, they couldn't do a thing. It didn't take Colebank long to figure out her heated discussion with Tara had made her the first law enforcement casualty of the investigation. She realized it the next time she called Gaskins and Berry to ask what their day's agenda included—and no one called her back.

————————

Whoever Josie Snyder was, she had very good sources. Even the police thought so. They followed Josie's online harassment of Rachel and Shelia. Trooper Berry felt certain she knew something about the case. He tried unsuccessfully to get a warrant to learn her identity, prompting Josie to go dark for a while.

Then after nothing but stony silence since November 21, Josie came alive the evening of December 16 with a series of colorful tweets. They were addressed to Mia Barr, but everyone familiar with the case knew they were *really* subtweets for Shelia and Rachel.

At 6:31 that evening Josie tweeted: *failed lie detector. no shit no one gonna come out and say the truth how ya purposely od ur bff.*

Josie clearly believed Shelia and Rachel had killed Skylar by causing her to overdose.

Josie tweeted again at 6:59: *oooh no no! Hiding from po po.*

Nine minutes later, at 7:08, possibly in reply to a text message from Mia Barr, Josie's third tweet was nothing if not ominous: *no but one failed, one hiding out so the one that failed doesnt take care of business like she has witnessed #bffscaredofbff.*

There was no mistaking what Josie meant: she thought Rachel was in hiding so Shelia wouldn't kill her. Of course that really meant Josie had no clue that Rachel had run *to* Shelia, not away from her.

thirty-two

About a Girl's Car

On a regular basis all four officers—Colebank, Spurlock, Gaskins, and Berry—would gather around and watch the surveillance video again and again. After Colebank was "excommunicated," as she jokingly calls it, the male officers continued the practice. One day they blocked out half a shift and huddled around a large-screen computer monitor. Over and over, they watched the surveillance video that showed Skylar sneaking out her bedroom window. They played it from the beginning, in slow motion. They played it backward just as slowly. They looked at every single frame, trying to figure out what they had missed. Because surely there was something there—something so obvious they couldn't see it.

Over the course of the next several weeks, the officers continued watching the video, looking for that tiny clue that would tell them whose car Skylar got into that night. One morning, Spurlock, Gaskins, and Berry turned on the video at 8:00 A.M. when their shift began and then studied different car makes and models for hours online.

"We were so burned out, we actually went to the sergeant's office where he has a bigger screen, to blow up a screen shot," Berry said. "The coffee didn't taste good anymore."

The three men were so specific in their search for details, they looked at the gas caps, the back glass in the cars—everything they could think of to try to find a match to the car in the video. By ten that night, the men began to argue over their theories and the minor differences in vehicle models they found online.

"Let's stop right here," Spurlock said. "Let's go home, take a night, sleep on it, and start out fresh tomorrow."

"Okay, sounds good to me," Berry said. Gaskins agreed and the three men headed home.

———————

Chris and Alexis Berry had been married for four years when he was reassigned to the Morgantown Detachment. Alexis had given up her dream of going to medical school to become Chris' wife, because she was crazy about him. But his work on Skylar's case began to take a huge toll on their marriage.

Berry spent more hours at the office than he ever had before. That wouldn't have been as hard on Alexis if Berry hadn't also brought his work home with him. Many times, he wouldn't get home until midnight—and yet she'd still wake up to find him texting. Again. It was the same thing every night. At first she didn't believe him when he told her who he was texting.

"Who are you texting at two A.M.?" Alexis asked.

"Gaskins," Berry said.

"Sure you are."

But then he'd show her his phone, and Alexis saw he was telling the truth. She couldn't stop worrying, though. He looked horrible. She knew Spurlock and Gaskins were equally rundown, because she'd become acquainted with the women in their lives, too.

That's how Alexis knew she wasn't the only worried wife. The men were exhausted—and it showed. They had dark circles under their eyes. They were eating on the fly, when they bothered to eat at all, so they all lost weight.

"When we work, we work," Berry would often tell her.

———————————

That night—the night they all worked so long the coffee didn't even taste good anymore—was awful. Berry couldn't stop thinking about the case, mulling it over in his mind as he drove home. He knew Alexis was probably going to be "mad as a wet hornet" when he arrived. He was right.

"It was an awful night," Alexis agreed.

Then inspiration hit him like an early fall frost.

"It just clicked," Berry said. He'd been watching the video all day long, looking at every possible make and model of car and—nothing. But the minute he sat down with his wife, it hit him: Shelia told police she picked Skylar up and later dropped her off at the end of the street, but they had never seen Shelia pick Skylar up the first time. *Damn,* he thought. *Colebank was right all along.*

He didn't waste a second. He called Gaskins and then added Spurlock so they were all on a three-way phone call.

———————————

Gaskins was a few miles away, pacing in his kitchen. Even from upstairs, his fiancée Kelly Wilkes could hear Gaskins talking to himself. They usually only had a few hours each evening to spend together. At one time, that had been because of Kelly's schedule. She managed a fast-food chain and was going to college at night. But ever since Gaskins got this case they'd hardly seen each other.

So their relationship suffered, too. At first, Kelly expected Gaskins home for dinner a little late. Then she realized if she waited for him, dinner would be burnt to a crisp.

"Well, I'll see you when I see you," she finally learned to say. She ate alone many nights, watching episodes of *Law & Order.*

At other times Kelly tried to call Gaskins but got no reply. "He might not answer me for a couple of hours and I'd be worried he'd be out there dead," she said.

Like Alexis, she was frustrated by her man's constant texting—especially when they did sit down to a meal together. "Get off there," Kelly would tell Gaskins. "Dinner's gonna get cold."

Upstairs in bed, Kelly could hear Gaskins below, still talking to himself as he paced around the living room. She knew he was obsessed by the case and figured by the time he'd solved it, the floor covering would be worn out.

Oblivious to Kelly's worry and only able to think about the missing girl, Gaskins continued to pace, trying to figure out what he'd missed. He knew if he thought long and hard enough, retracing every step of their investigation, replaying the entire case from start to finish, he could find the answer. For the next hour or two, that's what he did. He remembered how everyone believed at the outset that Skylar left with a boy, or because of a boy—either a random stranger she met online or in the Wendy's drive-through lane where she worked, or a boy she'd been sneaking around to see, without her parents' knowledge.

Pretty early on, they ruled out the theory Skylar left with a stranger. That left only boys she knew, so they had looked at Dylan Conaway, at Eric Finch, at Floyd Pancoast, at Dylan's cousin, Kevin Willard, at...so many boys Gaskins couldn't remember all their names. There was only one problem: none of those boys drove a car like the one in the video and, in fact, no one could remember seeing Skylar with a boy, or hearing her express interest in a boy—any boy. So no, it hadn't been a boy at all.

Gaskins thought back to Shelia and Rachel, to how they had picked up Skylar and then dropped her off—supposedly at the end of the street. It was Shelia who had given the police names of other boys they might want to look at. But those leads were dead. They went nowhere. There hadn't been a party at the Conaway home, either, or anywhere else. For once, it seemed like the teens were telling the truth, when they said there had been no parties in Blacksville that night.

He believed someone out there knew something, but they were just too scared to talk. Then again, there was the troubling fact that

Skylar wasn't seen coming home on camera. That took Gaskins back to square one, to Shelia and Rachel, and he realized there was only one answer left: it was Shelia's car. Nothing else added up.

Walking the floor, ruminating on all he knew, Gaskins was methodically working out the kinks of the case when Berry's call came through.

"That *has to be* Shelia's car!" Berry was practically yelling. "The girls are *definitely* lying!"

———————————

The next day at work, everyone involved celebrated the first major crack in the stone wall Shelia and Rachel had erected. They did so after gathering around the video again—this time backing it up to 11:00 P.M., the time Shelia said she and Rachel picked up Skylar.

Sure enough, no one saw anything like that on the video— because no car showed up to get Skylar then. The vehicle they had been searching for so long and hard, had been there the entire time, just like Colebank originally suspected. It was a silver Toyota Camry—and it didn't pick up Skylar until 12:31 A.M.

thirty-three

Contents under Pressure

Berry knew he was taking a chance. The idea might come to nothing, but it was worth a try. He knocked on the door of the Neeses' apartment, trooper hat in hand.

Dave answered. "Come on in, Chris."

Berry could tell Dave was down. Without Skylar, Thanksgiving had been rough for the Neeses and as Christmas drew near, both of them had grown increasingly sad and weary. Berry wondered how much more they could take.

"Dave." Berry nodded as Dave stepped back. "I have an idea."

Mary was sitting on the couch, staring at the TV. Dave sat down beside her. Berry stood, shifting from foot to foot.

"Time to shake some trees," Berry said.

"See what falls out," Dave replied, sitting forward on the edge of the couch. He liked the idea already.

Berry had told him before that "shaking trees" often results in a big break in an investigation. When leads dry up, go out and do a "knock and talk"—the police equivalent of a cold sales call. Start asking questions and make yourself as much of a nuisance as possible, then sit back and see what happens. Berry knew Shelia and Rachel were hiding something, but he hadn't been able to make them talk yet. He felt like they were beating him. Berry couldn't take that, because Berry *hated* to lose.

"I know those girls aren't telling us what they know," Berry said. "I just have to find the right buttons to push. I wanted to arrest them both for obstruction, but Ronnie didn't think we had enough."

"Those girls have been lying since day one," Dave said.

"What Dave said," Mary said, turning away from the TV for the first time. "I cut Shelia off a long time ago."

"It may be worse than either of you think." He looked at the recliner. "I know they read the TEAMSKYLAR 2012 page. I want you to use that. Mind if I sit down? I need to tell you some things. It won't take long."

———————

Mary sat at the computer, trying to compose her thoughts. She was optimistic, but she would try anything if it would bring Skylar back.

In the months after Skylar disappeared, bits and pieces of Mary's memories began to surface. For instance, she remembered that Skylar had rejected the idea of applying for a job at Chick-fil-A, where Shelia then worked. Instead, she got a job at Wendy's, joining her childhood friend, Hayden McClead. Soon after, Skylar got Daniel a job there, too.

Skylar and Daniel had always been tight, but with all three of them working at Wendy's, Skylar and Hayden grew close again. Hayden— like many of Skylar's friends—didn't like Shelia. She wouldn't hang out with Skylar if Shelia was around.

To Hayden and other teens, it seemed like Shelia was always testing the limits in uncomfortable ways. She liked being more outrageous than her peers. Hayden recalled a specific party held in Blacksville where Shelia really pushed the limits.

Everyone was getting high, and Shelia and another girl, Janet,[28] were kissing. Some boy began snapping photos, so Shelia and Janet

---

[28] Not her real name.

started a striptease for all the partygoers. Hayden and Skylar were disgusted and sat back in a corner, trying to pretend it was no big deal.

Thinking about the stories Skylar had told her and the ones she later heard from Hayden, Daniel, and others, Mary realized that while she and Dave had tried to accept Shelia and think of her as a daughter, they never completely succeeded. In the years since Skylar and Shelia first met at The Shack, Mary and Dave had seen Shelia mostly in the summer and a few times during the school year. In eighth grade, Skylar and Shelia's visits became more frequent, with Shelia staying overnight at the Neeses' or Skylar sleeping over at Tara's place in Blacksville.

In ninth grade, everything changed. Mary said that as time went on, she and Dave finally began to notice little things about Shelia they had always overlooked. Shelia was their daughter's friend, and they wanted to see only the best in her, but her effect on Skylar hadn't always been positive.

For instance, there was how Skylar treated her own cousin, Kyle Michaud. Two years older, Kyle had been there the day Skylar came home from the hospital. Carol had only Kyle, and Mary had only Skylar—so Skylar and Kyle grew up as close as siblings. But once Shelia came to UHS, Skylar wouldn't even talk to Kyle when she saw him.

As Kyle later put it, they passed in the hallway "for more days than there were words exchanged between the two of us."

He'd told Mary how acutely he felt the effects of Skylar's withdrawal from family and friends. One day was particularly vivid in his memory. He'd driven his father's car to work and was waiting in the parking lot to give Skylar a ride home, as he did two or three days a week. Only that day in December 2011, she didn't show.

A couple of years apart in age, Skylar was a sophomore that year, Kyle a senior. They had already drifted far apart. On the days Skylar rode home with him, she'd wear her earbuds, blast the music, and only answer direct questions. Otherwise, they didn't talk.

Top: Skylar enjoying her birthday with her family. (From left: Aunt Carol,
Cousin Kyle, Skylar, and her mother, Mary.)
Bottom: Skylar and her protective older cousin, Kyle.

He waited for ten or fifteen minutes, then went back into UHS,
looked around the cafeteria and checked her locker. No Skylar. She
could be anywhere. School had been out for twenty-five minutes. On
his way back to the car, he called his father.

"I don't know where Skylar is, Dad," Kyle said. "I'm telling you now, I'm not gonna get yelled at because she disappeared."

"All right, then. Come on."

When he arrived home, his aunt Mary was just leaving. He told her Skylar had never shown up after school.

"Oh, she's okay. She went with Shelia." Mary stopped, her coat half on. "She didn't tell you?"

"Nope," Kyle said sullenly. But he wasn't surprised.

That's when Mary remembered what Kyle had said: "Shelia's a bad seed." That memory helped Mary realize that since Shelia moved into town, Skylar had been growing away from the older cousin who had once been like a big brother.

It was also unnerving how often Shelia lied about one thing or another—Mary remembered how she even covered for Shelia with Tara. But it was a sexually explicit Facebook message that really made Mary reflect on Shelia's character. She and Dave had been appalled and angry when they stumbled onto it.

Mary remembered that it happened not long before Skylar disappeared. In a rush to meet up with Shelia, Skylar had forgotten to log out of her Facebook account on the family computer. When Dave went online, the page was there in plain sight. The message from Shelia to Skylar described in graphic detail one of Shelia's sexual experiences. It was so worrisome that Mary and Dave printed it out and drove to Tara and Jim's townhouse to show them. But Shelia denied she had sent it. She blamed it on Shania, saying the other girl was pranking her. Tara believed Shelia, and brushed the entire matter aside.

Mary started typing. Maybe if she wrote everything down, she could make sense of it all. The words came slowly at first, but she discovered the more she wrote, the better she felt. She realized she wanted to share her thoughts with the world—and she did that in the form of a letter on Facebook.

It appeared on Mary's personal Facebook page in mid-December. Before long, everyone in the two Facebook groups had shared it. Some people later claimed Mary Neese's honesty, clarity, and directness led to Rachel Shoaf's confession soon after.

Mary's written words showed how six months of lies and stonewalling had radically changed her and Dave's view of Shelia and Rachel. *The time has come to tell the full Skylar story from beginning to end as we know it to this point,* Mary began. She recapped the circumstances of Skylar's disappearance and described the discovery of the apartment surveillance video.

The grieving mother discussed how the unreliable tips and sightings were all they had to give them hope. They'd continued hanging MISSING posters around town for two months, *until I could no longer take it.* Then Mary stated something that only a mother would know: *Skylar could not stay away from me that long, let alone her friends.*

Law enforcement confirmed Mary's maternal instinct: *Skylar's two best friends... were not telling the whole truth. They have continued to withhold information... and have been caught in multiple lies to [the] authorities.*

Her moving public plea concluded on a dramatic note: *This is truly the ultimate betrayal.... These girls are more guilty than originally suspected.... It looks like foul play has occurred and murder has not been ruled out.*

A former UHS guidance counselor, Monongalia County Commissioner Tom Bloom had known Dave since he was a high school student himself. Bloom was deeply moved when he read the news about Skylar. He had known her during her freshman and sophomore years at UHS. Bloom called Dave Neese as soon as he read the original *Dominion Post* article about Skylar back on July 10.

"Dave, I'm not sure what I can do, but man," Bloom said, "I just want you to know I'm here for you."

"Thanks, Tom," Dave said.

When Becky Bailey posted her online petition in early December, Bloom was one of two people who immediately reached out to her. Chuck Yocum, a former student of Tom's, offered to add some legal language to the petition.

Bloom called House of Delegates member Charlene Marshall, who introduced Skylar's Law to the state legislature in January. Marshall had long thought the AMBER Alert system needed to be revised. In her view the current law wasn't doing enough to help bring home missing children.

"We're getting complaints about you," Gaskins told Berry one day as the younger trooper hung up his hat. "But at least we're getting results."

"Big surprise," Berry said, grinning. "From out Blacksville?"

He was used to it. Berry's first posting had been at the Martinsburg Detachment in West Virginia's eastern panhandle. The city had become a suburb of metropolitan DC, and criminal activity there was confined more to the city than the outlying rural areas. There, Berry had learned more aggressive policing techniques than were common in some other parts of West Virginia—because the criminals were more violent.

Even though he solved crimes at a high rate, once Berry transferred to Fairmont, twenty miles southwest of Morgantown, he found the interview techniques he had used in the suburbs of DC didn't translate well. Still, his superiors knew he was a good investigator, so when a rash of bank robberies occurred in Monongalia County, Berry had been sent to the Morgantown Detachment specifically to work the robberies. Then that case intersected with Skylar's disappearance.

As the months wore on with no leads on Skylar, however, Berry knew they had to break something loose to get results. So he had begun to aggressively question people, just like he used to in Martinsburg. The result was "pissing people off," as he later put it. He knew of a few people in the Blacksville area who disliked him, for sure.

So when he came into the office that day and Gaskins told him the sergeant wanted Berry to exclusively investigate some Westover bank robberies across town, Berry assumed that was the reason. He'd been talked to many times before about upsetting the locals.

It wasn't. It was something else entirely.

"Seen TEAMSKYLAR 2012 recently?" Gaskins said, a small grin playing on his lips.

Berry nodded. They both knew he had. Gaskins knew his way around a computer, but Berry was the go-to guy for all things social media.

That's when it hit Berry: he was being taken off Skylar's case.

Dave's version of why Berry was removed was more colorful. He said Gaskins called him the morning after Mary had posted her long letter and yelled into the phone: "Get that shit off the internet now!"

Dave said he called and tried to get Berry put back on the case, to no avail. With that, Berry became the second law enforcement casualty.

Teenage girls are notorious for primping, and Shelia and Rachel were no different. Makeup, hair, clothes, everything had to be just right before they snapped the selfies that showed up all over social media before and after Skylar's murder. By the time they hit high school, the girls were experts at managing their images.

Skylar's murder didn't change that. If anything, as the police grew closer to the truth, the two teens tried even harder to maintain the appearance of normalcy. Rachel was finding it an impossible task.

Evidently Rachel's descent began not long after she murdered Skylar, signaled by the daily crying spells many students saw at school, cutting herself while at home, smoking more and more weed, and being reprimanded by school officials. There are allegations Rachel was using harder drugs, too, and some people say she and Patricia were fighting more frequently. Along the way, her school attendance also grew spotty.

If possible, Rachel's behavior grew even more erratic. As Christmas approached, her parents reached the end of their rope. They may have planned to hire a good therapist for their daughter. If so, they never got the chance.

———————

Rachel wasn't the only one who was acting out. So was Shelia. She and Rachel cut classes so they could be together, and spent their days hanging out at friends' houses, smoking weed.

Shelia had always pushed the boundaries, but usually backed down once Tara made it clear Shelia wasn't getting her way. But something had changed, and Crissy said Shelia was vocal and disrespectful whenever she challenged Tara's authority. Equally odd, Tara didn't say a word in reply.

That was the part Crissy found weird. "It was like Tara was afraid of Shelia," Crissy said. She then related how Tara had confided she was giving Shelia weed and alcohol to calm her, after Shelia grew outraged one day and grabbed her mother's arm so hard Tara thought it was broken.

———————

Shania knew how much her friend Shelia missed Skylar, so she slaved over the homemade Christmas gift. She wanted it to be the perfect present; she planned to give it to her when Shelia came to pick Shania up for a sleepover a few days before Christmas.

Shania was a little nervous because she wasn't sure how Shelia would react. Would she be happy or burst into tears? She had copied dozens of photos she knew Shelia would love, of Shelia's friends and family. There were shots of Shelia with Shania or Skylar, or all three girls together, an assortment of posed shots and selfies. Shania labored over the fabric-covered collage for hours, carefully assembling it. She had far more photos than would fit, so she wrapped up the loose photos together, so Shelia would have them, too.

When she was done the collage looked fantastic, and Shania felt it helped memorialize their missing friend. Shania believed her present would provide Shelia with something tangible, something to hold onto—until Skylar returned.

Shelia's reaction to Shania's handmade gift was exactly what Shania had hoped for. Shelia loved her present, and she and Tara took turns looking at all of the pictures Shania didn't have room to place in the collage.

"Thank you," Shelia said, giving Shania a big hug.

Shania didn't give the moment much thought until a week later, when she was back at Shelia's house. Shania saw the collage, but not a single photo of Skylar remained. Shelia had removed them all, and tossed them into the gift bag with the rest of the photos.

thirty-four

Nervous Breakdown

"Don't take my suitcase out of the car because I'm going back to Dad's," Rachel said.

Her mother was trying to remove the luggage when Rachel chimed in, right after they returned home from celebrating Christmas with Patricia's family. When Rachel saw her father's Jeep in the driveway, she didn't even plan to go inside with her mother. She wanted to leave as quick as she could, to go see Shelia.

"Your dad is sick again," Patricia said, "so he's moving back in and I'm going to take care of him."

Rachel didn't know it but Patricia and Rusty had concocted the story for their daughter's benefit before she and her mom began the drive back from Virginia. Patricia texted Rusty on the way back, telling him they were *almost home.* The last thing she wanted, Liz says, was to have another fight with Rachel. *You better hurry, because she's getting upset,* Patricia texted him.

She noticed the closer they got to home, the edgier Rachel became, as if she might explode from nervous energy. Patricia suspected part of it was because Rachel had been separated from Shelia for so long. That was the reason she wanted to take Rachel away. The police had warned her from the start and Colebank told her Shelia was a pathological liar who was no good for Rachel. The rest of Rachel's anxiety probably stemmed from the fact the FBI wanted to question her the following day. Again. Patricia might be a screamer but most any mother would be, after all she'd been dealing with for the last five months. She wanted to scream again when she thought back to that day when Liz told her what Rachel said: "I had to make sure Tara didn't mind if I came to lunch with you," Rachel had told Liz.

Trying to keep Rachel away from that girl—*and her mother*—had proved an impossible task. She remembered the day Rachel had jumped from the Jeep and run to Tara—and Rusty hadn't even told her. The whole time she thought Rachel was at the State Police office, taking her polygraph test. If it hadn't been for Liz, whom Rachel later confided in, she never would have known. Patricia felt her blood pressure rise just remembering that terrible day. Rachel could have been killed. Patricia couldn't understand why Rachel would feel she had to run away from the police when all they were trying to do was find Rachel's friend. To find Skylar, the girl Rachel had asked Patricia to let come live with them a year ago, when it looked like Skylar's family might be evicted. It hadn't come to pass, but Patricia had been touched by her daughter's compassion.

Who was this girl who defied her own mother, all while doing whatever Shelia and Tara asked her to, as if she was their puppet? Patricia couldn't understand why Rachel didn't try to do everything she could to help the police. Who was this girl? Where was her Rachel?

Patricia was no fighter. She knew that. She had never overcome her tendency to cower when someone threatened her. It was a hold-over from her own childhood, and she couldn't do anything about it. Not so Rachel, who was much stronger and whose behavior had become more aggressive lately. Patricia dreaded the showdown that would occur if she and Rachel were alone when she figured out the ruse, when her daughter learned what was really going on.

Rusty had already arrived when Rachel realized her parents were actually trying to prevent her from staying with her father, but in Rachel's overwrought state, his presence provided no restraint.

Patricia cringed as Rachel began shrieking. "You're ruining my life!" she screamed at her parents in their driveway on December 28, 2012. "You're ruining my life!"

No matter how much Patricia and Rusty urged her to calm down, Patricia knew Rachel had gotten so worked up that she wouldn't. Even if she had wanted to, which she didn't, she couldn't have stopped the tornado whirling within her. Her teenage world as she knew it was imploding. Rachel couldn't contain five months of pent-up feelings a minute longer.

Since September her father's house across town had been Rachel's refuge from the recent strife between her and her mother. But more important, living with her dad was the only way she could be with Shelia. He let her see Shelia whenever she wanted to—unlike her mom. Even though Patricia had recently tried to keep her away from Shelia, just like the police told her to, Rachel would have none of it. She had to be with Shelia, see Shelia, have Shelia tell her what to do and say, every time the police came by with more questions. Shelia's sense of calm and control were what helped Rachel fend them off.

Patricia wasn't a fool. She knew Rusty wasn't just Rachel's father. He was her friend, her buddy. He knew how much she needed Shelia, and he didn't see the harm in Rachel being with her. But now? Now they were telling Rachel he was moving back in. She knew it was a scheme to keep her from seeing Shelia. Why was he willing to work with her now, Patricia must have wondered, when he never had before?

Rachel's screams were loud enough for the entire cul-de-sac to hear. Just as Patricia suspected, she saw through their act.

Trying to keep their private lives out of the public eye, Rachel's parents quickly guided her toward the front porch. Once inside Rachel's anguish only increased.

Amidst the drama, neither Patricia nor Rusty noticed Rachel's iPod. She held the device in her hand, FaceTiming everything live to

Shelia. If they had realized that, they might have been less worried about what their neighbors could hear and more worried about what Shelia might witness.

Patricia Shoaf has authorized her best friend Liz to share the details of Rachel's meltdown. Unlike earlier reports claiming Patricia was on top of Rachel on the floor, Liz says it was the other way around. Rachel punched Patricia in the eye and threw an unlit candelabra against a wall. In the ensuing melee Patricia and Rusty were both injured when they fell down the steps trying to get their daughter under control.

While Rachel raged in the background, Patricia called 911.

In the audio recording, she sounds remarkably calm. "I have an issue with a 16-year-old daughter of mine. We can't control her anymore," Patricia said. "She's hitting us. She's screaming. She's running through the neighborhood."

It sounds like Patricia is talking to Rachel next, when she says, "Give me the phone. Give me the phone."

Rachel's screams punctuate the 911 call, until Patricia is heard telling her, "No. No. This is over. This is over."

More screams erupt from Rachel before Patricia tells the dispatcher, "My husband's trying to contain her. Please hurry."

As Patricia hung up, Rachel bolted upstairs and into her bedroom. She locked the door and began kicking holes in it. Rusty ran after her but she shoved her dresser in front of the door.

At this point, Rachel's screams were so loud a neighbor went to his window to see where the noise was coming from. That's when he heard Rachel threaten to take her own life.

"You've ruined my life," Rachel insisted between sobs. "I'm going to kill myself!"

Rusty managed to get inside and, despite her threats, by the time police arrived Rachel was subdued, sitting on the living room couch.

According to 911 logs, the State Police arrived at 7:10 P.M., two minutes after Patricia called. Rachel sat there without moving while the two troopers explained to Rusty and Patricia how they could take their daughter to the hospital and ask for a mental hygiene hearing. Rachel was eerily silent.

Patricia wanted Rachel arrested but the troopers explained only deputy sheriffs have that authority. Instead, they encouraged Rachel's parents to seek medical help. Patricia and Rusty took their advice, loaded Rachel into the family car, and drove her to the hospital.

————————

Shelia told Shania all about Rachel's breakdown, but she framed it as a violent family fight. She said Rachel's screams grew so shrill that Tara rushed into Shelia's bedroom to investigate. By then, Rachel was yelling, "Help me! Help me!"

Shelia raced to the emergency room and waited four hours, trying to find out what was happening to Rachel. Her December 28 tweets, *wow literally worst night of my life* and *ugh hope my girl @_racchh is okay <3 loveee youuu* show Shelia's concern.

Shania later said by the time Shelia was allowed to see Rachel, "her face was all bruised and knotted and swollen, and she had marks all over her."

Loved ones who saw Patricia in the days following Rachel's breakdown say her face was so badly discolored it took weeks for the bruising to disappear.

thirty-five

"We Stabbed Her"

Patricia knew Rachel was going to miss her December 29 FBI interview, so she called Angotti and explained that Rachel was in Chestnut Ridge Center, the local psychiatric hospital. By then, Rachel's attorney knew the reason the police were so insistent that Rachel come in again for questioning: Rachel's story had changed. But Shelia's hadn't, at least not quickly enough.

"You need to bring Rachel to our office the minute she's released. Not home," Angotti told Patricia.

Liz says Patricia was told to go directly to Angotti's office because the FBI and the U.S. Attorney's Office needed to talk to her before Shelia began controlling Rachel again.

Due to cutbacks in the mental health system, unless a specific diagnosis merits a longer stay, the average length of time for anyone who has been committed to a psychiatric facility is three to seven days.

So on January 3, 2013, Rachel Shoaf walked out the front door of the local mental hospital a free individual, finally ready to take her polygraph test. Rachel was just in time for the climax, as the curtain opened on Act Three.

By then, police had heard rumors Skylar might have been killed in Pennsylvania. So the U.S. Attorney's office took the lead in coordinating case interviews. The office rescheduled its December 29 meeting with Rachel, the FBI, and the WVSP. When Corporal Gaskins got word Rachel was being released from Chestnut Ridge, he was glad the teenager was going straight to her attorney's office for another interview. He hoped they would get the truth this time—and he couldn't wait to hear what it was.

Patricia and Rusty had looked forward to taking Rachel home, but once Angotti told them the federal government was calling the shots they found themselves being told what to do. They were eager to help if it meant Mary and Dave would learn the truth, too, and have the closure they deserved. So on that cold January day, the Shoafs drove their daughter straight to her attorney's office downtown. Once there, Patricia and Rusty waited in the lobby while Rachel met with John Angotti, FBI Special Agent Rob Ambrosini, and Corporal Gaskins.

The State Police corporal was replaying the details of the case as he wove the cruiser through traffic. All the way across town, through the slush and snow still on the streets after the recent snowfall, he mulled over what Rachel might say. Gaskins had known the two girls were keeping a big secret, and the entire time he'd been working the case, he had hoped it would be that Skylar's death had been accidental. He still believed that was true.

Gaskins hoped Rachel would tell them what really happened to Skylar so law enforcement would have some answers. Perhaps they would finally learn if Skylar's disappearance was connected to the bank robberies. Had Darek killed her to cover up something she had learned? Or maybe it really was as simple as an overdose, and Rachel and Shelia had managed to keep quiet. Gaskins thought of all the hours he and Berry had logged and all the time Colebank and Spurlock had put in. He thought about the dozen or so extra city, state, and federal officers who had helped and, along the way, become engrossed by the case. Now everyone would learn the truth.

Gaskins walked into the law offices, his face a mask. He greeted Rusty and Patricia, who sat waiting in the lobby, and went back to the conference room, where Ambrosini was waiting. The men said their hellos, exchanging small pleasantries about the weather or work, then took their seats at the conference table. The tension in the air was palpable.

When Angotti led Rachel in, she looked nothing like the girl who had stonewalled everyone for four months. She was shaking and she looked terrified. Rachel took the seat Angotti held out for her and immediately drew her legs up against her chest, hugging them tightly to her.

As soon as she began talking, Gaskins knew something was different. She no longer mentioned being too stoned to remember details. She wasn't flippant or careless. Clearly this girl wanted to talk. Rachel Shoaf was finally ready to tell the truth.

We're going to find out, he thought.

"I need a wastebasket, because I'm probably going to throw up," Rachel said.

———

While Ambrosini, known as one of the most skilled polygraph examiners in the FBI, led the interview, Gaskins waited for the teen to say she and Shelia had given their friend some kind of drug, an overdose. Or Skylar had fallen and hit her head, and when they couldn't wake her up, they'd gotten scared and left her behind. The seasoned investigator was expecting anything other than what he heard that day in Angotti's conference room.

"Was there a party?" Ambrosini asked.

Rachel shook her head back and forth, indicating *no*.

"Did she overdose?"

Again, Rachel shook her head.

"Did she choke?"

Another shake of her head.

Ambrosini and Gaskins looked at each other. They needed to change tactics, since they were getting nowhere.

"Well, what did happen, Rachel?" Gaskins asked.

Something like a tiny grin, brought about by sheer terror, appeared on Rachel's face. "We stabbed her."

All three men almost fell out of their chairs. Ambrosini and Angotti were speechless. So was Gaskins.

He looked up from his written notes, staring directly into the teenager's eyes. "I'm sorry, I don't think I heard you right."

"Shelia and I, we stabbed Skylar," Rachel said, her voice quivering and barely audible.

The pencil fell from Gaskins' hand.

"Are you saying you killed Skylar Neese?" Gaskins asked in disbelief.

She nodded.

Rachel Shoaf bared her soul, finally relieved of her heavy burden. She told them everything, including the way Skylar managed to grab Rachel's knife and used it to try and defend herself.

"I have the scar on my leg. Wanna see it?" With that, Rachel pulled up her pants leg—revealing a three-inch scar near her ankle.

After 181 days, Rachel held nothing back. She told them everything—everything except the reason they killed Skylar.

All Rachel would say is, "We just didn't like her."

———

After Gaskins and Ambrosini finished taking Rachel's statement, a shaken Angotti called Rusty and Patricia back to a private room. There he told them he knew the girls caused Skylar's death, but he didn't know any details. Angotti said they would need several hours with Rachel and suggested the police bring Rachel home after she led them to Skylar. After Rachel's mind-blowing revelation, Angotti honestly didn't know if Rachel would even make it back home or if the authorities would keep her. Until she actually led them to Skylar, several variables were up in the air, including whether Skylar was buried in Pennsylvania or West Virginia.

"I'm afraid your daughter is directly involved in the murder of Skylar Neese," Angotti finally said.

Stunned, Patricia's mind began spinning, as she reflected on all the lies Rachel had told her since Skylar disappeared. She thought of Rachel's future—and the life her beautiful, talented daughter had thrown away. One part of Patricia's mind couldn't accept what Angotti was saying. The other part knew it was true. Patricia crumpled to the floor, weeping.

Gaskins and Monongalia County Prosecuting Attorney Marcia Ashdown both knew after six months outdoors, exposed to the harsh elements, the crime scene and Skylar's remains weren't likely to yield much evidence for court. The best police could hope for was that there would be enough left to identify.

"Going to be a lot of snow in the woods," Ambrosini said as he and Gaskins were getting ready to go. Ambrosini's backup had arrived and was waiting in the parking lot outside the law offices. "Might not even be able to search."

Angotti had Rachel in his office, awaiting Gaskins' signal. It was time for Rachel to give them more than words—leading police to the body was the only way to prove she was telling the truth.

Driving the first of two cars, Gaskins thought Ambrosini might be right. Conditions didn't look promising. The farther out of town they drove, headed northwest, the more the snow piled up on the sides of the road. Rachel rode in the back seat of the lead car so she could direct Gaskins where to turn when it came time. Angotti sat up front with Gaskins. The second car, with the two FBI agents, trailed close behind the State Police cruiser.

During her confession, Rachel claimed Shelia disposed of the knives, their bloody clothes, Skylar's purse and iPod, the shovel, and the other tools the two girls had used to try to hide their crime. When Rachel said she had no idea where any of those items could be, she seemed sincere. But she had agreed to lead police to Skylar's body in exchange for a plea deal.

On the way there, after passing through Blacksville and turning off onto a narrow gravel road, Gaskins knew they were about to cross into Greene County, Pennsylvania. No one else was surprised, since most of the twisting back roads in that part of the county snaked back and forth between West Virginia and Pennsylvania. Rachel had been up there partying many times before, so she was pretty sure the spot was in Pennsylvania.

Both cars turned onto Morris Run Road, a narrow country lane composed of asphalt and gravel. The entire terrain was bathed in white that cold January day as gravel crunched softly under the vehicle tires. Less than two miles in, along an isolated stretch, Rachel told them to stop. The officers, the lawyer, and the suspect got out. All eyes were on Rachel, as she surveyed the white forest, first turning this way, then that. But it was two seasons later, in the dead of winter, and everything looked much different than it had in July. Finally, she admitted she couldn't tell where she and Shelia had left Skylar.

Gaskins and Ambrosini discussed how to proceed. In those kinds of conditions, who knew how long it would take to find Skylar? If they found her. They hated to admit it, but they had no choice: they would have to wait until the snow was gone.

———

The neighbors who saw Patricia and Rusty drive away not long after Rachel's return didn't understand why they would leave their daughter, newly released from a psychiatric hospital, home alone. They had heard Rachel's suicidal threats, and could only assume Rachel must be greatly improved for her parents to feel it was safe to leave Rachel behind. Evidently, they didn't see the strange cars scattered around in nearby driveways, or the police officers crouched down inside those unmarked vehicles, so the neighbors had no way of knowing Rachel was anything but alone.

Rachel texted Shelia saying her parents were gone so she could come over—just as Gaskins and Ambrosini had instructed. Then she sat back to wait, trying not to let her frayed nerves get the best of her. It had been a very long day—but it was far from over.

After five full days at Chestnut Ridge, she had left the hospital, gone to Angotti's office and told them about killing Skylar, agreed to help police catch her best friend saying something incriminating, and then led them to the place where she and Shelia had killed Skylar. Rachel knew what she needed—the best actress face she had in her repertoire—and it had better be in place before Shelia arrived.

The authorities say Shelia, of course, didn't know any of that. So Shelia probably stared out the passenger window as her mom drove toward the Shoafs' neighborhood, thinking about Rachel's hospitalization. It must have really unnerved her—God only knew what they'd done to Rachel while she'd been in that place, or how they had tried to brainwash her, but she was out now, and Shelia was anxious to see her best friend and lover. Since it was the first time she and Rachel had been separated since Rachel started falling apart, Shelia would have had a ton of questions. She was also worried Patricia and Rusty wouldn't let Rachel hang out with her. Not now.

She didn't know how much time they'd have. It was evening, and Rachel told Shelia her parents wouldn't be gone long. Tara planned to drop Shelia off and wait for her, killing time by circling the block until Shelia came out again. The cul-de-sac was tiny, and Tara didn't want to attract any attention by parking too close to the Shoafs'. She knew the neighborhood was full of gossips, so word would easily reach Patricia's ears. Or what if Patricia and Rusty sensed Shelia and Rachel were up to something and turned around and came right back? When they pulled in front of Rachel's house, Shelia breathed a sigh of relief: neither Shoaf vehicle was there.

Shelia had tried at least twice to see Rachel inside Chestnut Ridge. She was so persistent, security had to turn her away repeatedly. The first time was on a day set aside specifically for family visitation. Usually friends can visit, too, but only with permission from the patient or—in the case of minors—the parents. Patricia had left strict orders: "Family ONLY."

Shelia learned this when Tara dropped her off and she went inside the red-brick medical facility, where she was told her name wasn't on the list of approved visitors. It didn't make any sense. Before, she would have *been* family. Shelia wasn't sure what was going on. Still, she tried and tried—but failed to get past security.

When Patricia arrived to visit her daughter, she was surprised to see Tara waiting outside in her car. She immediately asked why Tara was there—where Tara was, so was Shelia—and sure enough, when Patricia walked into Chestnut Ridge, there was Shelia.

"What are you doing here? I told you only family," Patricia told Shelia.

Without waiting for an answer, she turned to the security guard and warned him not to let Shelia in.

"She's not getting past us, ma'am," he assured Patricia.

Shelia tried again two days later. Again she was turned away.

Mother and daughter were together on January 3, when Tara dropped Shelia off at the curb in front of the Shoafs' house, then began to drive slowly around the development. Rachel answered the door and Shelia slipped inside. Some people think Shelia had no clue what a busy girl Rachel had been earlier that day, that she didn't have any inkling Rachel had told authorities she and Shelia had savagely stabbed Skylar to death. They assumed Shelia didn't know Rachel had spent hours confessing to her lawyer, the State Police, and the FBI, and that nothing seemed amiss because Rachel wasn't in custody.

People speculate Shelia didn't know Rachel had agreed to gather evidence against her best friend, or that everything they said and did was being recorded on audio- and videotape.

They might be wrong, though. Shelia may have suspected all of that when she noticed Rachel's new accessory: she was wearing a really fancy watch.

"Nice watch, Rach," Shelia said. "I've never seen you wear a watch before."

Those people also believe Shelia, apparently like some of the neighbors, didn't notice the extra cars, either, or the officers inside those vehicles who were listening and watching the two girls' exchange.

Outside was another matter. From their respective positions in the unmarked cars, Gaskins and his entourage were listening and watching what was going on inside the Shoaf home. Every few minutes, Tara would drive by, and the officers would have to stop writing and duck down, hoping Tara couldn't see them.

"Man, I hope she can't tell the windows are fogged up, and figure out what we're doing," Gaskins said.

"That would be bad," Ambrosini replied, laughing.

For the entire time Shelia was inside with Rachel, the game continued: the officers would listen and watch and try to take notes—and then Tara would drive by again. By then it was so dark they knew she couldn't see them, but they knew she might be able to see some of the LED lights from their equipment inside the vehicles. Of course, writing soon became difficult in the dark, but they didn't have much longer to wait, because Shelia came out a few minutes later.

Despite all their efforts to catch Shelia in her lie, she didn't say anything that would directly incriminate her. It was clear to the state troopers and FBI agents listening outside that the teens were involved in a conspiracy—just as Rachel had said—but bugging Rachel and Shelia's "reunion" only produced one useful piece of information: the two girls spoke of "sticking together" in the coming days and weeks. Otherwise, the police got nothing else that helped their case.

However, this incident may have had an unintended consequence. Rumors that Rachel wore a wire started circulating in May, soon after the arrests. They persisted even after both Rachel and Shelia were found guilty of Skylar's murder. Every member of law enforcement directly involved in the case denied the rumor at the time. The FBI audiovisual surveillance was probably its source.

At the moment of their reunion, Shelia was oblivious to all of that; her only care was telling the world how happy she was to see Rachel— *her* Rachel—again. When Shelia left, she happily tweeted, *FINALLLLY GOT TO SEEE @_racchh <3*. She attached a selfie of the pair.

In that revealing photo, the pair of matching smiles seems forced and one can see the stress Rachel was under, her eyes rimmed with dark circles and a look of exhaustion in her expression. Shelia said as much with her very next tweet: *and i don't even care how bad we look*. Shelia never expected that tweet to be the last one she ever sent directly to Rachel.

Soon after leaving Rachel, Shelia was no longer happy. Police believe that's because Rachel's parents told Tara their daughter needed to stay away from Rachel—Shelia wasn't allowed to try to call, text, or chat online with Rachel. That if Shelia tried, it would be of no use anyway, since they were taking Rachel's cell phone and other electronic devices.

People who have tracked the girls' tweets believed it could have been something else entirely; that somehow that night, Rachel told Shelia that the police were onto them, so she needed to be careful. They speculated Rachel could have handed Shelia a small piece of paper as she told her goodbye at her front door, or she could have called her on the phone right after that and given her a heads-up.

Whatever happened, Rachel's parents did confiscate her cell phone. Then they left town. While Rachel was in Chestnut Ridge, Rusty and Patricia began reflecting on her behavior during the last six months, and how she had gone from being respectful to hateful and argumentative. They remembered how she seemed to be keeping secrets and looking to Shelia and Tara for approval. They wanted to get Rachel away from Shelia—and her mother. Rachel had grown far too close to Tara since Skylar's disappearance, and Tara seemed to be trying to control Rachel as much as Shelia had been. United in their approach to parenting in a way they never had been before, Rusty and Patricia were determined to do whatever they could to make that happen. Under no circumstances were they going to allow Rachel to have any communication with Shelia. Or Tara.

Back home in the warmth and security of her mom and stepdad's townhouse, Shelia's next tweet, -_____-, shows clearly her world wouldn't stay warm and cozy for long. The emoticon depicts a mouth and two squinty eyes, and is teenspeak for any feeling from dislike to hostility. The longer the line, the greater the displeasure. The line Shelia tweeted was quite long, indicating she was very, very upset.

She also tweeted, *i dont have time to be wasting my time.*

thirty-six

All That Remains

It had been another bad day for Shelia. At 8:30 that morning, she had tweeted, *first time ive ever been completely speechless.* That was followed almost immediately with, *holy fuck.* Shelia wasn't easily rattled, but something had stunned her.

Just after noon she had tweeted, *someone please explain to me why i get myself into situations i can't get out of ?* And fifteen minutes later she retweeted something that she also felt: *I am so sick of everything like I don't even know how to deal with reality anymore.* She was feeling sorry for herself, but not as sorry as she would feel when the day ended.

Shelia's eyes were wide when she opened the front door and found Gaskins and three other state troopers on the stoop. "Can I help you?"

It was Friday, January 4, the day after the FBI had bugged Rachel's house in anticipation of the teens' reunion.

Gaskins held up a sheaf of papers. "We have a couple of warrants."

Shelia punched a number into her cell phone. "They're here, Mom, the State Police. They say they have warrants." She sounded confused as she handed the phone to Gaskins.

"It's for electronics and knives," he said in answer to her question.

He listened as Tara asked them to wait for her to get home from work.

"We can do that," Gaskins said, turning his back to Shelia, voice lowered. "But we need to wait inside. To make sure Shelia doesn't hurt herself, or anything."

It was standard protocol for searches, to ensure none of the evidence, or the person being served, was harmed. Gaskins knew he had several good reasons to keep a close eye on Shelia.

Just then, two vehicles pulled up to the Clendenen house—a car with four FBI agents and a truck to carry the confiscated material.

"What's all this?" Shelia asked as the truck backed toward them.

Gaskins handed Shelia the phone.

"Mom? What's going on?" Shelia said. Her voice was shaky.

As Gaskins eased past Shelia, he heard her say, "But what do they want?"

Shelia sometimes had an oddly childlike quality about her, especially around her mother. Gaskins had seen it more than once during interviews, usually right before she started crying. More often than not Tara would shut down the interrogation at that point.

He called down to the lead agent in the driveway. "The mother will be here soon. She's on her way home from work." He then went inside to wait with Shelia for Tara. The troopers stood while Shelia sat on the sofa.

When Tara arrived fifteen minutes later, Gaskins sent a couple of his men outside to help her in. It was icy and he didn't want her to fall. When Tara got inside and saw the word "murder" on the warrants, she turned and gave Shelia a long, hard look. Gaskins thought her expression said it all: "Is this true?"

Shelia got up, took the papers from her mother, and her eyes grew big as she read the words. She didn't say a word. Neither did Tara.

Gaskins asked them both to wait in the dining room during the search. He stepped onto the porch and signaled the agents outside to get started.

In the kitchen, two agents opened all the drawers and after taking photos, bagged and tagged every knife they found. Meanwhile, Gaskins headed upstairs to Shelia's bedroom.

Outside, the driver of the truck checked his paperwork against the car in the driveway: a 2006 silver Toyota Camry, registered to James and Tara Clendenen. It was a match. He unhooked chains and began the process of impounding Shelia's car. Pulling a lever on the rollback truck's bed, it slid backward on a hydraulic jack, causing it to tilt down on the ground and effectively make a ramp. He hooked a winch to the front end of the vehicle and pulled it up onto the bed.

"This is it," he said to no one in particular. He began to unhook chains from his truck and drag them back toward the car. The FBI agents didn't even bother going inside. They were there for the car and only the car. The FBI had tests to run to see if they could corroborate any part of Rachel's confession. In fifteen minutes, the agents and the truck were gone—with Shelia's car.

To Gaskins, Shelia's bedroom seemed like any other teenage girl's: colorful and messy. Bob Marley posters hung on the walls. Closet and dresser drawers sat partially open and the bed wasn't made.

After he peered under her bed and lifted the mattress, Gaskins searched the desk and closet. He then checked the hallway bathroom. Finding nothing, he went back downstairs. Shelia and Tara sat on the couch in the living room, watching.

The search lasted two hours. Any electronic devices they had missed with the last warrant, as well as every knife in the house, were labeled and boxed up for transport. Gaskins noted that whatever Shelia might be feeling, she sure wasn't showing it.

"Can you leave me one knife?" Tara asked, "so I can make dinner?"

Gaskins shook his head. "I'm sorry, ma'am. We can't."

By midnight Shelia had somehow gotten access to another electronic gadget, expressing her feelings online by tweeting, *life fucked me yet again*.

Shelia wasn't thinking about what she had done to cause it. She wasn't thinking of the painful death of her "best friend." Shelia was thinking about Shelia. The interviews, the searches, the accusations were all just another conspiracy by the universe to inconvenience her. She was sure of it.

If Shelia thought her life sucked after the FBI took her wheels, she probably wanted to die when the authorities pulled the social rug out from under her and Rachel in early January. That's when they both left UHS and were home schooled. Liz says the U.S. Attorney's office took the action to protect other students from the two teen killers. Other people speculate that the girls received so many threats from fellow students they were removed for their own protection.

Whatever the reason, the fact remains that in early January Rachel and Shelia found themselves attending a virtual school inside their own homes. Separated from most social interaction and estranged from each other, their tweets indicate they put on a good front for the outside world.

Still, when either girl showed up to take a test at school, people talked. They were incensed after someone posted a photo showing Shelia attending the prom with her cousin, Lexy Eddy, at North Marion High. Although she couldn't have known it then, Lexy's decision to invite Shelia to the prom would jeopardize her own standing in the community.

Once Shelia and Rachel *were* arrested, Lexy found herself being harassed on social media and by her fellow students—who said she must have known about the murder, too, if she kept close ties to her cousin. Before long, Lexy closed all her social media accounts, withdrew from school, and began instruction at her Mannington home. The beautiful brunette was basically forced underground, where she refused to talk to anyone outside of her immediate family and a few trusted friends.

———————

The public took to social media to voice its disbelief and outrage. They wondered why the authorities would remove the two teens, only to let them intermittently return to school—and possibly endanger other students.

What the public didn't know is that the police were as frustrated as anyone else that two probable killers were roaming free, being allowed to travel out of state, or occasionally drop back in on UHS classes. But without any evidence, they couldn't arrest Rachel or Shelia. Many, many people confess to crimes they don't commit, and the police wanted to make sure Rachel's confession was rock solid before they made their move.

So the hands of the police and the prosecutor were tied, because while they had Rachel's confession, they did not have Skylar, so they couldn't confirm Rachel's story about the murder. Skylar's remains were still somewhere out in Brave. The police didn't have enough to convict Shelia, either. Not yet.

Their only option was to bide their time, allowing the public to believe they were idiots, and wait until they had enough evidence to convict Shelia, to back up Rachel's confession. In the meantime, they would wait for the DNA testing results from Shelia's car. Little did they know the long and winding trail that testing would take, or that it would be several months before the DNA would help police to prove conclusively that the girls had been involved in Skylar's murder.

———————

Ashdown did make one deal with Rachel. They needed evidence to back up her confession. People give false confessions quite frequently, sometimes intentionally, other times by accident. So police must gather evidence that corroborates a confession. This was crucial in Rachel's case because she had lied to the police for months.

Rachel had confessed—now they just needed her cooperation. To convince her to do that, Ashdown offered Rachel a plea of second-degree murder. In return, she had to lead them to Skylar's remains as soon as the weather was good—and she had to agree to testify against Shelia.

By January 16, Gaskins couldn't wait any longer. Snow had smothered the area for two weeks, melting off slowly. To the veteran trooper, the two-week wait was agonizing and had seemed to drag on and on. He waited as long as he could and finally decided to try again.

They would need two teams, but the second team wasn't free until later that morning. Gaskins wanted to get started early so they would have a full day if they needed it. Spurlock rode with him. A cadaver dog unit supplied by the FBI followed the two of them out Route 7 toward Blacksville. Gaskins took the same route as they had two weeks earlier.

Gaskins pulled his cruiser over at the same GPS coordinates Rachel had led them to before. It looked very different with the snow mostly gone. This time, the place was familiar. As they waited for the dogs to arrive, Gaskins remembered all the times he and Trooper Berry had searched the area. The two troopers had scoured the wooded mountains and had searched six mine shafts. One time in particular, they had hiked up the hillside and looked down a mine shaft. There they found a yellow size-medium T-shirt similar to the one Skylar had been wearing. They also found bones.

Worried about the find, they were relieved when they learned the bones were those of an animal. But the T-shirt was another matter. That took some time. But in the end, all tests came back negative.

When the cadaver dog and his handler were ready to go, the dog was turned loose and the search began. No sooner had they been deployed than Gaskins got a call over the radio. The second team was there and ready to go, but Gaskins needed to drive back to the detachment and lead the way. Otherwise, they might get lost.

Within minutes of Gaskins' departure, the dog's handler noticed the canine's collar had fallen off, along with the small GPS unit attached to it.

The agent called out, saying he needed to find the $300 piece of equipment. He retraced the animal's steps and discovered the unit stuck between some rotting pieces of wood. The agent bent over and started to pick up the unit, then suddenly stopped when he saw something that looked like it had been dead for quite a while.

There, buried under rocks, branches, and other debris, about fifteen feet from the gravel road, the team discovered human remains. Skylar had been buried just twenty miles from her home—and only a few hundred feet from the spot where a handful of devoted officers had searched, repeatedly, during the last several months.

On their way back to the search, once again on Route 7, Gaskins and Spurlock talked as they drove.

"This might be a long day," Spurlock said.

"Wouldn't it be nice if we got a phone call right now," Gaskins said. "Someone would say, 'Hey, we found Skylar.'"

"Yeah, it would be nice."

About two minutes later, Spurlock's phone rang. Gaskins could clearly hear what the caller said: "Morgan, we found her."

Gaskins and Spurlock could hardly contain their excitement.

"Rachel came through," Gaskins said. "She told us where we'd find the body, and we did."

"Now we can begin corroborating Rachel's confession."

Sad as it was for both men—not to mention Dave and Mary—the remains needed to be confirmed as Skylar's. The labs must find evidence that she had, indeed, died from knife wounds, and with any luck they might find evidence pointing to the killers—even though Gaskins already knew who the killers were. Rachel had told them, and had passed an extensive polygraph afterward. Gaskins now knew she had told them the truth.

Already ravaged by weather and time, the remains were unrecognizable except for one feature: they were clearly those of a small human being. Worst of all, the head was missing.

Only Gaskins, a member of an elite state crime-scene unit, and a veteran trooper who had worked more than thirty crime scenes across the state and had personal knowledge of the case, recognized the tattered remnants of clothing Skylar had worn her last day alive: a yellow print shirt and stained green shorts.

Feelings of relief that their search had come to an end mingled with a sense of satisfaction that Mary and Dave could find closure. Overwhelmed by all of the conflicting emotions he'd kept bottled up inside for the last five months, Gaskins couldn't keep from crying.

As so often happened in this case, social media broke the news that Skylar Neese was dead. However, the news was carefully hidden behind a smokescreen because police had been cautious about whom they shared their find with—and traditional news media was not among that group. Law enforcement at the scene knew at the time the remains were all that were left of Skylar, but they wouldn't release that information until all of the standard DNA tests were performed.

Still, some people outside of police circles figured it out. Josie Snyder was one of them. At 2:53 P.M. that same day, Josie took to her keyboard to send out a poignant tweet. She wanted the world to know what she knew, but at the same time, Josie wanted the message to be somber and subtle: *SKY is so gloomy today* :(.

Whoever they were, Josie Snyder's sources were solid. Her tweet about Skylar being found came in the early afternoon of the same day she *was* found.

For the next forty-eight hours, the crime scene was sealed off. But the presence of so many FBI agents and State Police troopers wandering around was bound to have caused a stir among the neighbors. All Gaskins and Spurlock hoped was that they could get all the goods on Shelia before she got word that Skylar's remains had been found.

Gaskins alerted Greene County authorities they would be bringing the human remains there. When they reached the county offices, Coroner Gregory Rohanna was given strict orders not to release any information about the body. Not to the media or anyone else. The police still had one suspect loose, and they didn't want her to know they were closing in on her.

thirty-seven

Skylar's Law

Dave learned the bitter truth the day Skylar would have celebrated her seventeenth birthday.

He had chatter and rumors from various people—Skylar had been killed, her murder involved knives, Shelia and Rachel were somehow mixed up in it—but all the puzzle pieces came together the night of the candlelight vigil.

That February 10 was a Sunday, and it was Mary and Dave's first birthday without Skylar. The day had been unseasonably warm for that time of year, in the low 60s. People kept coming, and before long there were far too many to fit inside Mary and Dave's modest apartment.

Mary had announced the vigil on Facebook and the radio and newspaper mentioned it, but they never expected this many. Friends, relatives, and complete strangers came. Some just came to pay their respects; others stayed the course of the three-hour event. Cars filled the apartment parking lot and lined both sides of the street.

Mary's sister, Carol, arranged for large containers of coffee and hot chocolate, set out on the retaining wall where Skylar had hidden her vanity bench the last night she snuck out. Carol also coordinated the efforts of the people who brought snacks and desserts, placing everything on a table on the blacktop parking lot.

It was particularly difficult for Mary, who missed her daughter terribly. Skylar should have been there that night. She wasn't, though, and she never would be.

As people arrived, Carol gave each one a candle for the Chinese lantern ceremony they had planned. People mingled in the parking lot because the grass was wet from the rain. And they kept coming. Eventually, there were so many people that Carol ran far short of the 150 candles she had brought.

At one point early in the evening, County Commissioner Tom Bloom pulled Dave aside, saying he had something important to tell Dave. Being in county government, Tom heard all the stories, especially from public employees, like politicians—and police officers.

He told Dave it *was* Skylar's remains that had been found in January, just like Dave had heard. The remains hadn't been positively identified yet, but law enforcement was pretty certain what was left of Skylar had been shipped to FBI headquarters in Quantico, Virginia. But he had worse news.

Tom had also heard that Rachel Shoaf had confessed. She and Shelia had stabbed Skylar to death. Tom emphasized that none of this information could be made public yet.

Dave was shaken, but not surprised. It felt like all the whispers of the last few months had been leading to this. A little later, he revealed what Tom had told him to Mary, who felt the evening begin to fall apart. She didn't do well in crowds to begin with, and this event...this news....Once again, Mary and Dave felt pushed beyond their limits.

The high point of the evening came when the lanterns were released into the starry sky in honor of Skylar. Because Skylar had been a budding environmentalist, they chose biodegradable lanterns. When someone suggested balloons early on, Mary said they were out of the question because Skylar believed balloons were nothing more than a pollutant—and a danger to animals. The large crowd lit their candles and held them aloft as the lanterns began ascending. Each one powered by its own individual flame, they rose and floated away in the night sky.

Dave remembered the evening as both sad and happy. They were touched by the concerns and well-wishes people expressed, but still couldn't quite accept the fact that their private grief had once again become a public spectacle.

As the gathering wound down, leaving mostly relatives and closest friends to linger, Dave decided he had no choice. He'd already tried telling people to ease up on their search efforts. What he couldn't say—because he wasn't supposed to know—was that the remains found on January 16 were most likely Skylar's.

Two people still at the gathering had been completely devoted to the search for Skylar: Mary's boss, Tammy Henry, and Becky Benson. Both women had pushed themselves until their health suffered. With what Tom had told him, Dave couldn't let them continue working so hard.

He took Tammy, who had been one of the most active searchers, aside privately and again tried to tell her to slow down. He said he and Mary appreciated it, but it was time to stop. The look in Tammy's eyes told Dave she wouldn't, so he told her that Skylar's remains had been found.

Then he went to find Becky. "This isn't going to turn out the way you thought it would," he said, also breaking the news to her about Skylar. Just like Tammy, though, he could tell Becky didn't want to believe him, either.

———

Mary and Dave had missed so much work since Skylar disappeared they didn't even have enough money to fill their gas tank. Yet they had been invited to address the House Legislative Committee in the middle of February 2013, a month after Skylar's unidentified remains were found. Gas or no gas, they were going to Charleston to help make Skylar's Law a reality.

Skylar's Law had been introduced with Delegate Charlene Marshall as the lead sponsor. The clock was ticking, the time fast approaching for the Legislative Committee to discuss the bill, and

Charlene believed its members should hear the story of Skylar's disappearance. She wanted them to know how badly Skylar's Law was needed.

Dave hoped Mary would join him, but she refused. And Dave—who realized his wife was a more mature copy of Skylar in temperament—understood he shouldn't push her. Mary felt she couldn't hold up through the ordeal. Her emotions were like a rubber band stretched to its breaking point. She couldn't listen to Dave talk about Skylar in front of all those people.

But one of them had to make the three-hour trip to Charleston. Thanks to Commissioner Bloom, Dave didn't have to worry about fuel for their old car. Bloom insisted on providing gas money for the trip.

When Dave arrived at the state capitol, he went straight to Marshall's office. Bloom was already there.

"Dave Neese, I'd like you to meet Delegate Charlene Marshall," Bloom said, introducing Dave to the tireless eighty-year-old representative from Monongalia County.

Dave shook Marshall's hand. "I want you to know, Delegate Marshall, that I'll always cherish the photo of you and Skylar," Dave told her.

The senior statesman thought the grieving father was confused, because she didn't recall ever meeting Skylar.

"You probably don't remember. Skylar was your special page when she was ten."

Marshall felt the hair on her arms and the back of her neck stand up.

"Mary and I, we were sitting up in the balcony that day," Dave said. "Skylar gave you your lunch. She was so pleased.... You were like a hero to her."

Marshall felt tears welling up as she tried to remember the child page. "Well, she did something for me then, and now I'm trying to do something for her," she said at last.

When Bloom and Marshall offered to pay for Dave's lunch, he politely declined, but Marshall insisted. She knew he had a long day ahead of him and what he was up against. He needed enough energy to get through it.

Dave had to tell the committee about his missing daughter, and it would be the hardest speech of his life. He had to address the legislators as though Skylar was still alive, even though he was grappling with the reality that she wasn't.

He told Mary he would simply pretend that Skylar was still alive. It was their only hope of passing Skylar's Law.

―――――――――

Dave addressed the committee, and though his voice caught with emotion several times, his words were convincing and moving. Skylar's Law, he said, needed to be passed for other potentially endangered children. He explained it was a small but crucial amendment to existing AMBER legislation. It would mandate that police contact the AMBER Alert system, which would be required to treat all missing children and teenagers—regardless of how they came to be missing—as actual kidnapping cases unless an investigation proved otherwise.

Dave's trip to the capitol was successful, as Skylar's Law was overwhelmingly popular with the legislators. As it wove its way through the legislative process, Skylar's Law came up for a vote in each chamber. Each time it passed unanimously.

When he heard the news, Dave called Mary immediately. "It passed! It passed the House 98–0 and the Senate 34–0," Dave told his grieving wife.

thirty-eight

Finding Skylar

When the news of Skylar's remains finally broke on Wednesday, March 13, the U.S. Attorney's Office in Wheeling made the announcement. It confirmed the FBI was directly involved in Skylar's identification, which explained in part why the process had taken so long. But the four-sentence press release explained little else.

March 13, 2013

FOR IMMEDIATE RELEASE

Body Recovered in Pennsylvania Identified

WHEELING, WEST VIRGINIA—United States Attorney William J. Ihlenfeld, II, announced today that the body recovered in Wayne Township, Pennsylvania, on January 16, 2013, has been scientifically identified as that of Skylar Neese. Neese is the Star City, West Virginia, teenager who was reported missing by her parents in July of 2012. The testing of the body was conducted by the laboratory of the Federal Bureau of Investigation.

The investigation into the disappearance of Neese and her subsequent death is ongoing.

With Skylar's remains positively identified, authorities were one evidentiary step away from arresting Shelia and Rachel.

———————

Daniel Hovatter was among the growing number of people who were rapidly learning that Skylar was gone. Mary had broken the news about Skylar's remains in a Facebook message back in February, and Skylar's close friend had been absolutely heartbroken. Like the Neeses, he had not learned of Rachel's confession, either, but when he was told it looked like her remains had been located, he knew immediately who was responsible.

By the time the news of Skylar's murder was made public on March 13, Daniel's world was falling apart, so he did the only thing he could do to cope with the intense pain he felt: he went home, locked himself in his bedroom, and lit up a joint. Then he cried and cried—for days on end.

———————

Skylar's other childhood friend, Hayden McClead, heard the same time Daniel did in February. Her mother, Katrina, and Mary were close, so when Katrina learned the news from Mary, she told Hayden. For the next month, Hayden's world was suspended in silent grief. Never having faced something this awful before, she simply didn't know how to feel. While she had been told Skylar was probably dead, she didn't want to believe it. She continued to go to class, mired in a cloud of numbness and denial—until March 13.

Hayden was listening to her chemistry teacher's lecture during fourth period that day when she felt her phone vibrate. Someone had sent her a message on Facebook. *R u ok?* The words confused her. She wondered what they meant and why anyone would be worried about her. Just then, her mom's picture appeared on Hayden's cell phone screen. Hayden left the classroom to take the call, worried that something bad must have happened.

Katrina broke the news to her daughter as gently as she could: Skylar's body had been positively identified. Hayden could no longer ignore the truth. Still, she was so shocked when the reality set in, she could barely speak. One singular thought kept repeating inside her head: *Shelia and Rachel did it.*

———

Across the county, Shania Ammons' volleyball coach pulled her from class to deliver the news in person. Shania went from sobbing to wailing. She was so upset that school officials were afraid to let her drive herself home, so she called her grandma and talked for a while until she calmed down. Then she walked out of Clay-Battelle High School and went straight home, stopping long enough to text Shelia with the news. She was sure Shelia would want to know.

Shelia didn't cry that day. Shania didn't think it odd because she and Shelia had cried together, back when Skylar first disappeared.

Back at the home she shared with her grandparents, Shania told her grandmother she was headed over to Shelia's.

"If you're going, then I'm going," Linda said. The slender but forceful grandmother wouldn't let Shania go by herself, because Linda had her own suspicions about Shelia.

"My family didn't believe her story," Shania said, "and they tried really, really hard to keep me away from Shelia. It was a constant fight, an every-single-day fight. But I still hung out with Shelia. They didn't keep me away from her."

Ironically, on that March 13, Shania and Linda already had plans to join Shelia and Tara for dinner. So they all went to Martin's Bar-b-que Joint in Morgantown together. Shania remembers the meal being sad and awkward.

Shania said Shelia asked her who she thought had committed the murder. Shania answered honestly.

"I don't know."

———

The high school cafeteria could be called a precursor to today's social media sites: a hotbed for the same kind of gossip and innuendo that pops up on Facebook, Twitter, and Websleuths. Many students first heard rumors about Skylar's murder in the lunchroom—some true, some false. One particularly disturbing rumor began floating around after Skylar's body was found, but long before Rachel and Shelia were arrested.

This dark story especially affected Jordan Carter. She had never given up hope that her one-time summer playmate would come home. Perhaps because the color purple was used at Skylar-themed events after she disappeared, Jordan would think of Skylar every day when she drove home from school past a local bar called the Purple Cow Lounge. Jordan was always looking at the faces of people she passed—hoping one of them might just be her missing friend.

After the news broke about a body being found, Jordan was sitting at a table in the UHS cafeteria when a snippet of conversation caught her attention.

"You know Rachel and Shelia killed her, right?" one teen asked another. "You know they cut off her head and dumped her in the woods."

Jordan was speechless with horror.

·

———————————

The snow was coming down hard on March 18, almost a whiteout, as FBI Victim Specialist Tessa Cooper navigated the black SUV toward Brave. Dave rode in the passenger seat, with Mary in the back. It was a quiet ride.

No one had expected so much snow in mid-March. A week earlier the sky had been clear, the temperatures in the high 60s. That day, thick flakes fell in a torrent. Looking out the window, Dave thought the snow wouldn't be around long, not with the ground so warm. He knew these roads; he and Mary had driven them a dozen times at least, back when...when Skylar was still missing. Now Tessa was going to show them where Skylar had been found.

As they rode north, Tessa talked to them about what they were going to see. She had become Mary and Dave's primary liaison with law enforcement and the prosecutor's office. She explained what they should expect, helped alleviate worries, and provided an outlet for the pent-up emotions.

"Nothing about the site jumped out. Nothing obvious," Dave later said. "She was trying to prepare us [for] the fact that they dumped her like a sack of garbage."

Based in Charleston, Cooper served the entire state, counseling victims of terrorism and crimes like murder, kidnapping, and child abuse. It was heart wrenching but important work, and she had been doing it for over a decade.

Tessa pulled over at a wide place in the road and turned the car off. Mary and Dave got out, and Tessa said, "Over here." She led them to a scattered pile of branches and leaves and debris at the base of a tree about ten feet off the road.

In silence, Mary and Dave both cried, their arms supporting each other in their shared grief. Dave felt the snow pelting his face and thought of his little girl, *their* little girl, and what she must have gone through that night. Again, he told himself that he should have been there for her.

―――――――――

Riding home, temporarily cleansed by tears, Mary spoke: "How did you all find this place?"

"Rachel told them," Dave said. Even though the prosecutor's office hadn't officially told them about January's confession, several people whom Dave believed were in the know had already laid it out.

"Through investigation," was all Tessa would say, but it looked to Dave like she was nodding as she said it.

Riding back in silence it occurred to Dave that he should try to remember how to return to the spot. Then he realized he didn't need to. He knew Mary would know the way if they wanted to come back, but at that moment he also couldn't imagine why either of them ever would.

Gaskins couldn't get Skylar Neese out of his mind. He kept replaying the day they had found her. The crime scene unit had been on site for nearly forty-eight hours after they found the remains. Gaskins, several other state troopers, and FBI agents had carefully sifted, bagged, and tagged anything that might contain clues to how this person— who Gaskins was convinced was Skylar—died. Or who might have been responsible, or where the knives and shovel were. Most worrisome was that they hadn't found her skull.

For over two months, Gaskins' thoughts kept coming back to that. He had since moved on to other cases, but he couldn't forget about her missing head. By March 29 temperatures had climbed to the 60s. When First Sergeant Chad Tierney asked Gaskins to take him out to see the site, Gaskins jumped at the opportunity.

"That shovel might still be around there," Gaskins said.

As he drove, Gaskins and Tierney talked about the case. Most likely, scavengers were responsible for her head being missing. Gaskins knew bodies that are left outdoors for months are always victimized a second time—first comes the death and then the ravages of wildlife and weather. In earlier cases Gaskins had worked, he'd found bones as much as a quarter mile or farther from the victim's body.

He also thought about how Rachel's confession had taken him completely by surprise. He and Berry had known for months that Shelia and Rachel were withholding information, but they never believed the teens had stabbed their friend to death. That's when he realized the bank robberies were completely unconnected to the murder.

The lack of real evidence, coupled with Rachel's confession, had taken the pressure off the Conaway boys. They ceased being primary suspects. Gaskins could no longer see any reason for their involvement.

When they arrived at the site, Gaskins showed Tierney where they found Skylar. Then he led the way up a little road that was more like a footpath than one vehicles would travel. It curved around the mountain and led up to a pond. Gaskins told Tierney about the mine shafts he and Berry had searched, and the T-shirt they'd found.

The two troopers were walking back down the road when Gaskins glanced over. Scanning the field, he saw an odd glint in the sunlight. "Man, that doesn't look right."

Gaskins and Tierney kept walking. "It might be the skull," Tierney told him.

"It can't be that easy."

But it was. As they drew near, they could tell it was a human skull. Gaskins couldn't believe it. He was so excited he could barely find the right screen on his phone to call Berry.

"Grab my camera. Grab my crime scene stuff. Get out here right now."

Berry had to restrain himself as he drove the familiar route. He knew the road so well he could easily drive much faster than the speed limit. Still, Gaskins was waiting, and so was Skylar—all of Skylar could be returned to Dave and Mary.

When Berry arrived, he took photos from every angle. Then they gently placed Skylar's skull inside an evidence bag and took it to the Greene County coroner.

Not long before Rachel pled guilty, she invited Wendy Evans for a sleepover. Wendy had been friends with Rachel since they were freshmen but over time their friendship had faded. Because they hadn't done anything together in many months, Wendy was surprised but pleased to receive Rachel's invitation. Ever since Shelia came onto the scene, Rachel had been different. Wendy thought Rachel was trying to rekindle their friendship, so she was excited about the upcoming visit.

However, that night Rachel dropped a bombshell. "I have something to tell you," Rachel said once they were alone in her bedroom. "You know all those rumors, about Skylar, about the FBI pulling me out of classes, going around school? The police caught Shelia and she's probably going to jail. I just found out she killed Skylar."

Wendy stared at her friend as though she couldn't believe what she was hearing. "What do you mean? Weren't you both with Skylar that night?"

"I know!" Rachel said, a look of sincere shock seeming to spread across her entire face. "So she must have gone back and done it after she dropped me off, right? That's the only thing I can figure. I can't believe all these months I've actually been friends with a murderer!"

"How did she kill her?"

"I don't know—but I could have been next! What if it had been me instead?" Rachel looked truly terrified at having been such close friends with a girl who turned out to be a murderer.

Wendy was stunned. "Wow!"

"I know, it's like—all those jokes, about being a murderer—those kids were right! Right?" Rachel gave Wendy an incredulous look, her brows raised high.

Wendy had never liked Shelia, who seemed sketchy and rolled her eyes a lot. In fact, Wendy had harbored her own suspicions the previous fall. She believed Shelia could do such a terrible thing, but not Rachel, who often wrote her very best friends little notes in class, telling them how amazing they were, how much she loved them, and loved being with them. No. Rachel would never have killed Skylar. She was far too sweet to hurt anyone—much less murder them.

It was a Twitter exchange—over baby turtles, of all things—that left people chattering.

The short series of tweets among Shania, Shelia, and her cousin, Lexy Eddy, was intensely scrutinized in light of Rachel's plea and Shelia's arrest. People trying to interpret it said the tweets were a sign of Shelia's deep pathology. A thread on the local Topix Morgantown site called it "disgusting."

The tweet exchange took place about 9:45 in the evening on April 9, 2013:

Shelia: *my father is telling me to kill my wittle baby turtles.*

Lexy: *that's the solution. you wouldn't have to worry about em anymore.*

Shelia: *-_-*

Shelia then retweeted Lexy's *wellll do ya have a hammer on ya?* and added *HAHAHA exactly what he said.*

Shania chimed in, and Shelia retweeted it: *@slexy_@_shelia let me hit them with a hammer.*

The troubling tweets ended with Shelia's, *it's not that i don't want them. it's that they're fucking green dude*

Normally, this kind of "conversation" would be seen as absurd. But the people who were combing through Shelia, Rachel, and Skylar's Twitter, Facebook, Snapchat, and Instagram records were looking for evidence of anything that would indicate the two teens had killed Skylar.

What would have been taken for silliness before Skylar's murder became an example of callous neglect at best, sadism at worst.

When asked about the exchange, Greg Eddy shed some light on his daughter's baby turtles—and therefore, the tweets about them.[29] Greg said Shelia bought the tiny creatures from a pet store. Over the next few weeks, though, she discovered her new pets were sick, so she said she wanted to take them to a vet's office, to have them put to sleep. When Shelia told her father that, he said it would be ridiculous to pay so much money when she could easily take care of

---

[29] Greg Eddy otherwise declined to be interviewed.

the turtles herself. He suggested she hit them with a hammer, which would be quick and painless.

Greg's explanation certainly sounded plausible, and from her own tweets, Shelia seemed to be in a light-hearted, joking mood, typing *wittle* for *little*. She also said they were green, which could have been a reference to their being sick.

While Shelia was talking about humanely putting her baby turtles down, or merely taunting the world she knew was watching her online movements, Rachel was packing a suitcase and preparing for what she knew would be a final visit to her grandparents' home.

thirty-nine

The Close of the Day

Not long before Rachel and Shelia were taken into custody, Governor Earl Ray Tomblin put pen to paper on April 29 and approved the pending legislation that transformed one angry mother's late-night Facebook rant into Skylar's Law. Governor Tomblin didn't know it, but with his official seal on the new law, he gave the Neeses the only happy ending they would ever have. Skylar's Law is now being used as a model by several other states to help reform their own AMBER Alert systems, and the reform stands to provide a beacon of hope for parents of presently and future missing children.

On May 1, four long months after Rachel's confession, Shelia Eddy and Rachel Shoaf were arrested for the role they played in Skylar's death.

When people heard about the Shoaf family's beach trip just before Rachel pled guilty on May 1, the online discussion boards lit up. Busybodies who knew nothing beyond the pictures that showed up online and Rachel's tweets characterized it as a last mother-daughter fling. Other people questioned the competence of the authorities charged with investigating and prosecuting the case.

Even though the police already had Rachel's confession, and she had passed an extensive polygraph exam afterward, they still didn't have any hard evidence to arrest her. They were still waiting for the results of the DNA analysis. So the authorities had no reason *not* to let Rachel leave the state. Until the police had enough evidence to charge her with murder, she was free to come and go at will.

Despite the public's misperceptions, the trip was taken for one reason: so Rachel could say goodbye to her maternal grandparents, who lived in Virginia Beach. Because Rachel's arrest was imminent, the Shoafs knew she wasn't going to see her grandparents for a long time, if ever again.

The online community's reaction to the Virginia Beach trip once again highlights social media's uncertain connections to the truth. For instance, Rachel's tweet *sunday is the day when me and my mom get drunk together and its a great time* made their beach trip sound like one nonstop party. In truth, this tweet occurred after Patricia let Rachel have a sip of her mimosa. Rachel tweeted it because she wanted to appear cool, like Shelia and Tara. Liz says Rachel also did it because she was trying to prove to Shelia that her mother was cool, too. Another person close to the Shoafs said Rachel tweeted the lie to make her mother angry. She succeeded.

All through the late winter and early spring, Rachel had been trying to shore up her image as a happy innocent for her friends, her fans, and the strangers who were becoming more curious about her. She said once her name was cleared, she was moving to Canada or England, where no one knew the rumors and she could study acting. Once she simply tweeted, *i just cant wait to get the hell out of here and start a completely new life.*

Some of Rachel's tweets seemed manufactured, as if they were designed to portray her days as normal, when instead they masked her hidden life. On January 16, for instance, she tweeted, *my life is beyond boring right now.* Rachel just wanted people to think she was no different than she ever had been.

Rachel's other tweets held a ring of denial and exhausted depression: *can i sleep til im 18 then wake up? that'd be perfect* and *i can't remember what's a dream and what's reality anymore.*

But sometimes, like someone hiding behind a translucent window sheer, reality has a way of becoming visible. This happened on February 10, when Rachel tweeted, *happy birthday skylar.* Later that same night, she tweeted, *i hate the shit i think about at night.* By the next day, she seemed to be shaking off her dark thoughts: *yeah, there are plenty of things i regret from my past. but im on a completely new path now and i really wish people could appreciate that.* Amidst all of this, Rachel had to face constant harassment, some of which she responded to reasonably (*seriously why can't you guys just mind your own business*) and some with a burst of anger (*GOD I HATE YOU GO AWAY*).

She did receive occasional support from a friend or two (*@_racchh rumors are rumors and that's all they will ever be, people who matter won't believe them anyways!*). Some of Rachel's friends believed the teenager just *couldn't* have done anything so heinous as kill one of her BFFs. Other friends simply thought the legal system accorded her the same right as everyone else: namely, that she should be viewed as innocent until proven guilty.

Rachel tweeted fairly regularly about her life with Mikinzy. There was her January 13 *so proud :')* *@mikinzyboggs* tweet. Two weeks later, on January 29: *mikinzy is so fun to talk to cause he's so curious about life and how people think.* Rachel seemed to value the relationship, and in early March she even tweeted *thank god i have a reliable boyfriend lol seriously.*

Unbeknownst to Rachel, Mikinzy wouldn't be hers much longer. By the time Rachel pled guilty to second-degree murder, they had broken up again.

As previously arranged, Rachel Shoaf turned herself in to Monongalia County Circuit Court on Wednesday morning, May 1. After being processed, she and her lawyer went straight to Judge Clawges' courtroom, where she pled guilty to second-degree murder.

Neither Shelia nor her mother, Tara, had a clue this was happening. By late morning, they were enjoying a meal together at Cracker Barrel.

Corporal Gaskins was not at the hearing. He was on standby, waiting for a call from the prosecutor's office to pick up Shelia. He had already called Tara's cell phone company hoping they would release her location without a warrant. They wouldn't.

Shortly after the hearing ended, Gaskins received a call from the assistant prosecutor.

"It's going to be on the radio soon," Perri Jo DeCristopher told him. "Time to get Shelia."

With Gaskins and Spurlock driving lead, two cruisers rushed to the Clendenen house in Canyon. When they arrived, no one was home. Gaskins and Spurlock talked over their options.

Gaskins looked at Spurlock and shrugged. "I'm going to call her."

To their surprise, it was that easy. In the course of their brief conversation, Tara said she and Shelia were eating at Cracker Barrel.

At one point, Tara asked, "Do I need to get my attorney?"

"Probably should," Gaskins said, and then he downplayed it, trying to ensure Tara didn't grow nervous: "Well, you guys enjoy your meal. Call us when you're done."

As soon as he hung up, Gaskins said, "Let's get to Cracker Barrel."

The cruisers took off, lights flashing and sirens blaring. Gaskins knew speed was important; Tara and Shelia might be gone by the time they arrived. When Gaskins learned that Trooper Tierney was just leaving the detachment, he radioed Tierney.

"Turn around, block the Cracker Barrel entrance," Gaskins ordered. "Nobody gets in or out."

Tierney rushed to Cracker Barrel and did just that. He got out of his car and walked toward the restaurant. He didn't know what Tara and Shelia looked like, but he approached two females who were leaving the restaurant.

"Are you Shelia's mom?" he asked Tara.

"Yeah," Tara said.

"Well, you can't leave," Tierney said.

When Gaskins and Spurlock pulled up, Tierney was standing with Tara and Shelia on the sidewalk. Gaskins could feel eyes on him and he and his partner jumped out. Sure enough, several people were watching from inside as Gaskins spoke the words he'd been waiting months to say.

"Shelia Eddy, you are under arrest for the murder of Skylar Neese."

Tara sat down on the curb. Gaskins handed her a copy of the arrest warrant.

"I think you need to call your lawyer now. Your daughter's being arrested for murder. She's coming with us."

As Gaskins handcuffed Shelia, she asked plaintively, "Mom, is everything going to be all right?"

"Shelia, I don't know," Tara could barely manage, as her trembling fingers punched the number for Mike Benninger, Shelia's lawyer.

forty

Rachel Cops a Deal

Shelia's arraignment hearing had been brief, less than thirty minutes, but because she was underage, few people outside of the courtroom knew about it. The public only learned that an unnamed juvenile was facing charges related to Skylar's murder, and that juvenile was in custody. A great many people had already concluded that girl was Shelia Eddy, thanks to details released after Rachel pled guilty to second-degree murder. By then, Shelia was being transported to juvenile detention.

Judge Russell Clawges, Jr., presided over Rachel's May 1 plea hearing. Prosecutor Ashdown had talked with him weeks before. Ashdown wanted Clawges because of his reputation for conducting smooth trials with a minimum of drama. A high-profile case like this one needed to be free of "hitches and mistakes," a confidential source explained.

They wanted to schedule a ninety-minute block of the court's time, which was tricky. It had to be on a day that the prosecution, the defense, and the judge all had an open ninety minutes. By early April they had sufficient evidence to corroborate Rachel's confession and arrest Shelia—but it took nearly a month to schedule the hearing on the court's docket.

The prosecution team wanted to sweep through the proceedings with one quick hearing, to keep the news as quiet as possible. They planned to begin with a juvenile hearing to transfer Rachel to adult status, and then move through Rachel's plea hearing, where she would plead guilty to murdering Skylar. A typed note telling the public that court was in session was the only sign anything was happening, as Judge Clawges began.

By the time the proceedings ended ninety minutes later, Mary and Dave had finally learned the answer to the single most important question of the last ten months: What had happened to their daughter?

According to Rachel Shoaf's admission in court, she had "unlawfully, feloniously, willfully, maliciously, and intentionally caus[ed] the death of Skylar Neese by stabbing her and causing fatal injuries."

Judge Clawges asked Rachel several questions to determine if she understood the severity of her situation. He inquired if she understood her rights, her waiver of indictment by a grand jury, her waiver to appeal the court's ruling, and her possible sentence. Rachel was composed and subdued, but said she understood everything.

Rachel Shoaf, now technically an adult for the purpose of criminal prosecution, would be held at the Northern Regional Juvenile Detention Center in Wheeling, West Virginia, until she was sentenced.

It was one secret Rachel couldn't keep: on May 1, the entire Morgantown community and everyone beyond its borders seemed to have heard the news. Star City Police Chief Vic Propst was driving his cruiser when he heard the newscaster say Rachel had pled guilty. Propst was so shocked he had to pull off the road. The veteran officer couldn't stop the tears that began streaming down his cheeks.

Propst wasn't the only officer to learn of Rachel's arrest on the radio. Chris Berry was headed home in his Jeep when the announcement came over the airwaves. He went to the fridge and popped the top off a cold beer. As he took a long, slow swig, he thought, *By God, we did it. We caught 'em. It's done.*

Naturally, the UHS student body also heard the news. Shock, disbelief, glee, and a host of other emotions passed across students' faces that day. When the news broke that their two fellow classmates—or even childhood friends—had killed Skylar, many students struggled with the realization that Rachel and Shelia had been lying all along. Rachel's singing talent was one reason that her confession of murder so devastated UHS students and faculty. Everyone had expected her talent to take her far, far from West Virginia—not keep her locked up there.

Students waiting in the hallway outside of Mrs. Farley's classroom heard about Rachel's confession after one student began reading the May 1 news on his cell phone. No one remembers who that student was because once the words "Rachel," "confessed," and "Skylar's murder" began to be repeated in the narrow corridor, the news spread like wildfire.

"Everybody knew that Rachel had pled guilty," Jordan Carter said. She had been standing on one side of the hallway, and remembered the first thought she had: "I knew it."

She couldn't help but notice the girl directly across from her: pretty, popular Grace Bonner,[30] one of Rachel's closest friends and a fellow Young Life member. "Grace's hand flew up to her mouth," Jordan said. "She just stood there with a blank look on her face, and then ran out."

Grace wasn't the only stunned student. Jordan remembers that everyone in that hallway had a reaction. Comments like "I knew it,"

---

[30] Not her real name.

"I can't believe it," and "We went to school with murderers!" tumbled down the corridor.

Just then, Mrs. Farley appeared. "I know what you all just found out, but put it aside, we've got to get to work," Jordan recalled her saying. The teacher unlocked the door to her classroom and the students filed in quietly. But throughout the class, students continued murmuring about how Rachel Shoaf had confessed to the most disturbing crime that had ever taken place in their small town.

Learning that Rachel really was a murderer was especially painful for one of her closest friends. Wendy Evans heard about it when her mother texted her: *Did you hear that Rachel Shoaf pled guilty to killing that girl?*

Wendy paused in the hallway, leaning back against a locker. After composing herself, she somehow managed to compose her reply.

No I didn't but it's good to know.

Shocked, she hadn't known what else to say.

Wendy realized that Rachel had been a liar all along. She felt many of the same feelings that Rachel's friends and teachers had expressed—surprise, sadness, denial—but when she suddenly remembered what happened near the end of their sophomore year, a couple of months before Shelia and Rachel killed Skylar, she felt sick to her stomach.

She hadn't thought about it much then, because kids say stupid things all the time, but Skylar's murder cast the statement in a whole new light.

"At this point," Wendy recalled Rachel saying, "I wouldn't mind if she died."

Wendy was a step or two away from the conspiracy and murder, but close enough to see the dynamics among Rachel, Skylar, and Shelia, so she had a unique perspective. "I just think they were all bad for each other. Rachel was bad for them both, Skylar was bad for them both, and Shelia was bad for them both."

Wendy felt like someone had knocked all the wind out of her. She leaned against her locker, hoping it would keep her from falling. *Wow! Rachel had been lying all along.* Wendy didn't remember walking to her next class or sitting through another lecture. All she could think about was Rachel and that night in her bedroom. At the time she had hoped Rachel's invitation signaled a desire to renew their friendship, but afterward, when she didn't hear from Rachel again, she didn't know what to think.

She wondered if Rachel was spreading rumors about her; she knew Rachel could be a backstabber. She recalled all the times she herself had heard Rachel talk about people when they weren't around—only to become sugary sweet when they were. Still, Wendy never thought Rachel would literally stab someone in the back.

After Mrs. Farley's class, Jordan went to her computer class. One student had pulled up on screen the actual written plea released by the media. "We all crowded around to look. It was surreal to see her actual signature," Jordan said.

Seeing Rachel's own handwriting on the legal document acknowledging her part in Skylar's death "made it real," Jordan said. But she still texted her mom, "to see for sure." Jordan's mom, Erin Carter, Googled the news and confirmed that Rachel had indeed confessed to the murder of Skylar Neese.

Throughout the next week, students discussed the news. Some students weren't surprised at all. Then there were the others—students like Grace Bonner and the rest of Rachel's crowd—who were totally caught off guard. They felt betrayed by Rachel, who was one of their own.

It didn't take long for students to begin worrying about other deaths: the fatal car crash that killed one girl, the suicide of another, the murder of two other students. Those connections caused them to wonder what was going on at UHS.

"Kids thought, 'Holy crap, there's something wrong with our school,'" Jordan said.

Students have been saying the new high school is cursed for a while now, and Skylar's murder didn't help diminish that belief. Since opening in 2008, UHS has been plagued with problems. Over the brief Thanksgiving break that year, shortly after everyone moved in, the sprinkler system went off, showering the inside of the new school. No one discovered the standing water for a couple of days. Students were told to stay home for another week while the pipes were fixed and the mess cleaned up. A few weeks later a gas leak developed, and classes were again canceled while repairs were made.

While infrastructure problems might be expected at a brand-new facility, UHS has also been troubled by student deaths, including auto accidents and at least two documented suicides. More troubling are the homicides: Skylar was the fourth student to die from homicide in four years, which helps explain why UHS teens would have been even more traumatized than usual, when they learned her killers were two fellow students.

Eventually the murmurs about Skylar's murder lost steam, and students stopped saying, "I told you so." They started accepting facts. But life wasn't the same; their youthful idealism was forever shattered. The realization that they had been lied to for almost a year, along with the accompanying feelings of betrayal, was traumatic—and it would remain that way. Even eight months after Rachel's plea, many of those students still were unable to talk about Skylar's murder or Rachel's role in it.

Grace's experience seemed to exemplify their pain. Finally, after all of the jokes, rumors, and innuendos, UHS students knew for sure that a murderer had walked among them. Students like Grace haven't really moved past their feelings of betrayal and loss.

That first day in May, Grace returned to class just as last period ended. Several people asked her if she was okay. Jordan said Grace's head bobbed up and down, but she couldn't say a word.

At first Daniel was ecstatic when he heard the news. But then he began feeling sad and angry. He just wanted people to stop talking about what Rachel had done. He tried to tune out the loud snippets of gossip going around UHS, so he could be alone with his thoughts. All those times he had ribbed Rachel, getting digs in at her so she would tell him the truth about Skylar, were for real. He meant every one of them. At the same time, deep down he didn't really want to believe that Rachel herself could have done something to hurt his Skylar. Not kind and compassionate Skylar, who refused to even kill a bug.

As Daniel walked into Mr. Kyer's class and headed for his seat, the drama teacher stopped him. With one arm around his shoulder, Kyer guided Daniel away from the other students and over to the side of the room.

"Daniel, um, I want you to know," Kyer tried to say, then stopped. He took a deep breath. "Look, I'm sorry for what I said that time about you accusing Rachel without proof."

Daniel looked at Mr. Kyer's face and wondered if his favorite teacher had been crying. He remembered how much Mr. Kyer had looked forward to having Skylar as a student that year. How much fun he and Skylar—and Rachel—would have had in class together.

"That's okay, Mr. Kyer," Daniel said. "She lied to you, too."

"Yes, she did," Kyer said, so softly Daniel almost didn't hear him. Then Kyer turned away.

Students in Kyer's class were some of the hardest hit by the news. Several students said it was difficult to even get anything done following the news about Skylar's murderers, but his was not the only class to suffer. Other students said many teachers who were close to Rachel had particular problems dealing with the news.

Barry Kolar's chamber choir was one such class. He had known Rachel since she was a small girl. Not long after Rachel pled guilty he was cleaning out his inbox when he came across an email from his former student and protégé. It contained a video attachment that Kolar hadn't yet been able to play. That day, though, he clicked on the attachment, opening it.

A student who walked in could see immediately how upset he was while watching the video of Rachel singing.

"I think I'm still in denial about it. Look at her," he said to the student. They watched Rachel sing, and listened to her lovely voice coming from the computer speakers. "Would you ever imagine her being a murderer?"

People all around the school were having difficulty understanding how a pretty girl with such a beautiful voice could stab anyone to death—let alone her best friend.

UHS had four guidance counselors at the time. Students reported extra counselors were brought in from other schools to help provide grief counseling, but many of these same students said they didn't see a counselor. However, some students did take advantage of the available counseling, which is good given that this was the only time they were allowed to discuss anything about the case while on school property.

Principal Shari Burgess issued her edict prohibiting anyone speaking about the news after it broke. Several students vaguely recall hearing Burgess announce the topic wasn't to be discussed during school hours, but no one can remember exactly what she said. They knew from their teachers' repeated reminders that discussing Skylar's murder—or Rachel and Shelia's arrest—was off limits.

In addition, at least three adults have said teachers are afraid they'll lose their jobs if they do talk. That's because Burgess decreed as much, they say. However, the UHS staffers also say Burgess told them county board of education officials created the mandate.

Which may or may not be true. A couple of people who work for the school system have said it isn't. According to an employee in

Superintendent Frank Devono's office, school employees probably weren't allowed to discuss anything until after the case was closed. That employee, who only gave her name as Beth, cited FERPA, the Family Educational Rights and Privacy Act, when stating this. That federal law prevents educators from discussing matters (specifically pertaining to a student's educational records) that could violate a student's right to privacy—a right that can be waived if student safety is in question or if legal authorities request certain information. Beth said she had no knowledge of the county board issuing the gag order.

Then there's the fact that several UHS students have died through violent means in recent years. If an entire student body is being silenced about Skylar, then what else might they be silent about? What dangerous undertow is this silence creating?

One parent believes if students and teachers were not allowed to talk about what happened, or what led up to it, then the police investigation was also affected—because facts about the case could have come to light much sooner, had people been allowed to talk about what they knew or suspected.[31]

It's entirely possible Burgess issued the edict due to the high number of threats and harassment directed at Shelia and Rachel. No one knows because to date UHS teachers remain silent on the matter.

---

[31] Material in this chapter originally appeared in "If You Talk the Talk, You Should Walk the Walk" by Daleen Berry (http://www.daleenberry.com/daleenberry/?p=998).

forty-one

Looks Can Deceive

Gaskins, Spurlock, and Colebank were preparing to leave for Parkersburg by the time Rachel's plea hearing ended. Shelia's wrists and ankles were shackled, but she still wore her street clothes. Not for long—the Lorrie Yeager Juvenile Center would provide her with an orange jumpsuit. Gaskins hoped she'd noticed the red and yellow "In Loving Memory of Skylar Neese" armband he'd hung on the rearview mirror just for her.

Having a female prisoner like Shelia in custody meant they needed to take extra precautions, so the two male officers asked Colebank to join them on the ride to Parkersburg. They also knew how hard she had worked the case, before the WVSP and FBI took it over.

"My hair is a mess," Shelia said.

Gaskins and Spurlock looked at each other, Gaskins shaking his head. This girl was incredible. She was on her way to detention for her involvement in a murder and she's worried about her hair?

"Seriously," Shelia said. "I have to look right when we get there."

"Do you have a scrunchie?" Shelia had asked the men. But once Colebank climbed into the back seat beside her, Shelia clammed up. She didn't seem to want to talk with Colebank nearby.

"Do you think photographers will be waiting for you?" Colebank asked in amazement, wondering how Shelia always seemed to think everything was about her.

"No one's going to be waiting, Shelia," Gaskins said. "No one cares."

He looked in the rearview mirror. Shelia was wearing an exaggerated pout, her lower lip protruding.

Colebank sat rigidly and stared straight ahead, as if Shelia's sheer presence was a personal affront to her. Gaskins knew the arrogant, self-absorbed teen had angered Colebank from the first time they'd met.

The female officer was ecstatic when she found herself riding in the back seat with Shelia, and said she was overjoyed to know Shelia was finally going to be locked up. She thought back to her first few days working the case, when her gut feeling told her Shelia and Rachel were behind Skylar's disappearance. She remembered the law enforcement seminar she and Spurlock later attended, when the presenter outlined the traits of a psychopath—and she and Spurlock, seated at opposite ends of a table—leaned forward and mouthed: "That's Shelia."

While she believed from the outset that the two killers would rate high on a scale showing sociopathic or possibly even psychopathic traits, no one else working the investigation wanted to—until the FBI did, after investigators consulted with the Behavioral Analysis Unit at Quantico, Virginia.

Her suspicions—and her gut feelings—were confirmed during an early autumn 2012 conference call with the BAU team. Using Rachel's diary, among other items from the two girls, the federal analysts called it: Rachel had sociopathic tendencies, while Shelia had psychopathic ones.

As Colebank thought back to the BAU's conclusion, she kept her hand on her Taser the entire way to Parkersburg. She knew it was entirely possible a troublesome teen like Shelia might give her a reason to use it.

When they arrived in Parkersburg, Shelia wanted to call her mother. "How much do I get to use the phone?" she asked.

Colebank had had enough and at that moment she couldn't keep quiet. "You get *nothing* here. You committed a crime. You *killed* someone," she said. "Don't expect royal treatment here. There are rules here. If they say you can use the phone, you can use the phone. You don't just walk up to a phone and call your mom."

Shelia was already crying as they walked through the detention doors, but at Colebank's words she cried harder.

The three officers escorted her to the processing area where she would receive her orange jumpsuit. They paused at a thick metal door with a small glass window, as a correctional officer told Shelia to follow him. It took a few seconds for Shelia to realize she was alone. Gaskins, Spurlock, and Colebank stood behind her, waiting for the heavy door to slam shut.

"Home sweet home," Colebank said. "Enjoy your stay."

Shelia's eyes grew large. "What?"

At that moment, Colebank felt "pure elation," and as the three officers left the building she went to have a celebratory cigarette before they got back on the road.

A few correctional officers were there, too, and had seen Shelia's arrival.

"Really, three of you?" one of them said. "What, is she here on drug charges?"

"No, she *killed* someone," Colebank said.

The other officers looked on in disbelief. "Her?"

Colebank was amazed they could be taken in by Shelia's tiny, delicate body and innocent-looking face. "Don't let her fool you. She will use her sexuality and her looks to get her way," she warned. "Do not fall (for) her ruse. It is an act. This is how she's going to be down here."

A couple of correctional officers laughed. "Oh yeah, okay."

Colebank could tell they didn't believe her.

"No way," another one said.

"Yep, way," Colebank said, feeling herself flush. *Why do people keep doing that? It's making me mad.* "We wouldn't have brought her down here today if she hadn't."

————————

After Rachel's plea and Shelia's detention, Twitter exploded. People were trying to make sense of what had happened. They truly wanted to understand the two teens' actions—even though not everyone had figured out that Shelia was the unnamed teen in Rachel's confession.

For example, @jsimp_93 tweeted, *How can you go on about your normal life after what you did? #dontunderstand*. People repeatedly said that Skylar's murder had shaken their faith in fellow human beings. Such was @lyssa_ruth's tweet, *Idk how anyone could hurt or especially kill their best friend*. ("Idk" is textspeak for "I don't know.") *It just shows us we can't trust anyone. #justiceforskylar*.

But the people who had believed all along that Shelia and Rachel had committed a terrible crime, and who had been harassed because of it, now fought back. @Hannahsgotalota tweeted, *To everyone who believed them, stood by their side, and told everyone how irrelevant their "rumors" were: go fuck yourself*.

Other people tried a lighter approach. Cheyenne Cowell tweeted, *Sometimes when I'm having a shitty day, I think "hmm. I wonder what Rachel Shoaf is doing" then suddenly I'm in a great mood*.

Interestingly, as if their jobs were done, Mia Barr and Josie Snyder had stopped tweeting in February—even though the public didn't find out the remains were Skylar's until March. Mia and Josie had either lost interest or they simply didn't think they were needed anymore. However, several other anonymous accounts stepped up to fill the void. Someone called @CountFistula tweeted a blast, that is, he retweeted Shelia's tweets—with added punchlines:

RT "@_sheliiaa *rest easy skylar, you'll ALWAYS be my bestfriend. i miss you more than you could ever know."* I just threw up. Twice.

RT "@_sheliiaa *hahahah good god you're such a compulsive liar. i mean seriously it'd probably kill you to tell the truth"* Pot, meet kettle.

RT "@_sheliiaa *i hate when people blame their own actions and choices on others."* Looked up 'irony' in the dictionary & found this tweet.

An anonymous account called @KillerGirlProblems also suddenly became active with tweets such as, *Just when you think you've gotten away with murdering your BFF, your accomplice rats you out. "UGH Y"* #killergirlproblems. Like many people on Twitter, @KillerGirlProblems also showed sympathy for Skylar's family: *Just wishing all the prayers & love in the world to the Neese family... how they have made it to this point is beyond me. #staystrong.*

Daniel's tweets showed that for him, life became much more difficult after Rachel and Shelia were arrested, rather than easier. His May 1 tweet called out Rachel and Shelia directly: *I have no sympathy for you girls. I just KNEW that you knew something, and I get called the jackass for believing that? #justiceforskylar* and *At one point, I considered you two some of my best friends. Now I just hope you rot in hell for this.*

A couple of days later he tweeted that he was going to see Mary and Dave. After the visit, Daniel was furious: *Hey Rachel, how's that scar on your knee doing? Mary told me everything. My girl didn't die without a fight, bitch.*

Understandably, Daniel spiraled into a depression, and on May 6, school authorities suspended him after finding illegal substances among his possessions. That evening he tweeted *I get so sad at night. <\3.*

Even though Daniel had been such a driving force in causing Rachel's story to crumble, at that moment he was completely unable to help himself.

Once people learned Shelia and Rachel had been arrested in connection with Skylar's murder, they began discussing whether Shelia
was a psychopath.[32] But that's not the way either psychologists or
law enforcement think about it. According to criminal profiler Ken
Lanning, people aren't simply *psychopaths* or *not psychopaths*. It's a
matter of how many traits of psychopathic behavior people have and
how strongly they have them. An individual can be more or less
narcissistic, more or less prone to lying, and so on. There are differ-
ing degrees of psychopathy, and someone with psychopathic tendencies can still have good behavior, or have positive feelings for other
people. In more extreme psychopathic types, of course, this isn't the
case.

According to Lanning, after he heard about the case and reviewed
letters Shelia had written from detention, she seemed to have psychopathic tendencies—to be a *psychopathic type* of person. However,
he warned, a label of *psychopath* should never be applied to a person
so young—especially not without extensive first-hand experience.

"You have to be careful about how much of this is really a diag-
nostic mental disorder," Lanning said, "and how much of this is just
characteristics, immaturity, that adolescents go through." Many people show psychopathic tendencies in adolescence and then simply
get over them as they mature.

UHS teens were no different, and as many of them looked back, they
began to question Shelia's behavior. Daniel found himself doing this a
lot. "Shelia just loved to run over animals for no reason," Daniel said
in hindsight. "I would never do that. I think it's horrible." According
to Daniel, she did it a number of times. It's hard to tell whether Shelia

---

[32] Also sometimes referred to as a *sociopath*.

actually did like running over animals or whether Dan just thought that, looking back after he knew she murdered his best friend.

Two other teens offered similar stories, but neither of them was in the car when the incidents happened. Their stories could have been simply the kind of rumors that go around when people discover murderers have been living among them.

Some friends said Shelia did seem to hit a lot of animals, but blamed it on country living. In the rural areas, everyone hit an animal, one time or another. The lucky people were the ones who didn't hit *large* animals, like deer.

However, what is interesting is how Shelia seemed to be able to manipulate other people in her world. For instance, she always put her books in her friends' lockers—because she said the lockers were too difficult for her to open. "She wasn't strong enough to open her locker," Shania said.

In light of this, it wasn't just running over bunnies that gave Daniel pause. There was also that time she talked him into stealing the answers to an exam.

"C'mon, Daniel, you know you need this grade," Shelia insisted outside in the hallway. Lunch period had just begun but she had asked Daniel to hang back for a minute. "We *have* to do this. We're gonna flunk, and our parents are gonna kill us."

She was referring to the class they had together sophomore year, AP English.

"Shelia, you know I can't do that. I'd rather just get grounded or something."

"They'll take your phone. You know they will."

Daniel thought about that. Taking his phone was the worst. Usually, when his folks were pissed off about something, they would freak out. He'd heard the lecture many times before: "You're not going to graduate. You're going to be a failure in life. Blah, blah, blah."

Seeing Daniel waver, Shelia pressed her advantage: "It'll be easy. He's never in his room at lunch. We can just go in real quick."

Shelia's idea was to simply walk into Mr. Kyer's classroom and steal the test answers or jot them down. They could memorize them that night, then ace the test tomorrow.

"This is freaky!" Daniel said. "We could get in *so* much trouble."

She put her lips to his ear and whispered, "Nobody will ever know."

"I don't know…"

She gently pushed his shoulder. "Let's do it now. In and out. We can be in the lunchroom in two minutes."

Daniel let Shelia persuade him to head down the hall to Mr. Lamb's classroom. All the other students and teachers were either at lunch or in class, waiting to take lunch next period.

"They're in the bottom drawer," she told him. "On the right." She clearly wasn't going in.

"Oh, sure," Daniel said, "make me go in and get my hands dirty."

"Don't be dumb. Someone's gotta stand guard."

Just like Shelia said, it only took a few seconds, and they were at lunch in a matter of minutes. Daniel felt guilty afterward. The worst part was, Daniel wasn't sure why he did it because he'd never done it before.

Daniel tried not to waste time dwelling on Shelia or the trouble, but it was really hard; he just wanted his Sky back.

forty-two

Skylar Comes Home

Mary Neese braved the summer heat and humidity to prove there is something stronger than the elements: a mother's love.

With the temperature hovering above 90 degrees, Mary and Dave led a solemn procession from Clay-Battelle High School to the place where their daughter drew her last breath. There, on June 23, family and friends dedicated a bench to Skylar along a narrow country road near Brave, Pennsylvania, at the spot where Skylar's body had lain for six months. The handmade bench read: "In Loving Memory, Skylar A. Neese, 1996–2012." The small crowd of about forty people who came to pay their respects tried to let their laughter outweigh their tears, as they hugged each other.

A pall was cast over the ceremony by Coroner Rohanna's steadfast refusal to let the Neeses spend ten minutes alone with Skylar's remains. Mary and Dave still did not have Skylar back yet, and the Greene County coroner put the blame on the FBI.

"We just received some of the remains back from the FBI within the last couple of days," Rohanna said. "I have not had the remains. The FBI has had them. But we're still investigating because we need to do the things we need to do."

A commemoration at what has come to be known as "Skylar's Site," an informal
memorial that formed at the place where she was murdered.
Photo courtesy Daleen Berry.

Nor had the federal agency released an official cause of death,
according to Rohanna. In addition, since Skylar's body had been
discovered in Greene County, he was the only person who could
make that call—which meant that his office was in charge of Skylar's
remains. Rohanna insisted they were staying right where they were,
and staunchly refused to let the Neeses into the building to see what
was left of their only child.[33]

At the informal gathering, Dave announced his plans to picket
the coroner's office in two days' time. He and Mary were tired of
being victimized by what looked more like a pissing contest than
anything real. The way Dave saw it, Rohanna was being a jerk just
because he could. The grieving father told members of the media
that he didn't care if he was arrested; he and Mary just wanted to say
goodbye to the daughter who had left them nearly one year before.

---

[33] Material in this section originally appeared in "Skylar Neese: The Struggle to Find
Closure Almost One Year Later" by Daleen Berry (daleenberry.com/daleenberry/?p=871).

By Monday the media had taken up the Neeses' cause and a second crowd had gathered for Skylar, this time at the couple's Star City apartment. Everyone was preparing to load signs saying "Free Skylar" into their vehicles and drive thirty minutes to the coroner's office in Waynesburg, Pennsylvania, when Dave's cell phone rang. The caller on the other end had good news: Rohanna was conceding defeat. All of Skylar's remains would be back in West Virginia within a few days. Mary and Dave felt lighter than they had in months.

Skylar was coming home.

On July 3, Mary, Dave, and Skylar's favorite aunt, Carol, drove a mile up the road to the Morgantown State Police detachment to tell her goodbye. The date of the private ceremony had been fiercely guarded to prevent the media from finding out, and all three of them had nervously awaited that day ever since learning what it would hold.

Mother, father, and aunt solemnly walked into the brick building, where Gaskins and Berry met them. Gaskins explained again, just as he had earlier, that Skylar's remains were in a sealed bag they weren't allowed to open. As gently as possible, he reminded them they wouldn't want to remember Skylar by her remains, but as the happy, beautiful daughter they had last seen the night she came home from work.

He explained they could sit inside the room with her as long as they needed. To protect the chain of custody, what was left of Skylar had been placed in an interview room with a two-way mirror. It was, he said, the best they could do.

Mary, Dave, and Carol entered the room and sat down on the three chairs facing the table that held Skylar. They told her how much they loved her, how much they missed her, and how happy they were she was finally home. They told her about all her friends—from school, from around the state, even some from around the globe whom she had never met—and how everyone was thinking about her. They talked to her about happier times, about how they wished they could hold her, and how they were going to make sure she got justice. They told her about the law named for her, and how they hoped it would help other teens. They sobbed and sobbed, not unlike the day Mary and Carol had wept together months earlier in the Neeses' Star City apartment.

Dave stood up then, towering over the bag with all that was left of Skylar inside. He leaned over the bag and kissed the end of it.

"Dave," Carol said, "you just kissed her feet."

In a year filled with weeks of darkness, it was a much-needed moment of levity.

"Well, hell, I can't tell," Dave said, blustering, as he walked down to the other end and kissed it, too.

Mary and Carol laughed and so did Dave, before they cried some more.

After being allowed to grieve privately at the detachment, Skylar's closest family members left feeling better—closer to closure than they had been before they arrived that warm July day. Finally, they could put her body to rest. Mary and Dave chose to have Skylar cremated, and her remains are held in an urn that doubles as a wall photo of Skylar's last school picture.

Her parents were finally able to give Skylar the service she deserved. The memorial was planned for July 20, not long after the first anniversary of Skylar's disappearance. Mary wore a ribbed purple blouse with black dress slacks for the day she would tell Skylar goodbye for good. Dave didn't own a single purple garment, so he wore the next best thing: a navy blue shirt. He knew Skylar would have approved.

Over two days, more than 1,000 people streamed through the Kingdom Evangelical Methodist Church sanctuary to pay their respects or attend the service. Many of them had never met the sunny, blue-eyed teen whose pictures played continuously on a large screen at the front of the room. They wore purple anyway, showing they had been touched deeply by Skylar's short life and tragic death.

Several of the people who had helped investigate and who were going to prosecute the case came, too, as did dozens of UHS students and faculty. People who were strangers before Skylar's disappearance also showed up, many of them just to meet and comfort Mary and Dave. More than one person drove several hours and crossed state lines so they could give the couple a hug, or offer them hope for happier days.

Teenagers lined up in rows to watch the poignant pictures of Skylar come and go. With their eyes glued to the screen, tears streaming down their faces, they all looked like silent statues. Many of them wore a range of Skylar purples; some were dressed in traditional black. None of them could leave the building without tearing up over the friend they had lost too soon.

During the memorial service, Pastor Kevin Cain shared Skylar stories he'd gleaned from friends and family. He told how Skylar was a strong source of support to other youths by being their counselor, their confidante. He told funny stories from her childhood and teen years that made those in attendance chuckle or even cry.

Mary and Dave were worried about how they would get through such a public display, but in the end, they held onto each other and wept openly, and with the minister's words, they allowed the long year of grief to gently wash over them. The service couldn't remove all of the pain and anguish they felt, but at least it helped to make it more bearable.

As he concluded, Cain turned the service over to Skylar's parents. Dave had been worried Mary wouldn't hold up well, but as they stood together she seemed, if anything, to look stronger. Not one to speak to large crowds, Mary Neese was the epitome of grace and dignity.

"I just want to say thanks to each and every one of you for all of the support you've given us this past year," Mary said. "We truly wouldn't have made it without you and words just can't tell you guys how much we love all of you. Thank you so much."

It was Dave's turn next. His voice was gravelly, his words unusually brief when he spoke. After repeating Mary's expression of thanks, Dave asked everyone to look at the large, framed photo of Skylar that

July 20 memorial service for Skylar at the Kingdom Evangelical Methodist Church.
Photo courtesy Daleen Berry.

also held her ashes. All eyes turned toward the front of the room.
"No one can ever hurt you again, baby," he said.

Not much is known about the day Mikinzy Boggs went to see his girlfriend[34] in juvenile detention, because he has refused to talk about it. People close to the story said Mikinzy was really confused about everything. After news about Rachel's possible involvement began spreading around the school, people said Mikinzy visited the counselor and even had several absences. Teachers say it was a bad

----

[34] Apparently Mikinzy and Rachel considered themselves a couple at this time.

time for him. Now more than ever, they believe the teenager needed answers: about why Rachel was in jail, why the media was reporting that she had confessed to murder, and when she was coming home.

When Mikinzy arrived at the Wheeling facility, he sat and waited to see Rachel. He probably didn't know what to expect, and he might have wondered if he would have to speak to Rachel through bullet-proof glass.

During that bittersweet visit Rachel revealed a secret to Mikinzy, and he made a promise to her in return.

At first Rachel was so happy she seemed almost giddy. "Oh, my gosh, hi! Great to see you!"

"Why are you smiling right now?" It didn't make sense to Mikinzy. He hadn't yet heard much news about the crime. "You don't belong in here, Rachel."

Rachel's answer was short and to the point. "Yes. Yes, I do."

"What do you mean? You didn't murder anyone. You would never do that."

"But I did. Shelia and I killed Skylar."

Mikinzy didn't know what to say, because he wasn't sure he heard her right. *Why would Rachel kill Skylar?*

"Why? Why would you do that?" he asked, shaking his head.

Everyone who saw Mikinzy and Rachel together before she confessed insisted the couple was crazy about each other, even though they frequently fought and were always on again, off again.

"Because she knew our secrets, and she was going to blackmail us," Rachel said calmly.

"What kind of secrets, Rachel?" Mikinzy asked. "What do you mean? I don't understand."

"She had a video of us making out. She knew we had sex together."

Mikinzy must have believed Rachel, because he told other people what she told him that day. But he didn't tell them how Rachel explained that she and Shelia had been girlfriends, that they had had a lesbian relationship, possibly while Mikinzy was dating her himself. Maybe she told him she was bisexual, maybe she told him she and Shelia hooked up during the off phase of Rachel and Mikinzy's on-again, off-again relationship. She did tell him she and Shelia had been lovers and that was why Skylar had to die.

At the time, Mikinzy was either still very confused, or deeply in love with Rachel, and she with him, because of what came next.

"Will you wait for me?" Rachel asked.

Mikinzy didn't hesitate. "Yes."

Near the banks of the Ohio River, another teenager was eager to impress upon her new inmate friends how badly she'd been wronged. Shelia Eddy reportedly told at least one other teenage girl housed with her at the Parkersburg juvenile center that Rachel was the backstabber who had squealed on her.

Then, even though it's a violation for inmates even to touch each other—much less have a sexual relationship—Shelia and that girl, Dawn, became lovers. For some unknown reason authorities can't explain, Dawn was then transferred to the same facility where Rachel was housed in Wheeling.

When Dawn confronted Rachel, calling her a snitch, Rachel grew so upset she vomited. Rachel begged Dawn to tell Shelia to plead guilty—so there wouldn't be a trial. Reportedly, Dawn intended to bully Rachel, but the two became friends instead, and Dawn's alliance to Shelia was quickly forgotten.

These details wouldn't have become public if Shelia's mother had not shared them with other friends and family. According to Crissy, Tara took a letter from Dawn to Shelia to Crissy's parents' home and read it to them. When her father heard the part where Dawn and Shelia were lovers, he told Tara he never wanted to hear anything like that again.

Crissy said that day was the last time her family heard from Tara.

forty-three

Her Day in Criminal Court

Four long and frustrating months after Rachel's guilty plea in May, Skylar's family feared the case had become as stagnant as a summer pond. The courts had done nothing. From the outside looking in, that's how it appeared both to the people closest to the case and to the public.

Despite initial rumors that Shelia would be transferred to adult status and Rachel would be sentenced swiftly, nothing further appeared to happen. The media would not even print or speak Shelia's name—much less speculate on what was prompting the delay.

As the summer heat pounded on, it became harder to tell which made people angrier: Rachel confessing to Skylar's murder or the media's refusal to name her accomplice. Eighteen weeks later, the people who followed Skylar's story got their wish: on September 4 Judge Clawges ruled Shelia Eddy would be transferred from juvenile to criminal court.

For the prosecution of Skylar's murder, that legal distinction meant Monongalia County now viewed Shelia as an adult. So did the State of West Virginia. That, in turn, meant both entities would hold the teen fully accountable for her actions. Equally important in the eyes of everyone following Skylar's story, the media could now print and speak Shelia's name—which news reporters did the minute Prosecutor Ashdown handed them a press release announcing the judge's decision.

For 426 days, from the day Skylar disappeared until September 4, Mary and Dave had never been far from tears. A question from a well-meaning stranger who recognized them in public would cause them to mourn their only child all over again. A passing headline about another missing child would suddenly force them to relive their own tragedy.

Regardless of how many people celebrated Shelia's new status, nothing changed for Mary and Dave. The Neeses continued to grieve. For the baby they brought home from the hospital, for the little girl who ran around naked in her family home, for the teenager who became the loyal confidante to so many of her peers. For Skylar Annette, the sixteen-year-old daughter who was lost to them forever.

So September 4, 2013, the day Shelia's alleged role in the murder became public, was a day to celebrate, but it was also a day for sorrow. That pivotal date initiated Shelia's slow march toward justice, but it also signaled the end of Mary and Dave's old life. In the end, the Neeses realized, it was an empty celebration.[35]

Trials are not about finding the truth. They are about judging guilt and setting the world right again. But after a crime as savage as the murder of Skylar Neese, people doubt the world can ever again *be* right. A promising young life was violently cut short in July of 2012, and all the possible futures of Skylar Neese—and *every benefit she would have brought to the people she had yet to encounter*—have forever vanished.

The murder is the central stone thrown into the pond, but the waves that ripple out represent all the lives irrevocably changed. Mary

------

[35] Material on this and the previous page originally appeared in "The Wait Is Over: Shelia Eddy to Be Tried as Adult in Skylar Neese Murder," by Daleen Berry (daleenberry.com/daleenberry/?p=929).

and Dave have suffered most from the killing of their daughter. So have their families, as have those of Shelia and Rachel. Skylar's friends, too, must go on without her. The teenagers at University High School, even the ones who knew Skylar only in passing, had bits of themselves torn away, as well. So did the teachers who trusted Rachel and Shelia, but who now felt betrayed. Even people not directly affected by the murder or its aftermath—in the Morgantown community and well beyond—were stunned by the betrayal of two "best friends" and may never again be able to trust in quite the same way.

Shelia's trial for premeditated murder could never undo the damage. People still longed for it to reveal hidden truths, such as whether some mental illness turned these girls into killers, or what Rachel really meant when she said they didn't want to be friends with Skylar anymore, or if Skylar was killed because they had to keep her quiet.

Shelia's arraignment took only fifteen minutes, but it contained all the elements of high drama. The court hearing was held September 17—eleven days before Shelia would turn eighteen.

Shelia wore the same orange jumpsuit, white socks, and sandals as the rest of the inmates. The only female prisoner in the courtroom stood before the judge, her wrists and ankles shackled.

The contrast between Shelia and her attorney couldn't have been more pronounced. Mike Benninger was as tall, broad, and dark as Shelia was short, slight, and fair. Their voices were a stark contrast as well. His boomed, by far the loudest in the courtroom. Distinct and certain, his voice allowed everyone seated in the wood-paneled room to hear him without the need to lean forward, fearful of missing something. Hers was soft and uncertain, almost childlike. Benninger's presence made Shelia seem even smaller than she was, as if she could not possibly have committed the crimes with which she was charged.

"Have you discussed the charges with your client?" Judge Clawges asked.

"I have, your Honor. Carefully," Benninger replied.

"Does she understand the charges against her?"

"She *absolutely* does," the defense attorney said.

Four times in a row, Shelia said, "Not guilty." To one count of first-degree murder. To one count of kidnapping. To two counts of conspiracy to commit kidnapping and murder.

Dave and Skylar's aunt Carol sat three rows back. Before Shelia could finish her first "not guilty," sobs were heard from their direction. People who came to observe, who had never met Skylar or her family, began to cry when they heard the sounds of grief coming from the Neese contingent.

In court, Shelia appeared to be chewing gum. Inmates do not normally chew gum while waiting to plead to felony murder charges. But the most distinctive aspect of Shelia's appearance was her emotional demeanor. Some people say they didn't see a single tear. Others said her eyes were rimmed in red, as if she had been crying at some point during the judge's questions.

Some people said Shelia was smiling while she waited for her case to be called. Dave Neese believed she smiled right at him, as if to reassure him that everything was all right. Or to taunt him. News media photos and online reports from observers all seem to indicate that most people believed Shelia had been smiling throughout the procedure. As if she was enjoying the attention.[36]

---

[36] Material in this section originally appeared in "Shelia Eddy Pleads Not Guilty," by Daleen Berry (daleenberry.com/daleenberry/?p=972).

forty-four

Judgment Days

By her second hearing, on October 15, Shelia wasn't smiling. At all.

A photographer later remarked that, unlike the first court appearance, he didn't see Shelia's pearly whites even once. Bespectacled, with her hair pulled back in an updo, she looked even younger than she had at her arraignment two weeks earlier. Extremely subdued, Shelia struck one observer as "possibly drugged," while another said she "looked like she was *trying* not to have an expression."

Whatever the reason for her September 17 arraignment smile, Shelia had apparently received a subsequent lesson in appropriate courtroom body language from her defense attorney. Whether out of nervousness or simply being unaware of how she appeared to onlookers, Shelia didn't seem to appreciate the gravity of the situation the first time she was in court. This time, she did.

Benninger filed the motions before Judge Clawges' September 30 deadline. Twelve motions were filed, ranging from a request for bail to a motion to change venue to motions for suppression of evidence. Shelia had waived her right to a speedy trial and was at the pretrial motions hearing at 9:00 A.M. to hear the judge's rulings.

In support of his motions, Benninger told the court he'd recently received the FBI report. He said it contained numerous "technical lab studies and photos." In addition, Benninger had "thousands of pages of documentation" he said supported his request to move the case out of Monongalia County.

Clawges wasted no time on one motion in particular. When Benninger requested bail for his client, Clawges ruled swiftly: "No."

Benninger also asked to have the trial moved to another county because of "substantial publicity and prejudice"; to bring in jurors from another area; to have Rachel Shoaf's testimony suppressed, due to her supposed mental instability; and to have all the charges dropped, citing prosecutorial misconduct.

Prosecutor Ashdown responded to the motions later that week, saying no misconduct had occurred and disagreeing that Shelia's chance at a fair trial has been hampered by excessive media reports.

As for the motion to move the trial, some Monongalia County residents already knew a lot about the case, but many hadn't even heard of it. Ashdown had gone to great lengths to prevent the media from revealing anything other than details that were a matter of public record anyway. She held no press conferences and made no public statements about teen killers or the plight of today's youth. She had been keeping a tight lid on the case since Rachel's confession in January.

What Ashdown didn't object to was the trial being delayed. Benninger requested this because he said his client's legal team needed time to look through all the documents from the prosecution. Then, the start of the trial was actually moved to an earlier date, since the court had an open date on the docket. But it never came to pass. On a frigid Friday in January, Shelia Eddy shocked everyone when she pled guilty to first-degree murder.

Anyone who saw Shelia's criminal case file would question how the teen's attorney could defend her. In the end, he couldn't.

"I have found negligible, if any, basis...to develop a defense," Benninger said. He looked through "every piece of paper, video, and audio," he received about the case, and met with or talked to his client or her family about thirty times. After digging through West Virginia, Pennsylvania, and even federal case law, Shelia's defense attorney said he found nothing that would allow him to mount a reasonable defense for his client. In the end, Benninger realized "there was little more that I or anyone else could do for this young lady."

Media from New York City and elsewhere flew in to cover the January 24 hearing, which was broadcast over a live video feed online. People dressed in purple—Skylar's favorite color—filled the courtroom. As Shelia was escorted in, she passed her mother and stepfather, her father, and other family members, as well as armed bailiffs wearing bulletproof vests.

Her hair was in a low side ponytail, but her blonde highlights had grown out, changing her back to a brunette. She wore large-framed glasses and an orange jumpsuit. Her hands and feet were shackled. Like her last court appearance, Shelia seemed to move slowly, almost as if she were drugged. Or afraid of what was to come.

By the time she took her seat at the defense table, her face was contorted and she began to cry. Oddly, it was one of the few times Shelia showed any emotion—causing many people to claim she cried crocodile tears. As Dave and others later said, "She wasn't crying for what she'd done, she was crying because she got caught."

Although Shelia Eddy pled guilty to intentionally killing Skylar Neese, she didn't utter one word about what she and her co-conspirator did—she simply pled guilty to all the charges Clawges read from his bench. Shelia said she understood what they meant. She said no one had pressured her to plead guilty. She even said her legal representation was good.

But the words Skylar's family most needed to hear—"I'm sorry"—were the ones Shelia couldn't, or wouldn't, say.

Or perhaps equally important, "Please forgive me."

Although Benninger read from a prepared statement and said his client and her family recognized the Neeses are in "a constant state of despair, loneliness, and sadness," the absence of those words from Shelia's own mouth left those in attendance dumbfounded. They wondered how Shelia could plead guilty to premeditated, first-degree murder—but remain silent when she was given a chance to prove her remorse.

In a room filled with the sound of weeping, Ashdown alluded to the motive behind the murder: Rachel and Shelia, she said, were "worried that Skylar would divulge their secrets. The kind of secrets girls have and…" Ashdown paused, "other things."

The prosecutor didn't elaborate, but it seemed to be a direct reference to Shelia and Rachel's *sexual* relationship. At first, Ashdown said, the two teens began to distance themselves from Skylar. But when they came to believe Skylar planned to expose their relationship, they murdered her.

Ashdown confirmed they lured Skylar into Shelia's vehicle, drove to the Blacksville area, and crossed the state line into Pennsylvania. They turned down a narrow country lane to an isolated area familiar to all three girls, where they planned to smoke weed.

At times while listening to Ashdown, Mary teared up and snuggled closer into the crook of Dave's right arm as he shook his head. The back of his neck was a florid red after the prosecutor described how Shelia and Rachel had hidden knives on their bodies and how the FBI had found blood in the trunk of Shelia's car.

"Relax, relax," Mary whispered in Dave's ear.

Ashdown continued, saying that instead of doing what Skylar thought they would do that night, Shelia and Rachel "both stabbed Skylar multiple times. Skylar fought back and tried to run but she was overcome by her attackers."

The prosecutor's next words were especially poignant. "They changed into clean, unbloody clothes and returned to their lives."

Judge Clawges accepted Shelia's guilty plea, saying she had waived her pre-sentencing rights. The family was invited to give an oral statement. Skylar's mother, Mary, didn't trust herself to speak. So her sister Carol spoke on her behalf.

"She's taken hopes and dreams from my sister," Skylar's aunt said. That's because Mary Neese was cheated out of seeing Skylar go to the prom, graduate high school, or get married. With Skylar's murder, Carol told the judge, Mary also lost any chance of becoming a grandmother. Everyone heard the sadness in Carol's voice and saw the tears flow down her cheeks, and more people in the courtroom started crying.

Moments after Carol returned to her seat, Dave Neese walked to the prosecutor's table and began reading from a prepared statement. His voice was small and quiet, in complete contrast to his bearlike size. When he stumbled over the words, the lead investigator, Corporal Ronnie Gaskins, reached his arm out as if to imbue Dave with the strength needed to go on.

Dave did, but not before he broke down sobbing. "My life and my wife's life has been drastically altered. We are no longer a family," Dave said.

Many people in the courtroom wept openly at Carol and Dave's words. No doubt Clawges was touched by what he heard, too, but in the end, that made no difference when it came to his sentence. *Miller v. Alabama* (U.S. Supreme Court, June 25 2012) requires "the court to impose a sentence of life imprisonment with mercy," Clawges told Shelia, "which means you would be eligible for parole after fifteen years."

The decision "is kind of binding on all of us," he added, since it means imposing "a sentence of life without mercy upon a juvenile would be a violation of the cruel and inhuman[e] punishment provisions of the United States Constitution."

So while Shelia received a life sentence, she will be eligible for parole in fifteen years. Clawges stressed the law allows for no more. However, that does not mean Shelia will find herself on the road to freedom that soon. The parole board must make that decision. One major factor that entity will consider is Shelia's remorse—or lack thereof—perhaps as evidenced by the words she didn't say to the Neeses that day.

Because of the nature of "this horrific and vile crime," the prosecution said it had one other request: "We are asking you here, today, to sentence this defendant to adult prison, for her very adult crime." Ashdown said Shelia should not return to a juvenile facility, especially since she was eighteen.

Judge Clawges agreed. He said that as soon as a bed became available, Eddy was to be placed in an adult prison. "If that's tomorrow, it's tomorrow," Clawges said. "If it's thirty days from now, it's thirty days from now."

In return for Shelia's guilty plea, the Pennsylvania and federal court systems both agreed to dismiss any pending charges they had against her.[37]

---

[37] Material in the preceding sections originally appeared in "Shelia Eddy Sentenced to Life with Mercy," by Daleen Berry (daleenberry.com/daleenberry/?p=1084).

forty-five

On Three!

After the plea hearing, Ashdown said Rachel confessed that she and Shelia started stabbing Skylar on "a prearranged signal." For months, people claimed that signal was a count: "One . . . two . . . three!"

At one time, such a notion seemed to be based solely on unrelated Twitter traffic on March 31, 2013, between Shelia and her cousin, Lexy.

In successive tweets, Shelia said,

still waiting "@slexy_Just waitin for you to make a move @_sheliiaa"
and

still. make a move "@slexy_"@_sheliiaastill waiting "@slexy_Just waitin for you to make a move @_sheliiaa"" o me 2"
and

@slexy_ on three

A little later, about 1:30 in the morning, Shelia tweeted, *we really did go on three.* Lexy, tweeted back, *"@_sheliiaa @slexy_ on three" that was a good idea.*

People repeatedly cited those tweets and others like them, saying the murder began after one girl gave the other a signal of "One, two, three." People claimed this March 31 exchange was proof Shelia's cousin knew about the murder. Social media chatter showed how early this speculation began. Although it may have begun earlier, on May 9, nine days after both girls were arrested, @KillerGirlProbz9 tweeted, *What are u guys gonna do, take to into the woods stab me on the count of 3?*

Similar speculation appeared repeatedly on Topix and Websleuths. PaulfromChas posted, *Looks like the "we went on the count of three" tweet was what it was rumored to be*, and Hillbilly_Chick responded, *Also, to me, that tweet says…others knew.*

Throughout this case, people laid blame first on one and then another family member or friend, saying they knew about the murder. Sometimes people pointed at those close to Shelia and Rachel and said they helped cover up the crime. Many, many teens were wrongly accused as murderers or accessories to Skylar's murder. But the authorities made no other arrests. Nor were they likely to—not when the real killers had confessed. Not when the evidence that Shelia and Rachel had acted alone was so strong.

Based on the tweets themselves, it looked as if people took Shelia and Lexy's words out of context. At one time, there was no valid reason to believe those tweets had anything to do with the murder. There was every reason to believe the cousins were discussing something the two of them did—not even remotely connected to Skylar's death.

However, it was also now likely Shelia was using something she knew she and Rachel had done as a way to mock her audience— whom she was trying to portray as having wrongly persecuted her. On February 4, 2013, she tweeted, *the littlest things can be blown out of proportion to something that is completely untrue. don't talk if you don't know what really happened.*

In her press conference after the hearing, Ashdown revealed the two teens really did count to three before they began stabbing Skylar.

Whenever three people are as close as Shelia, Skylar, and Rachel were, the relationship's dynamics can become extreme. Former FBI profiler Ken Lanning stated that alliances are always in flux, and at any given moment, two would be "in" and one would be "out."

Various friends of all three girls said this was *constantly* the case. A look at the trio's Twitter traffic during freshman and sophomore years verified this.

Lanning was so familiar with teen dynamics that he actually wrote the training manuals for the National Center for Missing & Exploited Children. Lanning said teen social alliances could be incredibly volatile and intense, and eventually "two girls together wind up doing something that possibly no one of them would have done by themselves."

At some point, the theory went, the trio broke down. It turned into two against one. The shifting alliance solidified, leaving Skylar the odd girl out—permanently. People were waiting for the trial to reveal what caused that final break, what the *real* motive was in Skylar Neese's murder.

Skylar's tweet on December 13, 2011, six months before her murder, provided a glimpse of that breakdown: *#whyareyousofuckingstupid #twofacedbitches #nevergettingoverit.*

Her tweet the evening of July 4, 2012, a day and a half before she climbed out her window for the last time, also showed signs that Skylar was angry at her two best friends and frustrated over being left out: *sick of being at fucking home. thanks "friends", love hanging out with you all too.*

The permanent two-against-one status leading to Skylar's death took shape as much as a year before her murder. Police learned this when Chris Boggs came forward after Rachel's confession. Boggs, a UHS student, posted on Facebook, *I knew those dumb bitches killed her!*

Mary, who saw Chris' post, sent him a private message. He replied, saying he and other students had heard both her and Shelia ask during class how to get rid of a body. Chris told Mary it happened in Dan Demchak's sophomore biology class.

Mary alerted Gaskins, who reached out to Chris. That led police to other UHS students—who agreed with Boggs' assessment. Students also claimed they overheard Shelia and Rachel making plans to kill Skylar. Some said they tried to warn their classmate, but when Skylar inquired about the warnings, Shelia and Rachel blew them off.

———————

Skylar's outsider status only laid the basis for her murder. Investigators look for a "precipitating event" that triggers a violent crime, something that turns a simmering situation to a full boil. In Skylar's case, three such events have come to light thus far. All three involved her and Shelia. First, the two girls argued and came to blows inside a movie theater in March 2012. Second, there was a known tiff that took place during their trip to the beach in June 2012.

The event that triggered the trio's problems came long before, on a hot August night in 2011, when Skylar witnessed Shelia and Rachel having sex.

———————

The disturbing video that captured the three girls playing a game about death six months before Skylar's murder shows "[c]learly there is some awareness of pain and suffering and different ways of dying," Lanning said.

Then, when Shelia and Rachel did kill Skylar, it was in "a pretty gruesome, horrible way, with a lot of personal attack against her and what they felt that she represented."

The long-time criminal analyst said that to "brutalize this person, to almost torture them, and then just leave them there…shows a certain amount of rage targeted at her and what she represents."

Skylar's death was gruesome. Investigators said her murder involved what police and prosecutors call "overkill." The act itself was extreme, involving anywhere from thirty to fifty separate stab wounds. Skylar's murder was *personal*: the victim's killers knew Skylar well and harbored deep personal feelings toward her.

Overkill can also indicate a murder driven by hatred, rage, fear, jealousy, loathing, disgust, or some combination of intense emotions—such as those that might have been fueled by a close, three-way friendship gone horribly wrong. Drugs or alcohol could have exacerbated those feelings, although no evidence of that emerged.

That many stab wounds could also indicate the two killers freaked out. "Somebody that young, they're going to freak out," Trooper Berry said. "They keep doing it and doing it, not knowing the whole time that the victim is dead. That's a typical reaction. I've seen it in other crimes."

Even if the murder was carefully planned, the intense emotion indicated the crime was not carried out simply to further an agenda (e.g., "Skylar was brilliant so she had to die") or to gain some advantage ("With Skylar dead, I can have her iPod").

Extreme violence, according to Lanning, could also indicate the killers didn't just want to do away with the victim—they wanted to obliterate Skylar. Possibly, Skylar reminded both killers of something about themselves they didn't like. It is entirely likely this was the case with both girls, albeit in different ways. For instance, it is no secret that Rachel felt intense anger toward her mother. Skylar, in many ways the responsible overachiever who called her friends on the carpet when they misbehaved, could have reminded Rachel of a mother figure.

Shelia, however, is another matter. Skylar could have reminded Shelia of what she lost, or willingly gave up, when she entered her boy-crazy stage. No doubt Shelia, whom Skylar believed had lost all self-respect, knew Skylar no longer respected or looked up to her, like she once did. Skylar's own words seem to confirm this, when she wrote about Shelia in her February 2, 2012, English journal: "*She transformed from an independent, free spirit into a needy doormat...*"

It wasn't "so much that they hated Skylar but that they hated what she represented," Lanning said. If Skylar served as a constant reminder of a past they wanted to forget—or a future they couldn't contemplate—then Shelia and Rachel might have believed killing Skylar would alleviate those negative feelings.

Lanning believes another factor to incite Shelia and Rachel's anger would have been the relationship Skylar had with her parents. She wasn't rich or spoiled, but "clearly her mother and father were two individuals who loved her and were devoted to her. Maybe that's what they resented about her. She was really this good person who reminded them of what they were not, and that's what made them angry."

—————————

So when Shania gave Shelia the photo collage as a Christmas gift and later discovered Shelia had removed all images of Skylar, it's possible Shania witnessed Shelia's attempt to block out any memory of Skylar, so she wouldn't have negative feelings whenever she saw Skylar's face staring back at her.

forty-six

The Affair

It was a lesbian love affair.

That's what people have been saying for more than a year now. As more and more months have passed, a growing list of evidence indicates they could be right.

At UHS, other teens called the trio lesbians long before Skylar's murder. The teens themselves joked about it through much of their freshman and sophomore years. Close friendships between teenage girls often inspire such rumors. Most of the time, that's all they are.

These days, girls stripping and kissing each other is quite common, especially at parties where alcohol and drugs are plentiful. When such behavior takes place in a semipublic context, it's often more about showing off than an authentic expression of sexuality. Any number of other factors could be at play, from a desire to be thought of as cool to exhibitionism. One teen called this kind of behavior "drunk girl games."

Over the months, many people spoke of pictures or a video the entire school is said to have known about. There was no indication from interviews, online research, or photographs that Skylar had ever been sexual with boys or girls. However, that isn't to say she didn't wonder about her sexuality—or whether she might be a lesbian—especially since there is no evidence that Skylar was interested in the opposite sex.

Skylar's own words seem to say she questioned her sexual orientation, which would be completely normal in today's world, or she thought she was a lesbian. In an essay titled "A Barren Heart," Skylar penned this poignant, undated piece sometime late in her sophomore year:

> The sun was scorching as I dragged continuously on. Sweat dripped down my face with each step I took toward what seemed a universe away. My muscles screamed with agony in response to even the smallest of movements and I begin to wonder if it's actually worth all I'm putting myself through. I'm stuck, forever trapped in endless nothingness. I've grown tired of nothing; nothing is all I've felt for months.
>
> My mind is my largest enemy. I detest my surroundings and refuse to face the fact that this desert is more desired than I am. "I want to see the world!" she would say. I was never invited, not that I had any desire to accompany her. I was content with my average life in an average city. Never had I yearned to explore the world or what it had to offer. She promised she'd return soon enough, a changed and happy woman. Soon enough has turned into never.
>
> Months passed and letters or photos went from rare to nonexistent. I kept telling myself to wait it out, for she's busy enjoying life and all will be normal soon. After four months with no communication I couldn't dull the pain with my own lies any longer. I knew she was gone. The desert had won, but I refused to be forgotten so quickly.
>
> Deep in the desert she resides with the area's natives. The thought of those people or the desert itself forces so much hatred through my body it hurts. This desert is nothing, has nothing, and offers nothing; a useless place. I'm getting closer and growing more and more excited to escape this wasteland with the woman I love. I arrive, ecstatic to see the beautiful face I've missed so much. Our

eyes meet, and I suddenly realize why she's still here. Her eyes
went hallow [sic], her face black. I am her desert.

Another undated poem from her sophomore Honors portfolio
speaks of Skylar loving someone. Given its tone and when compared
with Skylar's other writings, the poem seems to be give voice to her
feelings for Shelia:

Like an empty meadow / Filled with nothing but dry grass / It
smells of autumn air / I'm surrounded by beauty / I take it all in
at last / Here I am waiting / Too stubborn to understand / Time
passes slowly / Acceptance begins to come / That you will never
return / Loyal to you always / The love has me to [sic] captured
/ In your eyes I look / To you love, my heart belongs / Our love
cannot be broken

Lanning said the problems seen in Skylar's friendship with Shelia
could be from a change in the girls' attitude, or because "one of them
developed a little later than the other."

However, the relationship could also evolve, he said, "if one of
them found herself attracted to boys and the other found herself
attracted to girls."

————————

No one believes Rachel Shoaf. Her now-famous statement, "We didn't
want to be friends with Skylar anymore," has never seemed accurate
or adequate as a motive for murder. Everyone wants to know how,
and why, two bright and pretty teenagers were able to perpetrate
such a heinous crime against their professed best friend.

On February 26, 2014, everyone present in the Monongalia
County Courthouse waited to see if the redheaded teen, considered
by many to be the proverbial "lesser of two evils," would supply
new information, a substantial clue as to their reason to conspire,
kidnap, and kill their fellow UHS student. Was it a thrill kill? Were

they lesbian lovers terrified of being discovered? Was a boy involved, drugs maybe?

The courtroom atmosphere for Rachel's hearing was markedly different from Shelia's. A month earlier, the nine bailiffs had been edgy, no doubt because of repeated rumors of threats made on Shelia's life. That day, the bailiffs had scanned the crowd searching for would-be attackers. At Rachel's hearing, however, they were more relaxed. There was banter among them, even smiles.

The center section of the courtroom was filled with supporters of Skylar and her family. The left side, Rachel's side, was not nearly as full. There were few young people as nearly all of Rachel's high school friends felt angry toward her, betrayed.

During the proceedings Judge Russell Clawges kept his tone conversational but authoritative. Eventually he gave Rachel the opportunity to speak. Unlike her accomplice, Shelia Eddy, Rachel did not stay silent.

After scanning the crowd, her eyes came to rest upon the Neeses. "I am so sorry," Rachel began, her words soft, her voice quavering. "I don't know if there's a proper way to make this apology, because there are not even words to describe the guilt and remorse that I feel for what I've done."

"The person that did that was not the real me," she said, her delivery steady as she turned to Clawges, "not the person I am, not what I'm made of and not what I believe in."

As she spoke, Dave and Mary studied Rachel. Dave's face was etched with a deep scowl and his neck was flushed. Mary's eyebrows rose in surprise, or skepticism.

"I don't think I ever thought that this would actually happen. I became scared and caught up in something I did not want to do. I didn't realize the gravity of my actions and how many people I've hurt."

Mary Neese's expression, as she glanced at her husband, seemed to say, "Did you hear that?"

Rachel went on to admit that she "hurt the Neese family and those who love Skylar. I hurt my parents and shamed my family."

Rachel listed those she'd hurt—from her family and community to her "Lord and savior, Jesus Christ." Face in her hands, Rachel sank back into her chair. Her shoulders shuddered, as if she were crying.[38] One of Rachel's attorneys, John Angotti, spoke up. "There's nothing I can say here today to take away the pain and heartache that the Neese family has and will endure." He also said he believed the "case would not have been resolved without [Rachel's] confession and cooperation."

Angotti referred to Dr. Patricia Bailey's report and the result of her psychological evaluation of Rachel. Dr. Bailey recommended that Rachel be sentenced as a juvenile and remain in juvenile detention until she turns twenty-one. She should remain in the Northern Regional Juvenile Detention Center, Dr. Bailey's report said, and continue with her treatment. Because Rachel provided testimony, it would be detrimental for her to be in the same institution as Shelia.

Angotti went on to ask the court to accept Dr. Bailey's recommendations. He closed with a statement saying Rachel "understands and accepts" that she should be punished. "But more importantly," he said, "she hopes and prays for forgiveness, from the Neese family, her family, and the community at large."

Next it was the prosecutor's turn. Prosecuting Attorney Marsha Ashdown chose to begin with the victims' impact statements.

Speaking first, Dave Neese began by saying that while it was true Rachel led police to the body, "Rachel Shoaf also murdered my daughter in cold blood. Skylar would not be where she was if it wasn't for Rachel Shoaf. She should take her apologies and sit on them because that's about what they're worth to me and my wife.... Your honor, I ask that you give her forty years and plus, if you can."

Carol Michaud, Skylar's aunt, opened her statement by saying, "And still to this day we do not know why they did this, and that is

---

[38] Material in this chapter originally appeared in "Rachel Shoaf Sentenced to 30 Years for Killing Skylar Neese," by Geoff Fuller. (http://www.daleenberry.com/daleenberry/?p=1133).

a question we would like an answer to." Clearly filled with anger and anguish, she continued; as she spoke, sobs could be heard throughout the gallery. She ended by saying: "I hope you really and truly regret what you did, but it would never make us feel any better."

Dave's brother, Michael, followed Carol. He spoke with heart-wrenching detail of his experience after Skylar's murder. His testimony also moved many to tears. Overcome by emotion, he lost his place several times as he spoke. He concluded by saying, "The admitted murderer sitting here today has nothing but blatant disregard for human life and she deserves the maximum sentence."

Though Ashdown's account of the crime was not lengthy, it lasted just over five minutes, and was painful to hear, especially for Mary and Dave. "Rachel Shoaf estimated that Skylar was stabbed ten times before she died," Ashdown said. Her voice faltered at times and signs of fatigue were visible on her face. "And she explained that during the attack, Skylar Neese's neck made weird sounds, and they both continued to stab her until those noises stopped."

On top of that horror, Ashdown said Rachel and Shelia repeatedly coordinated their lies for police over a six-month period. They plotted before and covered up after. Rachel deserved an adult sentence, Ashdown said, for this "oh, so adult crime of cold-blooded, planned, premeditated murder.

"Murder by a stranger is a horror. . . . I imagine that Dave and Mary Neese wake up some mornings and there are an easy few minutes until the fact of Skylar's murder comes rushing back. And the unbearable must be borne again and again for the rest of their lives.

"Surely a sentence as a juvenile is unthinkable. If Rachel Shoaf has accepted full responsibility for her crime, she should not be asking to be sentenced as a juvenile. She should be willing to accept every day, every hour, and every minute of a proper adult sentence."

———————————

In the end, Judge Clawges agreed with Ashdown and refused to sentence Rachel as a juvenile. "That would by no means be justice in this case," he said, ordering her to serve thirty years.

No doubt aware of the community's horrified response to such a heinous crime, Clawges tried to offer some morsel that would satisfy them. "It is not my place to understand or to explain," he said. "I understand that nothing I have done or can do will make what has happened right for anybody. It is what it is and as far as I'm concerned, this matter is concluded."

Flanked by her defense attorneys, wearing her prison-issue orange jumpsuit, her wrists and ankles shackled, Rachel Shoaf shuffled out of the courtroom. Her face was puffy from crying, her shoulders tight as if expecting to ward off blows, and her eyes sought out those of her parents as she left.

At the small press conference after the hearing, a news reporter asked Dave what he would say to Rachel and Shelia if he could.

"I hope you have a rotten, rotten life because I—" He stopped abruptly, unwilling or unable to resume.

Ashdown talked more to the media about the case during those fifteen minutes in the press conference than she had in the last year and a half. Asked what kind of secrets the girls may have been hiding, she would only repeat "whatever secrets teenagers have." So it seems the secrets of Shelia Eddy, Rachel Shoaf, and even Skylar Neese are destined to remain unknown.

When asked which girl—Shelia or Rachel—bore the greater fault, she replied, "From my perspective they're equally responsible."

forty-seven

Society Is Naïve

People need answers, especially to difficult questions. It helps them make sense of life's most perplexing problems. Skylar Neese's murder is no different. Everyone who hears the story asks how the teen's two best friends could make calculated plans to brutally murder her—and then coldly carry them out.

But what if Rachel was telling the truth—or at least her version of it? Perhaps by that summer, the constant battles between Shelia and Skylar had become too much for all three of them. Shelia was sick of Skylar, Skylar was sick of being left out, and Rachel was sick of the constant fighting.

It's possible, probable even, that Rachel didn't want to be friends with Skylar anymore; people close to Rachel said that while she would fight, she dreaded fighting.

What about Shelia, though? She refuses to say a word about the crime, much less the motive behind it. So it's entirely possible her motive was different than Rachel's. At some point, though, Shelia convinced Rachel that it would be easier to end Skylar's life than end the three-way friendship.

From all accounts, Shelia could be mean and manipulative. Her Twitter feed alone proves that. Of course, Skylar could be mean, too.

However, there seems to be a basic difference between the two girls' meanness. Skylar acted mean when she felt justified in doing so, like the times she felt Shelia had slighted or wronged her. With Skylar, though, it wasn't who she was. Under normal circumstances, it was not in her basic nature to be mean to other people.

Skylar was a decent, good person who had a record of helping other people. She helped fellow students with their homework, she helped clean her aunt's house, and she worried about the environment, the rights of other people, and her parents. Skylar didn't have much money to give, but she had time and passion.

There may never be a fully satisfying answer to why Shelia and Rachel killed Skylar. Ken Lanning, the FBI profiler, said as much. According to Lanning, juveniles often commit crimes for reasons adults cannot wrap their minds around. He has heard numerous explanations from teens about why they committed some heinous crime, and said he is often surprised by what teens consider a valid reason to commit murder.

―――――――

If Shelia and Rachel's secret was a lesbian relationship, that is almost as empty as "We didn't want to be friends with her anymore." Even considering the unstable and explosive three-way relationship, it's possible neither Rachel nor Shelia would have cared at all if Skylar had exposed them.

However, if that exposure meant an end to their relationship as they knew it—if it threatened to tear the two lovers apart—that might have seemed like a logical motive for murder. At least in the eyes of two teenagers. In fact, a mentally challenged young gay man was murdered several years ago in nearby Fairmont, so it isn't a stretch to say homophobia remains a problem here.

Early in the investigation, it was believed Rachel Shoaf could have been afraid her church family would disown her if they found out she was having sex with another girl. Or that she would lose Mikinzy if he found out. Shelia would stand to lose, too, for being Rachel's lover, because her father's family is from the more rural Blacksville area, where homophobia is even more ingrained. But people who know Tara Eddy-Clendenen said they were sure she would have had no problems with Shelia if she was a lesbian, so there was that.

Or so it was thought, until recently, when Crissy Swanson shared information she gleaned from her mother. "My mom told me that Tara was very, very, very sure that her daughter would never be gay," Crissy said, adding that while talking about Skylar's murder and the lesbian rumors, "Tara said 'my daughter will never end up like somebody like that.'

"She said, 'You know her, all she's dated is boys, boys, boys . . . She'll never end up that way,'" Crissy said Tara told her mother.

Crissy believes this may be why Shelia felt she had to hide her relationship with Rachel. "Because neither parent would have agreed," Crissy said. "I thought she would love Shelia no matter what. That's her child."

Another question that begs an answer is whether Skylar was going to reveal Shelia and Rachel's secret. Did she threaten to, and if so, is that why they were so afraid? Why would they think Skylar was going to tell, if she had not done so in the year since she saw them having sex?

The easiest answer is: she did tell.

Skylar told Shania not long before school let out in 2012. Shania said Skylar told her about the two girls' sexual relationship a couple of months before they killed her.

Shania could have accidentally let the secret slip out, and perhaps told Shelia what Skylar revealed to her. Shania's grief has not subsided; she continues to experience difficulties from losing Skylar (to murder) and Shelia (to prison), and her tweets paint a picture of a very angry, depressed teenager. That's how Shelia found out, and could be why she said Skylar had to die.

In addition, one month after Rachel and Shelia had sex in front of Skylar, Skylar apparently did threaten to tell—or else Rachel and Shelia perceived her September 6 tweet, *id tell the whole school all the shit i have on everyone, which is a lottttt,* as a threat. One month later, they began joking in biology class about killing Skylar.

In late spring, after Shelia realized Skylar was telling their mutual friends about her sexual relationship with Rachel, she told Rachel, who, in turn, confided in Wendy, saying she wouldn't care if Skylar died.

Coming full circle, perhaps, just as Shelia and Rachel learned Skylar was talking about their lesbian acts, Skylar learned or finally began to believe the rumor about them wanting to kill her, which the *just know I know* tweet seems to confirm.

But what if it doesn't? Or what if, like Lanning said, there are several reasons for Skylar's murder—not just one simple one?

"The combination of the two girls together," Lanning said, "it may very well be that no one of them on their own would have done this. It was something about (that combination)...that played a role in this happening."

It wasn't the cause, and in Lanning's mind, the murder didn't occur because of one singular reason.

"You can't say, 'She did this because [Skylar] was going to expose their lesbian sexual relationship,'" Lanning said. "I just don't think it's that simple. It's a complicated series of things that all come together, and it's the totality of all of this that results" in murder.

Colebank also believes it's much darker than the two girls trying to keep their relationship secret.

"You get girls drunk, they're gonna make out," she said. "People know that and they don't care."

Colebank believes the lesbian sex didn't have anything to do with Skylar's murder. Instead, she believes "it was completely a thrill kill."

For both girls, who didn't have much in life to challenge them, the planning and execution of the murder was exciting. "They have everything they've ever wanted. They're given everything," Colebank said. "Nothing was a challenge for them. They could go out and party all they wanted, get any guy they wanted. They hated Skylar."

The idea of planning and then getting away with such a horrific crime was thrilling for both girls, Colebank believes, but it was especially exciting for Shelia, who sat back and played the innocent while the police chased all the false leads. The way both girls taunted the police in public, on Twitter, Colebank says, shows they "were enjoying the game."

Shelia loved watching crime shows like *Law & Order* and *Special Victims Unit (SVU)*, and Colebank believes it was a short walk for her to go from watching those shows to wondering if she and Rachel could get away with murder.

Colebank is the only officer who will say outright that Skylar's murder was a thrill kill. However, other officers who worked alongside her wonder if she might be right. The young officer has been right about a great many things in this case, so when she says she believes Shania Ammons was next on Shelia's list, it's a chilling possibility.

Shelia was treating Shania the same way she did Skylar, investigators later learned after finding a few text messages between the two girls. "Shania was Shelia's next victim," Colebank said.

For instance, Colebank related how Shania would text Shelia, saying, "Hey, let's hang out. I know this is rough on you."

"Yeah, we should hang out," was Shelia's reply.

When Shania said she would ask Tara if they could, Shelia would text Tara, saying, "Say no, just say no. I hate her. I don't want to hang out with her."

That, Colebank said, is exactly what Shelia did to Skylar.

Since she seems to be right about that, it's hard to ignore Colebank when she casually brushes aside another "gut feeling" she had. That one involves Shelia and Rachel having sex after they killed Skylar.

It's not the first time someone in law enforcement or the mental health field has brought up that possibility. Besides, sex is one tool Shelia used in her life on the edge.

Colebank says Shelia lives for excitement—and Skylar paid the price. It wasn't enough for them to kill Skylar, either. She believes

Shelia and Rachel then had to defame Skylar's memory by celebrating at the very site where they murdered her.

———————

Most likely, the female officer is right. While there were no beds available at Lakin when she was sentenced January 24, Shelia was transferred there not long afterward. Just as Colebank predicted, Shelia continues to use sex as a tool. Someone close to the case said Shelia's having sex with a male guard—who was then fired—got the teen killer an immediate transfer to the adult women's prison.

While in detention, Shelia has written letters to loved ones. Her own words indicate such behavior is entirely in line with her character. Lanning analyzed some of those letters and said Shelia lives in a make-believe world she has created. "She's already getting ready to move on," he said, referencing Shelia's desire to "go back to the old times" when she gets out of prison. Times that, for her, included riding around in cars, playing carefree games, and smoking weed.

Lanning said Shelia's attitude is not based in reality. "She acts like this whole thing was just a bump in the road. She's going through life and then [she murders Skylar], now she's got to figure out how to regroup."

Equally disturbing, she tends to blame her problems on two superficial factors. "So the two things that she suggests caused all of this," Lanning said, "are moving to Morgantown and meeting Rachel." These seem to her the biggest mistakes. If she could undo anything, it would be that—not scheming and killing Skylar, he added.

More important, Lanning's analysis found Shelia "seems to be in some kind of, almost, unwillingness to accept the reality of what she did."

This might explain why Shelia didn't tell the Neeses she was sorry when she had the chance at her plea and sentencing hearing. Not only does she not feel any guilt or shame for her actions, Lanning said; she "doesn't hint at any remorse over what she did."

People want to know why these girls killed Skylar, and in such a savage way. "It's not [a] simple answer," Lanning said, adding that it's anything but. "In my opinion, it's a convergence of a whole set of circumstances."

In addition, the expert behavior analyst believes Shelia is damaged in some serious way. "I think, rooted in that, is some type of flaw in this young woman's character. She's got some fundamental character flaw, whether it's genetic or whether it's rooted in some environmental problem. Most likely it's some combination of both."

While Shelia seems, at least on the surface, to be a typical teenager, "there's something wrong with her," Lanning said. "Lots of things that happened in this case happen every day in every high school across America, and no one gets killed."

———————

Colebank agrees. Not long after Shelia was transferred to Lakin Correctional Facility, *Dateline* aired an episode about Skylar's murder. Colebank was responding to a 911 call at CVS in Star City when a woman in her sixties recognized the young officer and mentioned the murder case.

"I don't believe it," the elderly customer said, "I don't believe those two sweet little girls did that."

That, Colebank told her, is because we live in a naïve society. The woman kept talking, and Colebank found it difficult to keep silent.

Why do people keep doing that? It's making me mad. Even though she wanted to, Colebank didn't give voice to her thoughts. *Walk away, you need to walk away from me right now.*

———————

Colebank's anger is justified. After all, she's one of the investigators who—along with Gaskins, Berry, and Spurlock—sacrificed countless hours to find the answers about Skylar's disappearance and then, later, unravel the mystery of her murder.

It's no wonder, then, after all this, that Colebank can't understand why people don't believe two pretty, fresh-faced teenagers could deliberately kill their good friend.

"Believe what you want," she says, "but it really happened."

Timeline of Events

1996

FEB. 10
Skylar is born.

2003

As second graders, Skylar and Shelia meet and become friends at The Shack Neighborhood House, a local community and youth center.

2010

SEPTEMBER
Skylar and Rachel meet when they enter UHS as freshmen.

OCTOBER
Shelia transfers to UHS from Clay-Battelle High School when her mother, Tara, marries Jim Clendenen and the family moves to Morgantown. She and Skylar are ecstatic to be in high school together, and soon Rachel joins their little group. Before long, the three teens begin to argue among themselves.

2011

LATE SPRING
Skylar, Shelia, Rachel, Floyd Pancoast, and Brian Moats are caught joyriding after curfew in Star City.

Aug. 16

Shelia and Rachel have sex in Rachel's bedroom while Skylar watches; Skylar and Shelia fight afterward and Patricia Shoaf separates the girls.

Aug. 21

Skylar angrily tweets she has learned a secret.

Aug. 28

Skylar angrily tweets to Shelia, saying she hates her.

Sept. 6

Skylar threatens to tell the whole school "all the shit" she has on them, if she could; believed to have meant Shelia and Rachel.

October

Shelia and Rachel are overheard asking how to dispose of a body in biology class, and mention Skylar's name at the same time. Another student tries to tell Skylar her two best friends don't really like her.

Nov. 27

Skylar tweets about the pain of losing a best friend.

Nov. 29

Skylar does not tweet to or about Shelia or Rachel for eleven days.

2012

Late March

Shelia and Skylar come to blows at the local Hollywood Stadium 12 theater.

May 10

Skylar tweets that obsessive girlfriends and ex-girlfriends are pathetic.

June 1

Shelia and Skylar leave for the beach, where they have a huge argument.

June 4

Rachel leaves for Young Life church camp in Rockbridge, Virginia.

JUNE 7

The Blacksville branch of Huntington National Bank is robbed, and police later suspect the robbery could be connected to Skylar's disappearance.

JUNE 7

Shelia and Skylar return from the beach.

JUNE 9

Rachel returns from Young Life very early that day, about the same time Skylar argues with an unnamed person on Twitter. Based on police reports that she, Rachel, and Shelia regularly argued online, it is believed Skylar was angry with one or both girls.

That night, Shelia and Rachel are seen arguing in the UHS parking lot about "something on Skylar's Twitter," and they decide Skylar must die.

JUNE 10

Shelia and Rachel put the plan to kill Skylar into action, beginning with an online search about the best ways to kill someone.

JULY 6

Skylar sneaks out of her family's apartment just after midnight.

Shelia and Rachel murder Skylar not long after she leaves her home.

Alarmed to learn Skylar did not show up for work, Dave calls 911. Shelia admits she, Skylar, and Rachel went joyriding the night before, but says they dropped Skylar off at the end of her street just before midnight. Star City police officer Bob McCauley responds to the 911 call and begins investigating Skylar's disappearance.

Skylar's parents, their landlord, Shelia, her mom, Tara, and Officer McCauley watch the apartment complex surveillance video. They see Skylar leave in a vehicle no one seems to recognize.

Chief Propst asks West Virginia State Police headquarters to issue an AMBER Alert for Skylar, but his request is denied.

Shelia and Tara help Mary and Dave canvass the neighborhood, looking for Skylar.

Online, word begins to spread about the missing teen.

Rachel and her mother visit Cheat Lake. That night Rachel writes in her diary, in a personal conversation to God, about something that went wrong the previous night.

JULY 7

Rachel leaves town to attend Catholic summer camp for two weeks.

Shelia and Tara help Mary and Dave canvass the neighborhood again, and Shelia begins to question the Neeses about what the police know.

JULY 8

Officer McCauley hands off the case to Officer Jessica Colebank.

JULY 9

Colebank conducts her first interview with Shelia.

The public learns Skylar is missing via TV, radio, and internet.

JULY 10

First print mention of Skylar's disappearance occurs in the Dominion Post, *Morgantown's newspaper.*

Dave's aunt Joanne organizes first coordinated search for Skylar.

JULY 13

First Websleuths thread about Skylar's disappearance is started by kmartin96, leading to a crowdsourcing of the investigation. Pisces_Sun later posts how people in Morgantown are not paying attention to Skylar's case.

JULY 15

Mary and Carol realize Skylar must be dead—or she would have come home by then.

JULY 16

The Blacksville branch of the Huntington National Bank is robbed a second time. State troopers Gaskins and Berry respond to the scene, which will later lead them to become involved in Skylar's case.

JULY 19

First police interview of Rachel Shoaf.

Gaskins and Berry interview Darek Conaway and other Blacksville residents about the area bank robberies. They return to the Conaway residence later with State Police, sheriff's deputies, and the FBI to search the house.

AUG. 6

Shelia posts selfie of her and Skylar along with the words, want my bestfriend back </3.

AUG. 16

University High School classes begin.

Daniel Hovatter is suspicious of Rachel and Shelia, and begins pressuring Rachel during drama class to talk. He doesn't let up throughout the fall or winter.

AUG. 17

Mary and Dave start TEAMSKYLAR 2012, a closed Facebook group.

AUG. 25

Dissatisfied with the status of the Star City Police investigation, Mary calls West Virginia State Police and asks them to get involved.

AUG. 27

Trying to see if Skylar's disappearance is linked to the bank robberies, Gaskins and Berry visit the Neese home and begin investigating Skylar's disappearance.

Police begin hearing vague rumors that the Conaway boys are involved, but later discover that isn't true.

SEPTEMBER

The Eddy and Shoaf families each hire attorneys. A major breakthrough occurs in the case when Trooper Chris Berry realizes the car seen on the apartment complex surveillance video belongs to Shelia.

SEPT. 7

First search warrant is served at UHS, and Shelia and Rachel's cell phones are confiscated.

First searches are conducted at the Eddy-Clendenen and Shoaf homes, and all of the girls' electronic equipment is seized.

NOVEMBER

A Midsummer Night's Dream performances take place at UHS; Rachel and Daniel have prominent roles. Upon hearing Rachel missed her opening night performance because she was with Shelia, Patricia confronts Rachel before show time.

The FBI and West Virginia State Police question Crissy Swanson, Eric Finch, and Aaron Roupe about Skylar's disappearance. The three teens are subsequently served with subpoenas for a federal grand jury.

Crissy tells Shelia she appeared before the grand jury.

DECEMBER

Shelia fails polygraph.

Rachel jumps from her father's car on the way to take her polygraph and runs to Tara's office.

DEC. 25

Shania gives Shelia a collage of photos with Shelia and Skylar as a Christmas gift.

DEC. 28

Rachel has a nervous breakdown and is committed to a local psychiatric hospital.

2013

JAN. 3

Rachel is discharged from the hospital.

Rachel confesses to her attorney, John Angotti, and the police that she and Shelia stabbed Skylar to death.

Snowfall hinders Rachel from leading police to Skylar's remains.

Rachel talks with Shelia while wearing a microphone, but Shelia fails to incriminate herself. There are no direct tweets from Shelia to Rachel from this day forward.

JAN. 16

Using GPS coordinates, police return to kill site after snow melts. They find Skylar's remains, where they discover her head is missing.

JANUARY

Skylar's Law is introduced to the West Virginia Legislature.

FEBRUARY

Dave speaks to House legislative committee.

MARCH 13

Remains publicly identified as Skylar's by the U.S. Attorney.

MARCH 29

Gaskins returns to the kill site and finds Skylar's skull.

MAY 1

Rachel turns herself in to authorities at the Monongalia County Circuit Court.

Shelia arrested in Cracker Barrel parking lot.

Rachel transferred to criminal court in closed hearing. After Rachel is assigned adult status, she pleads guilty to second-degree murder and is incarcerated at the Northern Regional Juvenile Detnetion Center in Wheeling, WV.

Gaskins, Spurlock, and Colebank take Shelia to the Lorrie Yeager Juvenile Center in Parkersburg, WV.

UHS students are stunned when they learn Rachel has confessed to killing Skylar, after news of her plea is broadcast on radio and TV.

JUNE 2

Mary and Dave begin to clean up the spot where Skylar's remains were found and create a memorial site in Skylar's honor.

JUNE 23

Memorial held for Skylar by family and close supporters at site of murder.

JUNE 24

Planned protest for Greene County coroner's office is canceled after coroner agrees to release Skylar's remains.

JULY 3

Mary, Dave, and Carol visit with Skylar's remains at Morgantown Detachment of WVSP.

JULY 10

Dave receives word the Greene County coroner will release death certificate so Skylar's memorial service can be held.

JULY 20

The public turns out for Skylar's final memorial service.

SEPT. 4

Shelia's status changed from juvenile to adult when she is transferred to criminal court; for the first time mainstream media reveals her identity in this case.

SEPT. 5–6

Shelia indicted on four felony counts during September term of grand jury.

SEPT. 17

Shelia pleads not guilty to all four counts at her arraignment.

SEPT. 30

Michael Benninger files motions on behalf of his client, Shelia Eddy.

OCT. 15

Judge Clawges hears motions in State of West Virginia v. Shelia Eddy.

DEC. 2

Shelia's trial date is rescheduled from February 11 to January 28.

2014

JAN. 24

Shelia pleads guilty to first-degree murder for her role in Skylar's death. She is sentenced to life in prison. She will be eligible for parole in fifteen years.

JAN. 29

Clawges signs the order to have Shelia transferred from juvenile detention to Lakin Correctional Facility for Women, the only women's prison in West Virginia.

FEB. 26

Judge Clawges sentences Rachel to thirty years in prison for her role in Skylar's murder. She will be eligible for parole in ten years. He sets a hearing for June 6, to determine if Rachel will also be transferred to Lakin on June 10, when she turns eighteen.

Red Flags for Parents to Watch for—and Prompt Actions to Take

1. **Your child is overly secretive.**

   Teens can become secretive as they gain more independence. Strive for an open-door policy, and encourage communication by talking to your child about your life and interests, too. Encourage your child to open up by getting involved in activities they enjoy, such as playing video games, reading the books they like, shopping for clothes, playing outdoor sports, or some other form of recreation, hobby, or social cause. As you interact on a regular basis, your child or teen will naturally open up and confide in you more.

2. **Your child asks you to "cover" for her friend.**

   Stay involved and supervise your child or teen's interactions, but don't lie for her or her friends. Explain to your teen lying only makes more problems and doesn't build good character, and if necessary, explain it to her friend, too. If you feel your teen may be headed for trouble or have friends who are, take them to the mall yourself and supervise them instead of dropping them off to run around on their own.

3. **Your child tries to sneak online.**

   One of the best pieces of advice for today's parents comes from parenting and law enforcement experts. They say one of the most important ways to protect children and teens is keep the computer in an open area of the home—not a bedroom. This helps reduce the likelihood your teen will begin chatting with an online stranger who could be a dangerous predator, or become involved in digital bullying.

4. **Your child seems to be on their smartphone nonstop.**

   Experts advise parents to limit their child or teen's use of these tools. This will automatically reduce the amount of time they spend with their friends through chats, texting, and phone calls. It will also limit their online surfing. Set up workable boundaries such as: "No calls after 9 p.m." or "You can only call or text friends we've pre-approved." There are also apps you can install to track your child's phone usage. Many parents have found great success with them. If you are concerned about your child's phone usage, you may want to randomly search its contents.

5. **You find out your child is behaving badly on social media.**

   Today's teens live on social media, and experts say it's causing them to become antisocial. The first way to prevent this is to explain the rules for acceptable online behavior. Second, set time limits. Third, learn what social media sites are popular with teens and create your own accounts. Assure your teen you will be watching her online behavior. If you see something suspicious like online bullying, put an immediate stop to it and discipline your teen accordingly. Download or purchase software or apps that help you monitor your teen, such as uKnowKids.com.

6. **Your child sneaks out at night.**

   Discipline promptly and firmly to avoid repeat behavior. Explain why you are taking a privilege and do not back down—no matter what. When you say "yes," mean it. Ditto for "no."

Parents who repeatedly give in because it's inconvenient to follow through with the promised discipline measures teach their children to be irresponsible. Require your child to earn back your trust. If necessary, take the lock off your child's bedroom door and be prepared to lock windows from the outside. Make sure your child knows sneaking out is unacceptable behavior.

7. **Your child has an unexpected, negative personality change.**
   If you notice any unacceptable behavior, such as hateful and disrespectful language or violent speech or actions, make it clear this will not be tolerated. If it only happens when your child is around certain friends, curtail the friendship. (A word of caution: If you do not see a clear connection, have a firm but loving heart-to-heart with your child. This could be a serious problem such as sexual abuse or drug use.)

8. **You find weed or other drugs (including alcohol) in your child's possession.**
   Many parents turn a blind eye to some amount of drug or alcohol use today. That's a big mistake. If your child is using, chances are she is well on the road to abusing one substance or another. Sit down and explain why it's harmful and discipline accordingly. Make it clear drug and alcohol use is unacceptable in your home. Follow through by not misusing alcohol yourself. If you as a parent have a known drug problem that you refuse to get under control, chances are your child will, too.

9. **Your child lies to you about who she is with or where she will be.**
   Tell your child lying is unacceptable, and explain why it causes other people to lose trust in her. Set the proper example by being honest with your child and other people. If your child has been dishonest while with her friends, curtail any association with those friends for a specific time. If the problem continues, cut off that friendship—in real time and online.

10. **Your child seems obsessed with one of her friends.**

Using gentle questions, try to find out what it is about the friend that your child likes. See if your teen feels like something is missing in her life. Try to fill that gap and draw closer to your child—while still acting like an authority figure, not her friend. More than ever, today's teens need parents who can set limits for them—and stick to them. They will respect you if you do this and don't break your own rules. Ultimately, they will be healthier and happier for it, and appreciate that you cared enough to intervene.

Acknowledgments

Telling this tragic all-too-true story has been an honor. It has taken tremendous time and effort from many people without whom this book would never have come to fruition. The entire creative team at BenBella Books has been fabulous, from Publishers Glenn Yeffeth and Adrienne Lang to Clarissa Phillips, Annie Gottlieb, James Fraleigh, Sarah Dombrowsky, Monica Lowry, Jennifer Canzoneri, and Lloyd Jassin.

A special word of thanks goes to Editor Erin Kelley, who took our "baby" and gave it just the right amount of tender loving care so it could face the world on its own.

In addition, we cannot thank our publicist enough. Michael Wright (and his partner, Leslie Garson) did an outstanding job, whether working with local or national media. He went above and beyond.

A handful of people deserve special mention: Mary and Dave Neese, who were courageous enough to share their story with us; Katherine Boyle, the best agent ever, and one we were so fortunate to find; Ken Lanning, whose analytical skills prevented us from being blinded by easy answers; Diane Tarantini, who provided an end-less stream of encouragement and whose eagle eye helped our words shine; and Kinsey Culp, who helped Daleen survive this journey.

We have tried to list everyone who was generous with their time and information, but if we forget anyone, it is no reflection on your contribution to this story, or your efforts to sustain us as we wrote it. Among this group are family and friends who supported us, fellow writers who loaned us their writing ear, the investigating officers who worked this case, and last but certainly not least, the teenagers who knew Skylar, Rachel, and Shelia. They were among the most courageous people to come forward with the knowledge that helped us piece together how this terrible crime happened.

They include Shania Ammons; Courtney Austin; Becky Bailey; Linda Barr; Trooper Chris Berry and Alexis Berry; Ted Bice; Commissioner Tom Bloom; Cathy and Mike Callison; Jordan Carter; Jocelyn Claire; Officer Jessica Colebank; Dylan and Debby Conaway; Jill Damm; Lexi Dean; Dan Demchak; Eric and JoJo Finch; Winston Fuller; Bri and Beth Gardner; Corporal Ronnie Gaskins; Shelley Gilbert; Julie Haught; Dyllan Hines; Kirsten and Tonya Hiser; Alesha Holloway; Becky Hood; Lauren Housman; Daniel Hovatter; Amorette and Penny Hughes; Candace Jordan; Sheriff Al Kisner; Kelsey Konchesky; Cameron Lancaster; David, Cheryl, and Morgan Lawrence; Fantasia Liller; Hayden McClead; Meredith Marsh; Delegate Charlene Marshall; Connie Merandi; Carol, Kyle, and Steve Michaud; Kristen Miller; Phyllis Moore; Cheri Murray; Joanne Nagy; Michael Neese; Cynthia Nelson; Chief Vic Propst; Destinee Pyles; Mary Beth Renner; Ashley Riffle; Sarah Robinson; Rick Stache; Crissy Swanson; Nancy Weber; Kelly Wilkes; Kevin Willard; Ariah Wyatt; Chuck Yocum; and all the people who talked to us, even if only anonymously.

However small or great, your contribution has been immensely important as we raced toward our deadline to finish this book. We cannot, no matter how much we try, thank you enough.